MIRACLES THAT NEVER WERE

Naturally,

Fred Acquistapace

MIRACLES THAT NEVER WERE:

Natural Explanations of the Bible's Supernatural Stories

Fred Acquistapace

Eye-Opener Books
Box 1531
Santa Rosa, California 95402

First Edition

99 98 97 96 95 94 93 92 91   10 9 8 7 6 5 4 3 2 1

Library of Congress Catalog Card Number: 90-085540

ISBN: 0-9628156-0-8

Printed in the United States of America.

To Ruth Acquistapace

This is dedicated to the one I love.
My wife of 36 years, Ruth.

Contents

Acknowledgments

Thank you to my wife Ruth who spent countless hours at the keyboard of the word processor typing my handwritten documents.

Thank you to Michelangelo for the cover illustration, "The Creation of Adam," which was painted in the Sistine Chapel, 1509-1512.

Thank you dear reader for taking the time to read this book. I trust it will inspire you to help yourself and others to a more rewarding life.

Prologue

I have spent thirty years reading, studying and researching the Bible. I find it a very fascinating book, but one not too well understood by most readers. In my research I explored many scientific fields. I compiled my book material from various sources, each of which supplied many explanations: biology, chemistry, geology, glaciology, history, hydrology, logic, medicine, meteorology, mythology, philosophy, physics, physiology, psychology, sociology, theology, and volcanology. While much of the material is complex, I am not interested in presenting technical or deep theological concepts. I intended to keep it plain, simple and easy to read.

Each story contains Bible references which I expect the reader to look up and read. Some of the references are quoted, but you should have the whole text before you as you read the story and its analysis. I used the King James version because it is the one most familiar to me and to most readers. You may, of course, follow along with any version you prefer. The subject matter of miracle stories is well known, but the explanations and analyses may be new to many of you. Bear with me as you read, and I trust you will gain a deeper insight into the meaning of the stories and the intent of the writers of the Bible stories.

As you read, look for an overall picture of the Bible. Try to see each story as a part of the whole book, not as a separate entity. Once you have such an overview you will find it easier to understand how and why each story became a part of the Bible. As you read, take time to think, make notes and look up references.

If you are like most people, you probably have a lot of questions. I trust you will find some answers you have been seeking—and some you may never have considered.

—Fred Acquistapace, 1990

Chapter 1

Orientation

It's a miracle! We hear this all the time but what do we mean by *miracle*? Webster defines *miracle* as "An event or effect that apparently contradicts known scientific laws and is hence thought to be due to supernatural causes, especially to an act of God." When the Bible stories were written, there were few known scientific laws. When we look at occurrences from the point of view of people in 500 B.C., we can understand why they called them miracles. Many miracles of yesterday are common events today. Even though we have more knowledge of science today, we cannot expect to know all there is to know. Future generations will increase knowledge beyond our wildest dreams. With this in mind let's look back and see how these stories came to be written.

The Jewish Bible, known to Christians as the Old Testament, originated from oral tradition to its present form over about 1,500 years. The Hebrews developed a written language about 1000 B.C. and they began writing their traditions. The earliest version was called *J* because it referred to God as Jehovah; it was a product of the Southern kingdom (Judah), from about 850 B.C. Many stories feature Aaron because he was their hero. The Northern kingdom (Israel), had a version called *E* because they referred to God as "El" or "Elohim." *E* was written about 750 B.C. and Moses was Israel's hero.

In 722 B.C. Assyria conquered Israel and many people were taken away captive. Those not taken went to Judah and took their traditions with them. Even though the two traditions were contradictory, they were both histories of the Hebrews and soon they were combined and became the *JE* version. *JE* became the official history of Israel shortly after 722 B.C.

13

In 622 B.C. the high priest found a book in the Temple and brought it to Josiah, the king. The book contained a code of laws which is now Deuteronomy 12-26. The king read this book and made it the law of the land. This material had been recently written but was attributed to Moses so it would have authority. Through a process we know as "legal fiction," the law was considered valid and could not be challenged. The new laws were recast into the older setting of the Mt. Sinai story. This addition was called *D* and was incorporated with the *JE* to form a new document called *JED*. The Deuteronomist who wrote *D* probably also wrote Joshua, Judges, Chronicles and Kings.

The largest source of the Pentateuch was from the priestly author and was called *P*. This priest was from the lineage of Aaron and made Aaron and his heirs God's chosen priests. Even though *JE* had made Moses the leader, now that Judah had been taken captive to Babylon, the Aaronic priesthood took charge. In *P*, Aaron became the older brother of Moses and the High Priest of all Israel by means of the legal fiction of the *P* document.

The newly instituted sacrifices and offerings were said to have been commanded by God to Moses and Aaron. Stories which told of sacrifices by Moses, David, Solomon and others were still in the traditions, but new *P* stories were written to show Aaron and his heirs making the sacrifices. *J* had a story of Noah taking seven pairs of each clean animal and offering sacrifices after the flood. *P* changed the story so Noah took only one pair of each animal and no sacrifices were made. Because of these changes there are two separate stories woven together as you will see in the flood story. *P* was written about 500 B.C., just after the end of the Babylonian Exile.

The final stage of blending the *JED* and *P* was accomplished by another Aaronic priest. This editor was called the Redactor, or *R*, and he put the Pentateuch in the order we have today. The *R* document was the product of Ezra about 444 B.C. With the power of his office and the backing of the Emperor, Ezra presented the Jews with the Torah of Moses, the first five books of the Bible. Read Ezra 7 and see how Ezra was empowered to write the Book of the Law. It was Ezra who gave the laws to the Jews but it was credited to Moses so it would have authority.

There you have the story of the Pentateuch. *J* written about 850 B.C.; *E* written about 750 B.C.; *JE* combined shortly after 722 B.C.; *D* written about 622 B.C. and combined into *JED*; *P* written about 500 B.C. All of these were edited by *R* about 444 B.C. into the form we have today. About 400 B.C. the Law became Scripture. The Books of the Prophets became Scripture about 200 B.C. The remainder, or the Writings, became Scripture about A.D. 90. That briefly is how the Jewish Bible was formed. A more detailed account of this material can be found in *The Interpreter's Bible* and in *Who Wrote the Bible,* both listed in the bibliography.

The New Testament was also the product of writing, rewriting, editing, interpolating, and finally by vote of Church councils. Paul's letters were the earliest New Testament documents written. They were written between 49 and 62, but the letters were not published until about 90. Mark's gospel was written about 70. Matthew and Luke were written between 80 and 95. John's gospel was written about 100. The last New Testament writing was the second letter of Peter and it dates from about 120.

As the Church grew and developed, new ideas circulated. The Church decided it needed a formal doctrine and an official book, so it began collecting stories. When the early Church formulated its doctrine, the gospels were edited to comply with the new doctrine. In essence it was not the Bible that formed the Church, but the Church that formed the Bible. When the Church was satisfied with its doctrine it selected what would be in the Bible and no more changes were allowed.

The twenty-seven books were selected from perhaps hundreds in use in various churches during the first three centuries of the Christian Era. There were about fifty gospels being used by early Christians and only four were selected. Many "Acts" and "Epistles" type books were in use and only those now included were chosen. In 367 Bishop Athanasius made a list and sent it to his followers as part of an Easter letter. Formal ratification came in 397 at the Council of Carthage. Finally the Bible was complete.

Close study of the Bible reveals several time periods where the number of miracle stories increased. When Moses and Joshua founded the nation there were many miracle stories. When Israel was struggling against idolatry, Elijah and Elisha were subjects of many miracle stories. During the time of the Babylonian Exile stories of Daniel and the three Hebrew children were told. When Christianity was introduced, more miracle stories were written. This indicates miracles were sporadic and not to be expected just anytime people wanted them.

If miracles were to hold a special place in the mind of man, they could not become too common. Augustus said, "The daily miracle of God has grown cheap by repetition." If man could call on God to do miracles any time man wanted them, God would be under the control of man. As we look at the stories we find several reasons for their inclusion in the Bible. Some fit the needs of the times, like those of Moses and the Exodus. Some miracles were written to add power and prestige to the priests or prophets. Some stories were written to inspire people during the Exile in Babylon. Some were written to add power to the message of Jesus and the Apostles. Each miracle story had a purpose and had a part in the religious drama as it was played out.

We will be discussing methods used to produce miraculous effects. We will see how natural phenomena appeared to be controlled by man's will. We will see how priests took control of the nation and used miracle stories to maintain that control. We have given a variety of explanations which may be new to you, but as you read them you will wonder why you didn't think of them yourself. Simple explanations frequently make more sense than some of the more complicated ones to which we have become accustomed.

In researching the miracles, I found the stories of healing to be the most fascinating, so I concentrated there. I focused on faith and found something very interesting. "According to your faith be it unto you," and "Thy faith hath made thee whole," and "Go thy way; and as thou hast believed, so be it done unto thee." Napkins and aprons could be taken to the sick and the sickness would be cured. Even those not present could be cured if they had faith. Do you see what this suggests? Healing isn't given—it is received. Healing comes from within, not from without.

I again narrowed my search and found many who were healed were "possessed with devils," tormented by an "unclean spirit," or a "dumb spirit." Now the search was focused not on the body but on the mind of the one suffering. I found many physical ailments stemming from mental disorders. I looked deeper and finally found the one word I had been seeking: hysteria.

Hysteria is the most common of all the neuroses. Hysteria is an emotionally caused psychiatric condition characterized by excitability, motor disturbances and simulation of organic disorders. More simply stated, hysteria can be caused by abuse, anxiety, duress, fear, guilt, hunger, minor accident, psychological trauma, rape, repression, stress, tension, sunstroke and many other conditions. Symptoms of hysteria include blindness, coma, deafness, dropsy, dumbness, fever, glossolalia, hallucinations of all the senses, impotence, infertility, multiple personality disorder, paralysis, skin disorders, trances, visions, and other common disorders. When I learned the causes and symptoms of hysteria, I knew I was on to something big.

The best part of hysteria is the cure. At the end of the 19th Century, Sigmund Freud was able to understand enough about hysteria to treat those suffering from it and cure them. Freud found hypnotism could be used to help in his cure. Today, psychotherapists help people with hysteria much as Jesus did two thousand years ago. The patient is put at ease with calm assurance or drugs. When the patient is able to accept the suggestion of cure, the symptoms disappear and the patient is well.

The fact that hysteric symptoms are mental allows the patient to receive instant relief. In hysteric blindness, the eyes are not damaged. In hysteric deafness, there is no physical impairment. In hysteric paralysis, there is no muscular atrophy. The Bible stories said those cured immediately resumed normal function. The man at Bethesda, paralyzed for 38 years, was able to rise and walk when he accepted Jesus' suggestion of a cure (John 5:1-9). You will find many other examples when you get into the book.

One reason for this book is to make people aware that many suffer from hysteric disorders. In 1861 Andrew Jackson Davis said, "The truth is, that accidents excepted, the great majority of human bodily diseases are of mental origin." About 80% of diseases are of mental origin and many are symptoms of hysteria. The person to see about a cure for hysteria is a psychotherapist. This could be the best news you ever heard, so don't be afraid to make an appointment.

When you finish the book you will know that over one-third of the miracle stories deal with hysteria. Because the history of the Jews was one of political upheaval and strife, the conditions were ripe for hysteria. Along with hysteria came a few who could relieve the symptoms and the results were miracle stories. Moses probably learned about hysteria in Egypt, but it doesn't appear that he taught anyone about it. Elijah learned about cures of hysteria and taught Elisha. Jesus knew how to relieve hysteria and was able to teach Peter, but the rest of the Apostles were unable to learn. Freud learned and taught his colleagues. We have a cure now, so if you or someone you know needs help, don't neglect to get the help you need.

It must be said that the only healings in the Bible dealt with hysteric symptoms. It cannot be stressed too much that no cures were recorded for people with real physical health problems. When John the Baptist was beheaded, no cure was offered. When Stephen was stoned to death, no cure was offered. When James was killed by the sword, no cure was offered. These were real physical health problems! The people were really dead. If you have a broken bone, see a doctor. If you have cancer, see a doctor. If you have high blood pressure, see a doctor. This advice is for those who need the help of a doctor so they won't just sit and wait for a miracle that will never happen.

Explaining the miracles is not intended to rob you of your cherished beliefs. It is only to help you understand what the Bible writers were trying to get across to the readers. We now can understand how and why the Bible stories were written. Even more important, we also know by and for whom the stories were written. The priests made up a religion based on fear, sacrifices, and offerings. It only makes sense when you know that the priests received these sacrifices and offerings for themselves. The tithes were demanded not for God but for the priests. The clergy today fail to explain this as they too often play the same game. When the clergy saw the tomb was empty, they moved in and have been living rent-free ever since.

It is important to understand that this is not a negative book. Knowledge leads to a positive attitude and it is with the goal of uplift that I present this material. By removing the supernatural element from the Jewish Bible, it is clear that the Jews themselves deserve all the credit for their survival as a nation. It is the intention of this book to commend the Jews for overcoming the adversity of three thousand years and maintaining their culture. Congratulations, I salute you.

If there is any error in understanding the miracle stories of the Jewish Bible, it lies with the Christian Church. How arrogant it was for Christianity to take a Jewish book, claim it as its own, and presume to tell the world what it means. It would make more sense to ask the Jews what their stories mean. The Jews don't believe Adam and Eve were the first two people on earth. They don't believe Joshua stopped the sun and moon. Jews don't believe Jonah was swallowed by a great fish, which Jesus said was a whale. Fundamentalists Christians have taught that miracle stories are fact and happened exactly as they were written.

Bernie Ward, a San Francisco talk show host, put it best when he said, "All the stories in the Bible are true—not necessarily factual—but true." I find this statement to be a great value in understanding the Bible.

As you get into the book, open your eyes to new insights and let your mind wander. Don't be too quick to say yes or no. It is the intent of this book to make you think. It is not intended to tell you what to think, but how to think. As this book is the product of inspiration, it is hoped that you too will be inspired.

Take a deep breath, get your second wind and make the most of your life. My desire for you is health, harmony and happiness.

STORIES
FROM
THE

OLD
TESTAMENT

Chapter 2

Stories From Genesis

1   Two Stories of Creation - Genesis 1 & 2

◆ Genesis 1:1-2:3, The First Story

In the beginning God created the heaven and the earth. And the earth was without form, and void; and darkness was upon the face of the deep. And the Spirit of God moved upon the face of the waters. And God said, "Let there be light": and there was light. And God saw the light, that it was good: and God divided the light from the darkness. And God called the light Day, and the darkness he called Night. And the evening and the morning were the first day.

On the first day God created light, but the light wasn't from the sun because the sun wasn't created until the fourth day. Where the light came from we are not told, but it could be divided in some way from the darkness. This story came from the Babylonian myth in which light was the first creation of the sun-god Marduk.

And God said, "Let there be a firmament in the midst of the waters, and let it divide the waters from the waters." And God made the firmament, and divided the waters which were under the firmament from the waters which were above the firmament: and it was so. And God called the firmament Heaven. And the evening and the morning was the second day.

This story is from the Babylonian creation myth in which a palace was built in the firmament for the sun-god Marduk. The first chapter of Genesis is by the author of the *P* or Priestly Code who wrote at the end of the Babylonian Exile, about 500 B.C. During the Exile, the Jews learned the creation stories of both the Babylonians and the Persians.

21

From these they formed their stories which we have in the book of Genesis.

> And God said, "Let the waters under the heaven be gathered together unto one place, and let the dry land appear": and it was so. And God called the dry land Earth; and the gathering together of the waters called he Seas: and God saw that it was good. And the earth brought forth grass, and herb yielding seed after his kind, and the tree yielding fruit, whose seed was in itself, after his kind: and God saw that it was good. And the evening and the morning were the third day.

Dry land was formed and on it grew plants and trees. There was not yet a sun to provide energy for the plants, but let's see what happened next.

> And God said, "Let there be lights in the firmament of the heaven to divide the day from the night; and let them be for signs, and for seasons, and for days, and years: And let them be for lights in the firmament of the heaven to give light upon the earth": and it was so. And God made two great lights; the greater light to rule the day, and the lesser light to rule the night: he made the stars also. And God set them in the firmament of the heaven to give light upon the earth, And to rule over the day and over the night, and to divide the light from the darkness: and God saw that it was good. And the evening and the morning were the fourth day.

Finally we have a sun, moon and stars. Now the plants can get the light and warmth needed to grow.

> And God said, "Let the waters bring forth abundantly the moving creature that hath life, and fowl that may fly about the earth in the open firmament of heaven." And God created great whales, and every living creature that moveth, which the waters brought forth abundantly, after their kind, and every winged fowl after his kind: and God saw that it was good. And God blessed them, saying, "Be fruitful, and multiply, and fill the waters in the seas, and let fowl multiply in the earth." And the evening and the morning were the fifth day.

Notice that the whales, fish and other water creatures, also all the birds of the air were brought forth from the water. What an interesting concept.

> And God said, "Let the earth bring forth the living creature after his kind, cattle, and creeping thing, and beast of the earth after his kind": and it was so. And God made the beast of the earth after his kind, and cattle after their kind, and every thing that creepeth upon the earth after his kind: and God saw that it was good. And God said, "Let us make man in our image, after our likeness: and let them have dominion over the fish of the sea, and over the fowl of the air, and over the cattle, and over all the earth, and over every creeping thing that creepeth upon the earth." So God created man in his own image, in the image of God created he him; male and female created he them. And God saw every thing that he had made, and behold, it was very good. And the evening and the morning were the sixth day.

Here God created man, male and female, but gave them no name. In Genesis 5:2 we read, "Male and female created he them; and blessed them, and called their name Adam, in the day when they were created." This was a different author and he said both man and woman were named Adam. In this version God was talking to someone else as he said, "Let us make man in our image." The Hebrew's God had no image after which he could pattern man. The source of this idea is the Babylonian Creation myth in which Marduk discussed the creation of man with other gods. In this first version of the creation story man was created after the animals but when we look at the next version we shall see something different.

> Thus the heavens and the earth were finished, and all the host of them. And on the seventh day God ended his work which he had made; and he rested on the seventh day from all his work which he had made. And God blessed the seventh day, and sanctified it: because that in it he had rested from all his work which God created and made.

God worked six days and rested on the seventh day, but what did he do on the eighth, ninth, tenth day and so on? There is no mention of God working again, so he must have taken an early retirement and turned all the maintenance over to mankind. The seventh day, or sabbath, was not of much importance to the Hebrews until after the Exile, so in the *J* version the sabbath is not even mentioned. This story was written by *P* shortly after the Exile and was intended to explain the origin of the sabbath.

◆ Genesis 2:4-25, The Second Story

> These are the generations of the heavens and of the earth when they were created, in the day that the LORD God made the earth and the heavens, And every plant of the field before it was in the earth, and every herb of the field before it grew: for the LORD God had not caused it to rain upon the earth, and there was not a man to till the ground. But there went up a mist from the earth, and watered the whole face of the ground.

This begins a second creation story, but this one says it took only one day to make everything. This version from the *J* source calls God the "LORD God" while the *P* source calls him just "God." Look at the next verse very carefully—it is very important: "And the LORD God formed man of the dust of the ground, and breathed into his nostrils the breath of life; and man became a living soul." This verse says that man was not created, but was formed, from the "dust of the ground." Creation is usually understood to be something from nothing, but in this version God starts with dust. Even though man is fully formed he was not alive, so God "breathed into his nostrils the breath of life; and man became a living soul." This can imply that life begins at birth, when a baby takes its first breath. One other point is important here, " . . . man became a living soul." From this the inference can be drawn that man does not *have* a soul but that man *is* a soul. Just as pieces of wood and nails become a box, a body and spirit, or breath, becomes a soul. This is one of the more thought-provoking verses in the entire Bible, yet few people ever ponder it.

> And the LORD God took the man, and put him into the garden of Eden to dress it and to keep it. And the LORD God commanded the man, saying, "Of every tree of the garden thou mayest freely eat: But of the tree of the knowledge of good and evil, thou shalt not eat of it: for in the day that thou eatest thereof thou shalt surely die."

This is the first law given to man and it carried with it the death penalty. Man had been on earth only a short time and already he was threatened with death for eating fruit from a tree. In the beginning God tried to keep Adam and Even from eating of the "tree of knowledge of good and evil." The Christian Church also tried to keep mankind from reading the Bible, their own "book of knowledge of good and evil."

> And the LORD God said, "It is not good that the man should be alone; I will make him an help meet for him." And out of the ground the LORD God formed every beast of the field, and every fowl of the air; and brought them unto Adam to see what he would call them: and whatsoever Adam called every living creature, that was the name thereof. And Adam gave names to all cattle, and to the fowl of the air, and to every beast of the field; but for Adam there was not found an help meet for him.

In this version God formed animals and birds from the same dust as Adam, who is named here for the first time. Even the fowl of the air were formed from dust rather than water as in the first version. It seems strange that God expected Adam to find a "help meet" from among the animals and birds, but that is what he had to choose from.

> And the LORD God caused a deep sleep to fall upon Adam, and he slept: and he took one of his ribs, and closed up the flesh instead thereof; And the rib which the LORD God had taken from man, made he a woman, and brought her unto the man. And Adam said, "This is now bone of my bones, and flesh of my flesh: she shall be called Woman, because she was taken out of man."

That was how woman came to be on the earth. She must have been very small but it didn't seem to bother Adam. After Eve, man and woman are taken out of woman, but here woman was taken out of man. This could be the first case of a human clone. Technically a clone would be the same gender, but for the sake of the story one was male and the other female. As Adam and Eve both had God as their father they were brother and sister to Jesus, who was also the son of the same father, God. To accept the story of Eve causing the fall of man into sin would make Eve responsible for the death of her brother, Jesus. Genesis 3 tells about a speaking serpent telling Eve about the forbidden fruit. "And the serpent said unto the woman, 'Ye shall not surely die.'" Adam and Eve both ate the fruit. They didn't die, but they did realize they were naked, so God made fur coats for both of them. What a strange story the Bible tells.

"Therefore shall a man leave his father and his mother, and shall cleave unto his wife: and they shall be one flesh." I can imagine the look on Adam's face when he heard this from God. He must have asked, "What is a 'father' and a 'mother'," for he had neither. This verse is the source of the phrase used in marriage ceremonies today. It is probably one of the more sexist remarks one can imagine.

The same kind of mentality persists in another ritual sentence: "I now pronounce you man and wife." Why is the male still man but the female now wife? Let's change it to "husband and wife."

Now that you have heard both stories of creation, which one do you believe? Which came first, man or the animals? Were man and woman created or formed from dust and bone? There is a clear dilemma that cannot be waved off by a sweep of the hand. The laws of logic require that one or the other—or both—be rejected. You cannot believe both accounts because if creation means something from nothing, and Adam was formed from dust and Eve from bone there was no creation. If Adam was made from dust and will return to dust as in Genesis 3:19, there is no immortality which the Christian Church has long preached. The Jews never did and still don't believe in heaven or hell; this shows they understood the story as it was written.

According to the latest scientific evidence, the cosmos came into being about twenty billion years ago, and Earth about five billion years ago. If God existed all these billions of years, and even more beside, it must have been very boring for him. All alone in total darkness God just waited and wondered what he would do. And you get bored waiting a half hour in a doctor's office.

As far as finding any miracle in this story of creation, the only one I find is the fact that some people still believe it to be true. There is nothing supernatural about taking myths from other cultures and using them as a basis for one's own stories. This is perfectly natural—it has been going on for thousands of years. We must be reminded that we are looking at another people's stories when we read the Jewish Bible that Christians call the Old Testament.

The Jews themselves never believed the stories to be factual. Why should we?

2   *The Death of Enoch*

◆ Genesis 5:19-24

> And Enoch lived sixty and five years, and begat Methuselah: And
> Enoch walked with God after he begat Methuselah three hundred
> years, and begat sons and daughters: And all the days of Enoch were
> three hundred sixty and five years: And Enoch walked with God: and
> he was not; for God took him.

It is amazing how much is made of such a short story that doesn't
actually say anything. All we are told about Enoch is that at sixty-five
years of age he had a son, and that when he was three hundred sixty-
five-years old, after producing other sons and daughters, he died. Because those before Enoch lived over 900 years each and Enoch lived
only 365 years, something strange must have happened, so stories were
made up to explain the early death. Hebrews 11:5 says, "Enoch was
translated that he should not see death," but I think the story was
translated into something that never happened. If the story had said
Enoch lived 965 years, everyone would have been satisfied. Evidently
365 years were not enough to suit them, so they decided to send him to
heaven. But remember, it wasn't the Jews who sent him to heaven
because they didn't have a heaven. The Christians made up the story in
spite of John 3:13 which says clearly "no man hath ascended up to
heaven." Isn't it amazing how the early Christian Church made up new
stories based on Old Testament accounts?

I can think of several reasons why Enoch "was not." He could have
run away with a woman from another area. He could have been killed
and eaten by wild animals. He could have been murdered and buried, as
Abel was. He could have developed amnesia and wandered away, fallen
into a deep valley or wandered into a cave and died. There are any
number of ways Enoch could have died, so there was little reason to
assume a miracle was necessary. Why look for a supernatural explanation when we have more than enough natural explanations?

Enoch is said to have "walked with God," so some assume they simply
walked all the way to heaven. When the same phrase is used concerning
Noah nothing is made of it because Noah lived 950 years. "Noah was a
just man and perfect in his generations, and Noah walked with God"
(Genesis 6:9). Noah didn't get a "translation" story as Enoch did. Noah
didn't get to go to heaven without dying. Noah didn't get something for
nothing—he had to build an Ark to gain his fame.

Much too much was read into the story of Enoch to be valid. There is
just no evidence to claim a miracle translation unless it occurs in the
translation from one language to another.

3   *The Flood Story*

◆ Genesis 6-9

> Noah was a just man and perfect in his generations, and Noah walked
> with God. . . . And God said unto Noah, "The end of all flesh is come
> before me; for the earth is filled with violence through them; and,
> behold, I will destroy them with the earth. Make thee an ark of gopher
> wood."

After billions of years of planning and deciding how to make a cosmos,
an earth, and man himself, God decided he did it wrong. God said, "It
repenteth me that I have made them," and decided to "destroy them with
the earth." What a fickle god we see here. Only one man's family is
suitable to be saved and start all over. Why didn't God just start with a
new earth and new people? Instead he chose some of those who let him
down the first time, so he lacked an excuse when it happened again. Noah
was instructed to build a boat 450 feet long, 75 feet wide and 45 feet
high. "And, behold, I, even I, do bring a flood of waters upon the earth,
to destroy all flesh." Now Noah saw why he was to build the Ark.

> "But with thee will I establish my covenant; and thou shalt come into
> the ark, thou, and thy sons, and thy wife, and thy sons' wives with thee.
> And of every living thing of all flesh, two of every sort shalt thou bring
> into the ark, to keep them alive with thee; they shall be male and
> female. Of fowls after their kind, and of cattle after their kind, of every
> creeping thing of the earth after his kind, two of every sort shall come
> unto thee, to keep them alive."

Now Noah learned that the Ark must be so big because it would have
to hold so many animals aboard and all the food for his family and the
animals.

So far, what we have quoted is from the *P* source; now we will look
at some verses from the *J* source.

> And the LORD said unto Noah, "Come thou and all thy house into the
> ark; for thee have I seen righteous before me in this generation. Of
> every clean beast thou shalt take to thee by sevens, the male and his
> female: and of beasts that are not clean by two, the male and his female.
> Of fowls also of the air by sevens, the male and the female; to keep
> seed alive upon the face of all the earth."

In this version the variance called for seven pairs of clean animals and
birds and one pair of unclean animals. The reason for the difference is
that the *P*, or Priestly Code, only allowed priests from the lineage of
Aaron to offer sacrifices. The *P* source only calls for two because no
sacrifice could be made. The *J* source was written earlier than the *P*
source and allowed *any* righteous man to offer sacrifices. Thus seven
pair of clean animals and fowls were needed because some would be

sacrificed. Don't be confused. Be aware that there is more than one source in these stories.

After the animals boarded the Ark and the only window closed, the Flood came. When the Ark finally came to rest "on the mountains of Ararat," Noah sent out a bird. The *P* source says "And he sent forth a raven, which went forth to and fro, until the waters were dried up from off the earth." The next verse is from *J*, "Also he sent forth a dove from him, to see if the waters were abated from off the face of the ground; But the dove found no rest for the sole of her foot, and she returned unto him into the ark." Seven days later the dove was sent out again and brought back an olive leaf. Seven more days and again the dove was sent out and it didn't return. So *P* sent out a raven and *J* sent out a dove. *J* doesn't say how long Noah was in the Ark but *P* is very specific. *P* says they went into the Ark on the 17th day of the second month and just a year later the 27th day of the second month they came out of the Ark. *P* is much more precise as we would imagine a priest making up a story would be.

In this fabricated story we find a copy of the Epic of Gilgamesh, a flood story the Jews learned from the Babylonians. To look at the story literally we see the Earth covered with water. The highest mountain was covered by 22 feet of water as "Fifteen cubits upward did the waters prevail; and the mountains were covered." The Ark rested "upon the mountains of Ararat" in present-day Turkey, about 600 miles from where Noah embarked. Many trips have been taken into the mountains of Ararat but no Ark has been found. None will ever be found because it is a fictional account.

Now let's look at what really happened and see how the flood stories came to be. We know that tribes of people around the world—even oceanic tribes—had stories of floods in which their hero and family were saved. How could so many different people have stories of a flood if it were not one actual flood over the whole earth? About 70,000 years ago there began a cooling trend that resulted in what American scientists call the Wisconsin Glaciation Period. This ice age reached its peak about 20,000 years ago. There were so many glaciers and ice sheets on the earth that ocean levels were about 300 to 500 feet lower than now. The Bering strait between Asia and North America was dry, and people used it to come to North America. The floor of the English Channel was dry and the British Isles were united with the European Continent. Continental shelves hundreds of miles from present shorelines were dry and became living areas for many people during the thousands of years of lower ocean levels. When the climate began to warm and the ice began to melt, the water ran back into the sea. The levels rose perhaps four or five feet during a century. Finally there came a time when certain groups of people had to move to higher ground. When mountain tops became islands, the only people who could leave became heroes. As in the story of Noah, they told their stories to their grandchildren.

Even oceanic tribes one day had to leave their islands, which became submerged, and these people too had stories to tell their grandchildren. The oceans reached their present levels about 8,000 years ago, and the stories came to the writers of the Bible from several sources. It is easy to see why all groups of people had flood stories to tell and why all of them are true or at least based on true events. The authors of the *J* version wrote their story about 850 B.C. and the *P* version was written about 500 B.C. There are variations in their stories, but the fact that the stories were combined and put into the Bible is what interests us today. We know that Egypt didn't flood to the point where everyone died. In the temples we find a continuity of their history spanning the time of the biblical Flood. It was during the early 1800s that scientists learned that the earth had been almost covered with water—not liquid, but frozen. About $\frac{1}{3}$ of the land surface of the earth was under ice sheets that averaged a mile thick.

Now that we know the natural reason for the Flood stories, why would we look for supernatural reasons?

4   *The Story of Babel*

◆ Genesis 11:1-9

> And the whole earth was of one language, and of one speech. And it came to pass, as they journeyed from the east, that they found a plain in the land of Shinar; and they dwelt there.

This speaks about the family of Noah because they were the only people on earth if the story of the Flood is true. They left the Ark and went on a to find a good area in which to build a city. When they found a site they set up housekeeping. Naturally they all spoke the same language. "And they said, 'Go to, let us build us a city and a tower, whose top may reach unto heaven; and let us make us a name, lest we be scattered abroad upon the face of the whole earth.'" All they wanted was a place to live and some way to help them find their way home when they wandered out of town: the tower.

The city must have been impressive: "And the LORD came down to see the city and the tower, which the children of men builded." The Lord wasn't happy with them so he decided to "confound their language," and "scatter them abroad upon the face of the whole earth." This story took place only about 100 years after the Flood, so there could not have been many people to scatter. Noah's family probably consisted of fewer than two hundred people. Nimrod was a "mighty hunter before the LORD.

And the beginning of his kingdom was Babel" (Genesis 10:9-10). Nimrod was Noah's great-grandson—about four generations. Noah had three sons and sixteen grandsons, allowing thirty years for a generation does not produce a crowd.

We don't know much about the language of that time. Nothing is told us about what language Adam and Eve spoke, what language God spoke, or what languages came out of the confusion of tongues. While some languages were written then, such as Egyptian, Babylonian, Sumerian and Akkadian, Hebrew was not a written language until about 1000 B.C. It is probable that some other tribes came to town speaking a different language and those events caused the story. Even today people with different languages get along and manage to learn some means of communication. What logical reason could there be to scatter when only a couple of hundred people existed? This story was simply invented to account for the diversity of languages.

There was no basis for a factual account, and all that was intended was a type of child's story to explain the diversity. Scientific evidence shows there were about one to two million people on earth then and that there were many languages spoken. Since there was no single flood where the population was reduced to eight souls, those people were already living in regions around the Mediterranean Sea and over to the Persian Gulf.

This fiction is not the story of a miracle but only a tale that was passed on through the years and found its way into the Bible.

5   *A Pharaoh's Plague*

◆ Genesis 12:10-20

> And there was a famine in the land: and Abram went down into Egypt to sojourn there; for the famine was grievous in the land.

Abram and his wife Sarai (that's Abraham and Sarah before their names were changed) went to Egypt because of a famine in their own land. Since Sarai was a beautiful woman, she and Abram concluded that if an Egyptian should want to take her they would have to kill Abram. So they agreed to say that she was his sister. Sarai actually *was* Abram's sister: "She is the daughter of my father, but not the daughter of my mother" (Genesis 20:12). Abram was right: "the Egyptians beheld the woman that she was very fair . . . and the woman was taken into Pharaoh's house. And he entreated Abram well for her sake: and he had sheep, and oxen, and he asses, and menservants, and maidservants, and she asses, and camels." Pharaoh wanted Sarai, and he was willing to give Abram a good price for her in animals and servants.

"And the LORD plagued Pharaoh and his house with great plagues because of Sarai Abram's wife." Now, there is a problem with a plague coming into Pharaoh's house. Abram deceived Pharaoh and accepted his offer, but rather than punish him, God punishes Pharaoh and rewards Abram. How could such deception be rewarded by a just god? We don't know what the plague was, but we do know plagues come and go independent of any specific moral conduct. It was pure coincidence that anything at all happened, but the writers made the most of it, and Abram won and got richer. What did Abram learn from this episode? He learned that crime does pay, and so, a little later, we will see him doing the same thing and again come out richer.

This story is derived from the *J* source and the same story was retold later from the *E* source in Genesis 20. It was proper for the Hebrews to borrow from the Egyptians because they were God's Chosen People while the Egyptians were mere pagans. We shall see with the story of the Exodus that the Hebrews again lie to the Egyptians and take everything they can beg, borrow, or steal.

There is no miracle in this story; it is only a tale of blessing to the Hebrew and curse on the Egyptian, a common theme in the Bible stories.

6   Smoking Furnace and Burning Lamp Dream

◆ Genesis 15

> In the same day the LORD made a covenant with Abram, saying, "Unto thy seed have I given this land, from the river of Egypt unto the great river, the river Euphrates."

Abram had just defeated Chedorlaomer, the king of Elam, and God decided to bless Abram again. Even though Abram had no children, God was going to bless his seed with all the land from the Nile to the Euphrates. To seal the covenant, Abram offered a heifer, a she goat, a ram, a turtledove and a young pigeon. The animals were cut in halves and put on the altar, and while Abram waited for God so they could walk between the halves, Abram fell asleep. "And when the sun was going down, a deep sleep fell upon Abram. And it came to pass, that, when the sun went down, and it was dark, behold a smoking furnace, and a burning lamp that passed between those pieces." It is clear from these verses that Abram dreamed the whole episode of the "smoking furnace and burning lamp." The fire in this story was the symbol of God and in his dream Abram believed he had made a covenant with God. It is usually in a dream or a vision that God appears to man. History shows Abram never possessed all this land. Abram's son Isaac never possessed it either. Jacob never got it. The promise never was fulfilled in all the history of the Bible. It was from this dream-story that the Jews claimed ownership of Palestine in 1948.

No wonder the promise never happened for Abram, Isaac or Jacob—it was only a dream. We read about this story in the Book of Hebrews, too, but the writer thought it was a true story. The author tells of the faith of these heroes and says, "These all died in faith, not having received the promises" (Hebrews 11:13). In Christian times these promises of physical land were transferred into promises of a heavenly land. No longer were the faithful to wait for something in this life—they were to wait as we are now taught: "We will have pie in the sky when we die."

There is no miracle of God's presence in this story. It was only a natural dream.

7   *Sarah's Conception of Isaac*

◆ Genesis 17:1-22; 18:9-15; 21:1-8

> And when Abram was ninety years old and nine, the LORD appeared to Abram and said unto him, "I am the Almighty God; walk before me, and be thou perfect. And I will make my covenant between me and thee, and will multiply thee exceedingly."

This is the *P* version of the story we just read.

> "Neither shall thy name any more be called Abram, but thy name shall be Abraham." And God said unto Abraham, "As for Sarai thy wife, thou shalt not call her name Sarai, but Sarah shall her name be. And I will bless her, and give thee a son also of her."

At that time Abraham was 99 and Sarah 90 years old. Much is made of Sarah's age but advanced age was nothing special in Genesis. Adam and Eve were both 130 when Seth was born, and we read they had more children after Seth. Noah, and probably his wife too, were 500 years old when they had their triplets, Shem, Ham and Japheth.

When stories are fabricated, anything can and usually does happen. Only the men's ages are given in Genesis 5, but we may infer that the women were about the same ages; those ages were often over 100 years. Let us not forget that we are not dealing with facts here, but stories written to show God's power by miracles. Priests made up these stories to show God's promises. The stories, in turn, showed God's power and gifts to those who obeyed him. The object was to inspire obedience. Obedience would produce devout followers who would also be blessed by God. In this *P* story God established his covenant with Abraham, and Sarah was promised a child to receive the blessings of God. We read of many women who were barren, and only after visitations of God or angels were they able to bear offspring.

I believe the reason for their barrenness was hysteria brought on by their anxiety, fear, and stress to bear sons for their husbands. In biblical times it was very important for a man to have male children, and this put tremendous pressure on the woman. When the wife was slow in producing children, she was made to feel guilty, and these emotions triggered hysterical barrenness in many women. So great was the demand for children that the Patriarchs had children by additional wives—handmaids of their wives—or even concubines. The Hebrew belief in immortality was that as long as someone remembered them after they died, it would be as if they lived again. Thus they had children in order to be remembered. There is an Egyptian proverb that says, "To speak of the dead is to make them live again." In this story Sarah said, "Shall I of a surety bear a child, which am old?" When she was assured the LORD could cause her to have a child, she believed it. When she calmed down and accepted the suggestion that she would bear a child, she overcame her hysteria and became pregnant. In stories found in the Bible, women who were long barren all bore sons who became great men. This is a clue that the stories were made up. Whether Sarah was barren and finally had a son or the story was copied from someone else, we are still dealing with natural occurrences.

Is it logical to seek supernatural reasons for natural childbirth?

8 *The Blinded Sodomites*

◆ Genesis 19:1-11

> And there came two angels to Sodom at even; and Lot sat in the gate of Sodom.

Lot invited them to his house and fed them,

> But before they lay down, the men of the city, even the men of Sodom, compassed the house round, both old and young, all the people from every quarter: And they called unto Lot, and said unto him, "Where are the men which came in to thee this night? Bring them out unto us, that we may know them."

Lot went out and tried to get rid of the people but they wouldn't leave. He even offered them his two virgin daughters but they wanted the two men instead. "But the men put forth their hand, and pulled Lot into the house to them, and shut the door. And they smote the men that were at the door of the house with blindness, both small and great." The two men then told Lot to take his family and leave town because they were going to destroy it. The two *angels* have now become two *men*.

This story portrays the men of Sodom as evil. They wanted to take the two men who were in the house of Lot and "know them." Though Lot would not give them the men he just met, he offered the Sodomites his two virgin daughters! But the people only wanted the two men. When the two visitors pulled Lot back into the house, they caused the crowd to be blinded. How the people were blinded we are not told, but several possibilities come to mind. The simple solution would be to throw some type of irritating dust in their eyes. It appears, however, to have been a natural event rather than a supernatural blinding. Sodom was built over petroleum deposits. Various gases and sulfur are commonly found with petroleum deposits. Sodom was destroyed by fire from an earthquake. It is likely that these gases burst out of the ground, and sulfur, or brimstone, was mixed with gases, irritated the eyes and the people were blinded. It was then that the visitors made Lot, his wife and their two daughters leave Sodom.

There are enough natural means to blind the people that we need not look for some supernatural reason.

Let's look now at what happened to Sodom.

9　*The Destruction of Sodom and Gomorrah*

◆ Genesis 19:12-29

> The sun was risen upon the earth when Lot entered into Zoar. Then the LORD rained upon Sodom and upon Gomorrah brimstone and fire from the LORD out of heaven; And he overthrew those cities, and all the plain, and all the inhabitants of the cities, and that which grew upon the ground. . . . And Abraham got up early in the morning to the place where he stood before the LORD: And he looked toward Sodom and Gomorrah, and toward all the land of the plain, and beheld, and, lo, the smoke of the country went up as the smoke of a furnace.

Sodom and Gomorrah were supposed to have been on the shores of the Dead Sea, but we don't know exactly where they were.

In ancient times the Dead Sea was called Lake Asphaltitis because of the asphalt around the area. Slime pits all around the area would collect asphalt, a good income-producing venture. Asphalt, or pitch, as it was also called, was used to seal boats, like Noah's Ark. With petroleum and natural gas below the city and asphalt all around it, we have a situation ripe for disaster.

The Jericho fault runs under the Dead Sea and through Jericho on the north and Sodom on the south. When an earthquake fractured the rock it allowed the gases and petroleum to reach the surface. It would only have taken a spark from an overturned lamp to ignite it and the disaster would be underway. The cities, the people, the trees, shrubs, and every-thing upon the ground went up in flames. The smoke was black "as the smoke of a furnace" and it probably burned for many days until the pressure was relieved and the supply of fuel burned out.

Other earthquakes along the Jericho fault may account for the destruction of the walls of Jericho later credited to Joshua. Earthquakes on this fault also accounted for blockages of the Jordan River as we will see when we come to Joshua. When the city was destroyed we do not know. The writer of this account told a story to make this point that the priests wanted to get across: When people break God's holy laws they are punished. To make it clear the Sodomites were shown as wicked and immoral. By showing their destruction to be the work of God, the moral of the story was easily understood by those who would later hear or read it. The power of the priesthood was the basis of this story, and we shall see many more like it.

There was no need of supernatural events to destroy Sodom and Gomorrah. The elements of nature were adequate to destroy the cities.

10   *The Story of Lot's Wife*

◆ Genesis 19:17-38

> Escape for thy life; look not behind thee, neither stay thou in all the plain; escape to the mountain, lest thou be consumed. . . . But his wife looked back from behind him, and she became a pillar of salt.

All she did was look back to see what was going on and she was turned into a pillar of salt. As Lot and his daughters hurried out of town, Lot's wife was behind them, and because they didn't look back how could they really know what happened to her? Wives customarily walk behind their husbands in oriental cultures even to this day.

When the story was written the ending was made up to suit the circumstances. No one knew what happened to Lot's wife, so the priests decided to make her disobey and be punished for her sins. She literally became the salt of the earth. She may have been overcome by the deadly gases from the ground. She may have been crushed by a falling building. She may have been killed by flying rocks from the explosions. She may even have decided to stay and died in the fire. We just don't know. There were many pillars of salt in the area because salt was one of the main business interests in that area. Even today some guides point out a pillar of salt and claim it to have been Lot's wife. Tourists will believe almost anything an apparently learned guide tells them, so the story still lives.

> When Lot and his daughters escaped . . . he dwelt in a cave, he and his two daughters. And the firstborn said unto the younger, "Our father is old, and there is not a man in the earth to come in unto us after the manner of all the earth: Come, let us make our father drink wine, and we will lie with him, that we may preserve seed of our father."

So both lie with Lot, conceive, and bear sons. These two sons become Moab and Benammi, and it is they who father the Moabites and the Ammonites "unto this day." In the Genesis stories we find such tales of individuals who founded entire nations. It is simply a case of priests making up stories to explain that cities were founded by their ancestors with the help of God.

In these stories we see the priests using supernatural explanations for natural phenomena. Stories showed the power of God and therefore their own power as representatives of God. Even in this story of incest, the end was shown to justify the means: such was the power of the priestly author.

No miracle is needed to account for the demise of Lot's wife. It is sad enough that she didn't even get a name of her own, but to make her a sinner besides is too much.

11 The Story of the Closed Wombs

◆ Genesis 20

> And Abraham said of Sarah his wife, "She is my sister": and Abimelech king of Gerar sent, and took Sarah. But God came to Abimelech in a dream by night, and said to him, "Behold, thou art but a dead man, for the woman which thou hast taken; for she is a man's wife."

Again Abraham claimed that Sarah, his wife, was his sister, and another king got in trouble with God.

> Abraham said, "Because I thought surely the fear of God is not in this place; and they will slay me for my wife's sake. And yet indeed she is my sister; she is the daughter of my father, but not the daughter of my mother; and she became my wife."

Here we see Abraham rewarded:

> And Abimelech took sheep, and oxen, and menservants, and womenservants, and gave them unto Abraham, and restored him Sarah his wife. And unto Sarah he said, "Behold, I have given thy brother a thousand pieces of silver. . . ." So Abraham prayed unto God: and God healed Abimelech, and his wife, and his maidservants; and they bare children. For the LORD had fast closed up all the wombs of the house of Abimelech, because of Sarah Abraham's wife.

Here we find only slight punishment for king Abimelech, while in Genesis 12 we saw Pharaoh and his house afflicted with a plague. This is the same story as Genesis 12, but from the *E* source, whereas *J* is the source of Genesis 12. Again the innocent king was punished, and God richly rewarded and even honored Abraham, the guilty.

What a system of morality presented in these stories. Though Genesis 12 is set in Egypt and this story is set in Gerar with a Philistine king, both are included in the Bible. In this story Sarah is 90 years old, still beautiful, and desired by a king. About 94 years later, Abraham's son, Isaac, and his wife, Rebecca, play the same game with Abimelech, king of the Philistines. The credibility of the Bible begins to suffer. The priests were trying to show that no matter what God's chosen heroes did, they were under his protection. If they lied, cheated, and stole he would still bless them.

We need not look for anything supernatural in this story because it was clearly a fabrication of the priests.

12   *Hagar and the Well*

◆   Genesis 21:1-21

> Abraham made a great feast the same day that Isaac was weaned. And Sarah saw the son of Hagar the Egyptian, which she had born unto Abraham, mocking. Wherefore she said unto Abraham, "Cast out this bondwoman and her son: for the son of this bondwoman shall not be heir with my son, even with Isaac." And the thing was very grievous in Abraham's sight because of his son.

This is a sad story because Hagar and Ishmael were thrown out of Abraham and Sarah's home because of Sarah's selfishness. It was Sarah herself, about eighteen years before, who had given Hagar to Abraham to be his wife (Genesis 16:2-3). Now Sarah didn't want them around so she told Abraham to get rid of them. Abraham gave Hagar and Ishmael bread and water and sent them packing. Ishmael was put under a shrub in the wilderness of Beer-Sheba and left to die. Hagar went a few hundred feet away so she would not have to see him die. As Ishmael cried out, God heard his cry and told Hagar that Ishmael was to become a great nation. At the same time, "God opened her eyes and she saw a well of water." Ishmael grew and became the father of the Arab nations while Isaac carried on from Abraham and became the leader of the Hebrew nation.

This story contains no miracle. The well was not specially created; rather, Hagar was already near the well and simply found it and saved herself and her son from thirst. If Hagar heard a voice, it was probably a hysteric hallucination caused by fear of death and anxiety about the welfare of Ishmael. In a state of hysteria some people experience hallucinations in any of the five senses. Hagar thought she heard the voice of an angel telling her to look around to find a well. Once she calmed down she did look around, finding a well that had been there all the time. Another explanation for the voice Hagar heard could be the most simple. Abraham could have sent someone to make sure Hagar found water for herself and Ishmael. Because of her thirst and fear for her life and Ishmael's life, she, as many others in the Bible, thought an angel visited and spoke to them.

This was not a supernatural manifestation of God because it didn't take a miracle to look around and see what was already there.

Chapter 3

Stories of Moses

13 *Moses and His Miracles*

◆ Exodus 1-2

> Now there arose up a new king over Egypt, which knew not Joseph. . . . And he said, "When ye do the office of a midwife to the Hebrew women, and see them upon the stools; if it be a son, then ye shall kill him: but if it be a daughter, then she shall live. . . ." And there went a man of the house of Levi, and took to wife a daughter of Levi. And the woman conceived, and bare a son: and when she saw him that he was a goodly child, she hid him three months. And when she could not longer hide him, she took for him an ark of bulrushes, and daubed it with slime and with pitch, and put the child therein; and she laid it in the flags by the river's brink. And his sister stood afar off, to wit what would be done to him.

So Moses was in the river and Pharaoh's daughter found him. Moses' sister quickly went to Pharaoh's daughter and said, "Shall I go and call thee a nurse of the Hebrew women?" And so Moses' own mother nursed him.

Moses was raised in Pharaoh's court for forty years, living in the lap of luxury. When he killed an Egyptian for smiting a Hebrew he left Egypt. He went to Midian, married a priest's daughter, tended his father-in-law's flocks and lived there for forty years. After the episode of the burning bush he went back to Egypt. He did his tricks for Pharaoh and led the Israelites out through the desert for another forty years and died just before they entered Canaan. The story of the birth of Moses was copied from the story of Sargon, a Babylonian king who lived about

39

2850 B.C. Sargon was born in Armenia, and his mother put him in a basket much like the ark of Moses and let it go in the Euphrates river. Sargon was found by Akki, a gardener. The Goddess Ishtar loved Sargon and made him king of Babylonia.

In *Moses and Monotheism* Freud says Moses was an Egyptian sympathetic to the Hebrews. While the story of Moses' birth told about his sister, there is no mention of a brother just three years older than Moses. When Aaron was finally mentioned he was to be spokesman for Moses because they had to negotiate with Pharaoh to get the Hebrews out of Egypt. I think Freud was correct about Moses. Moses needed Aaron to help negotiate with the Hebrews because he spoke very little Hebrew himself. With Aaron as a *political* brother, stories of the deliverance coupled Moses and Aaron until they finally made Moses a Hebrew and *blood brother* to Aaron. The name Moses was Egyptian, and though he married a Midianite woman his children's names were also Egyptian.

It was Moses who introduced the ritual of circumcision to the Hebrews. He borrowed it from the Midianites. His father-in-law, Jethro, was a Priest of Midian and much, if not most, of Moses' knowledge of God came from Jethro. This was a *J* story of the circumcision and the *P* story was in Genesis 17 where it said Abraham first practiced it. The *J* is 400 years older than the *P* version. The priests wrote *P* to show the ritual to be older than Moses by 500 years. To understand the Bible, it is important to know who wrote the various parts and when they were written. Then we can see why they were written. It was Jethro, the Priest of Midian, who taught Moses about Yahweh. Moses finally believed he met Yahweh on Mt. Sinai or Horeb. That was why Moses brought the Israelites to Mt. Sinai when he led them out of Egypt. It was there that he introduced them to Yahweh and put together a religion with laws; it was there that the Hebrew nation and religion was established. Abraham, Isaac and Jacob had nothing to do with the Hebrew religion. It was convenient for Moses to use their names as a means of extending Hebrew history. This then pushed it all the way back to Adam when they later formulated a genealogy. Moses had never heard of Adam and Eve—that was not written until centuries after Moses died. Moses was credited with writing the first five books of the Bible, but Hebrew was not a written language until 1000 B.C., around the time of David or Solomon, about 400 years after Moses died.

The priests used Moses as the lawgiver because that gave them power in their time when they wrote the laws. In their stories they showed that lawbreakers were punished and that those who kept the laws were rewarded. This gave them power over the people, helped maintain law and order, and kept the offerings coming in. With Moses as their founder, the priests could write their menu. It was the priesthood that decided what the people were to offer and on which days. It was the priesthood that received the offerings of the people.

These stories of Moses and the founding of the Hebrew nation were the last to have been written, and Moses had nothing to do with them. During and shortly after the Babylonian Exile in the 6th and 5th centuries B.C. the priests wrote these stories to gain power and prestige for themselves. "Now the man Moses was very meek, above all the men which were upon the face of the earth" (Numbers 12:3). I believe Moses would be appalled to see how the men of the cloth today are as proud and arrogant as any king or tyrant who ever lived.

Moses was not a product of the supernatural, nor did Moses use the supernatural. All that Moses did was done by sleight of hand, trickery, illusion or other natural means. Nothing miraculous took place in the life of Moses.

14 *Moses and the Burning Bush*

◆ Exodus 3

> Now Moses kept the flock of Jethro his father-in-law, the priest of Midian: and he led the flock to the backside of the desert, and came to the mountain of God, even to Horeb. And the angel of the LORD appeared unto him in a flame of fire out of the midst of a bush: and he looked, and, behold, the bush burned with fire, and the bush was not consumed.

Moses was about 80 at the time he saw this burning bush. It didn't even startle him when "God called unto him out of the midst of the bush, and said, 'Moses, Moses'." And he said, "Here am I." If you notice carefully, you will see miracles of all types in the Bible stories accepted as everyday occurrences. Even when the dead were raised only a ho-hum attitude is evoked as if it were nothing new or different. Here a voice called Moses and he simply answered, "Here am I." Then the voice said, "I am the God of thy father, the God of Abraham, the God of Isaac, and the God of Jacob. And Moses hid his face; for he was afraid to look upon God." What would *you* do if you heard a voice from a bush, let alone a voice that claimed to be God's? The most incredible thing that ever happened in his 80 years and all he did was "hide his face." Amazing how nonchalant the writers assumed their characters to be. What was really going on in the bush that Moses saw? How could there be a fire and nothing be burned?

An easy solution presents itself when one understands that the area was atop a petroleum deposit—and with petroleum there is natural gas. An earthquake would fracture the rock, allowing natural gas to seep up through the crack. Lightning, sparks, or flames brought to the site would ignite the gas as an "eternal flame." The flame was in the midst of a bush, and the limbs around the flame would have burned away. The fire would appear to burn the bush but it could not consume the bush. Such jets of flame that crown the escaping gases are not uncommon even today. In ancient times sun worshipers made up fables about them or even built temples or shrines over them. The voice Moses heard could have been a trick played on him by a fellow shepherd. It might even have been some Hebrew from Egypt who wanted Moses to help them get out of bondage. Most likely, it was a hysteric hallucination brought on by seeing the flame and experiencing anxiety or even fear.

It was not uncommon for people to hear voices. Even now we read about people who claim God speaks to them. This story of the call of Moses is a combination of *J* and *E* sources and occurred in the wilderness of Midian. Exodus 6:2-7;7 is the *P* account of the call of Moses and it took place in Egypt. In *P* there was no burning bush, but Moses did hear God introducing himself as the God of Abraham, Isaac and Jacob. In Exodus 3 God said his name was I AM THAT I AM. In Exodus 6 he said his name was JEHOVAH. In either case we have God calling Moses to tell Pharaoh to set the Israelites free. In Exodus 3 we saw Moses being told to take off his shoes. We will see this again in Joshua 5:13-15 when God calls Joshua and tells him to take off his shoes. It is important to recognize that this was a common formula for the call and commission of a servant of God. When Isaiah was called in Isaiah 6:1-8 the same type of call was given as Isaiah was selected to be God's servant and spokesman.

In all cases it was but a natural event being described. Though the stories were fabricated, they were possibly based on similar natural events—only the names were changed to exalt their own heroes.

15   *The Story of Moses' Rod*

◆ Exodus 4:1-5, 29-31; 7:8-13

> And Moses answered and said, "But, behold, they will not believe me, nor hearken unto my voice: for they will say, the LORD hath not appeared unto thee." And the LORD said unto him, "What is that in thy hand?" And he said, "A rod." And he said, "Cast it on the ground." And he cast it on the ground, and it became a serpent; and Moses fled from before it. And the LORD said unto Moses, Put forth thine hand, and take it by the tail. And he put forth his hand, and caught it, and it became a rod in his hand.

That sounds great to have a stick that became a snake and then was a stick again. According to the *Abingdon Bible Commentary:* "Snake charmers in the East do, even in the present day, by a sort of hypnotism, render snakes rigid so that they can be held in the hand as rods."

In a time and an area where magic and trickery were very important, people found ways to do all kinds of strange things. This snake-and-rod trick was done three times: in the wilderness (Exodus 4:1-5); before the elders of Israel (Exodus 4:29-31); and before Pharaoh (Exodus 7:10-12). The trick was common and was even done by Pharaoh's magicians in Exodus 7:11. In the show put on for Pharaoh we meet a new character. Aaron the Levite, supposed to be the brother of Moses, came to act as the spokesman for Moses. Moses complained and ". . . said unto the LORD, 'O my LORD, I am not eloquent, neither heretofore, nor since thou hast spoken unto thy servant but I am slow of speech, and of a slow tongue.'" According to Sigmund Freud in his book, *Moses and Monotheism*, Moses was an Egyptian. What he meant by "slow of speech" was that Moses couldn't speak Hebrew very well, so Aaron the Hebrew became his spokesman. The Bible said Moses and Aaron were brothers, but Freud says they were only political brothers in the cause of freedom for the Hebrews in Egypt.

This was only stage magic, done not only by Moses and Aaron, but also by the magicians of Pharaoh. Certainly God would not let the heathen Egyptians do miracles. Only natural means were used—nothing supernatural need be read into the story.

16　Moses and the Leprous Hand

◆　Exodus 4:6-12, 29-31

> And the LORD said furthermore unto him, Put now thine hand into thy bosom. And he put his hand into his bosom: and when he took it out, behold, his hand was leprous as snow. And he said, Put thine hand into thy bosom again. And he put his hand into his bosom again; and plucked it out of his bosom, and, behold, it was turned again as his other flesh.

This was all done while Moses was alone in the wilderness and was merely a rehearsal for his appearance before the elders of Israel. When he did this sign along with the snake-and-rod trick for the elders of Israel, they believed and agreed to follow him.

To accomplish this trick all Moses would have needed was a glove made up to look like a leprous hand. He could have put the glove inside his coat later to withdraw his hand with the glove on to look like a leprous hand. The glove and hand could easily and quickly have been hidden and withdrawn. People were easily fooled in those days. After elders of Israel saw the leprous-hand trick it wasn't used again on Pharaoh like the snake trick was.

"And it shall come to pass, if they will not believe also these two signs, neither hearken unto thy voice, that thou shalt take of the water of the river, and pour it upon the dry land: and the water which thou takest out of the river shall become blood upon the dry land."

Moses did not do this trick in the wilderness or for the elders of Israel. It was different from the first plague when the whole river was turned to blood. This was to be used only if needed, and it simply wasn't needed.

As in the other stories, no miracle is in evidence. Only sleight of hand was used—a purely natural exhibition.

17   *The Ten Plagues Collectively*

◆ Exodus 7-12

The story of the ten plagues is a long and involved story, and we shall look at several aspects to see if we can make some sense of it. We shall look at it collectively and at each plague separately, and we shall find some characteristics that will help us to understand the stories. First there is an overview of the whole story seen from the natural outcome of one spectacular event. Scholars have spent years studying history, geology, theology, volcanology, and whatever else was necessary to form a cohesive account of the Exodus. 1 Kings 6:1 tells us that Solomon's Temple was started 480 years after the Exodus began. As the Temple was begun around 1000 B.C., the Exodus would have been about 1480 B.C. As scholars studied this period of history they found something of great interest.

About 1477 B.C. the volcano on the Island of Santorini erupted and sent a column of dust, ash and smoke about twenty miles into the air. Hans Goedicke, an Egyptologist from Johns Hopkins University, believes this cloud drifted the 600 miles across the Mediterranean Sea and caused three days of darkness in Egypt. The iron oxides present in the dust that settled into the river turned the water red as blood. It poisoned the fish while it also drove the frogs onto the shore. Meteorological disturbances that accompany volcanic action also can produce high winds and heavy rains that could cause hailstorms. The winds may well have carried in the locusts that consumed any remaining crops not destroyed by the hail. Without anything for the livestock to eat, the flocks would starve. Insects such as flies, mosquitoes and gnats feeding on the carcasses would easily bring disease to remaining cattle and humans. There could have been so much death resulting from these natural causes that it would be called the killing of the firstborn of people and beasts. There is great merit to this theory, which is logical, well-timed, and covers all the plagues mentioned.

One other collective feature was the apparent ability of Moses and Aaron to have access to, and spend so much time with, Pharaoh. Not even the political favorites of a national leader get to have so much personal contact with a ruler, let alone one who is an obvious enemy. Why would Pharaoh have allowed Moses and Aaron to live, let alone cause such torment, destruction and death in Egypt? It would be unusual for someone to have an audience with a ruler once, let alone as often as Moses and Aaron did with Pharaoh. This is a hint to me about the credibility of the story. When we study Elijah later we will see the same accessibility to a king that suggests to me that the stories are make-believe. No king has that much respect for a friend, let alone an enemy.

I think the key to this whole series of plagues stories is in one verse: "And the LORD said unto Moses, When thou goest to return into Egypt, see that thou do all those wonders before Pharaoh, which I have put in thine hand: but I will harden his heart, that he shall not let the people go" (Exodus 4:21). That is the clue we need to keep in mind as we study each miracle story. Pharaoh had no choice in the matter. God is said to have hardened his heart. This gave power and prestige to the priesthood who proclaimed themselves to be the spokesmen of God. Here natural events are given an overlay of supernatural causes and said to have been miracles produced by God. Priests have put their imprint on history and claimed it as the doings of their gods.

Let's look at each plague separately and see how natural occurrences were made to look like supernatural events.

18   *The Nile Turns Red*

◆   Exodus 7:14-24

> And Moses and Aaron did so, as the LORD commanded; and he lifted up the rod, and smote the waters that were in the river, in the sight of Pharaoh, and in the sight of his servants; and all the waters that were in the river were turned to blood. And the fish that was in the river died; and the river stank. . . . And the magicians of Egypt did so with their enchantments.

Notice that the magicians could do just as Moses and Aaron did. They too could turn the water red, so we know there was some sort of trick involved. All one needed to do this trick was to put iron oxides into the water and it would turn red and poison the fish. When there is volcanic action around water, and iron oxides are present, it has the same effect today.

The Egyptians of that day were familiar with the annual flood cycle of the Nile. The water became discolored by decaying vegetable matter or by reddish soil from upstream. These discolorations were not harmful to the fish, however, so while it could account for the appearance it would not cause the fish to die. If a person really wanted to believe the story literally they would have to believe all the water in the 4,000 mile-long Nile turned to blood. It would take a lot more than seven days to clear the water from source to mouth. Also one must wonder what the Egyptians did for water for those seven days if "all the waters of Egypt," their streams, rivers, ponds and pools became blood.

When you decide to believe the Bible word-for-word there is no room for error, misunderstanding, mistranslation or make-believe. You have to take it as it is written no matter how farfetched it may be. One characteristic of these plague stories is that they all have natural explanations and yearly patterns, some of which still occur. As we will see with the other plagues, there is no need for miracles. Before we go on to the frogs, let's look at another verse, "And Pharaoh's heart was hardened" (Exodus 7:22). We will see this repeatedly as we proceed through the plague stories. You may have thought that Pharaoh decided to harden his heart, but as we go on you will see he had no choice in the matter.

Whether the water turned red because of natural causes or man-made causes, no supernatural occurrence took place.

19   *The Frogs*

◆ Exodus 8:1-15

> And the LORD spake unto Moses, "Say unto Aaron, Stretch forth thy hand with thy rod over the streams, over the rivers, and over the ponds, and cause frogs to come up upon the land of Egypt." And Aaron stretched out his hand over the waters of Egypt; and the frogs came up, and covered the land of Egypt. And the magicians did so with their enchantments, and brought up frogs upon the land of Egypt.

It may be supposed that the discolorations of the Nile were due to great quantities of decaying vegetable matter. This condition would be favorable to the multiplication of the frogs. Plagues of frogs were common to Egypt in September. After the Nile flooded, the putrid marshes would be excellent breeding places for frogs. Perfectly natural means produced great numbers of frogs many times over thousands of years. Why should this specific occasion be singled out as a miracle when the rest were not?

The only thing that would make a person think there was something peculiar in the story was the ability of the magicians to produce frogs. If this was in Egyptian literature it would be seen as a means of exposing Aaron for the trick he did. When it is in the inspired text of the Bible, it can only be accepted by the literalists as fact. If magicians could do what Moses and Aaron did, why wasn't it considered a miracle? In reality it comes down to a simple statement: When God's people did it, it was a miracle, when anyone else did it, it was witchcraft.

Pharaoh finally had had enough of the frogs, so he called Moses and Aaron. He said, "Entreat the LORD, that he may take away the frogs from me, and from my people." When "Pharaoh saw that there was respite, he hardened his heart." This time Pharaoh hardened his own heart, but God said he would harden Pharaoh's heart—remember this.

Why would anyone look for a supernatural source of frogs when nature can handle the job?

20   *The Lice*

◆   Exodus 8:16-19

> And the LORD said unto Moses, "Say unto Aaron, 'Stretch out thy rod, and smite the dust of the land, that it may become lice throughout all the land of Egypt.'" And they did so; for Aaron stretched out his hand with his rod, and smote the dust of the earth, and it became lice in man, and in beast; all the dust of the land became lice throughout all the land of Egypt. And the magicians did so with their enchantments to bring forth lice, but they could not.

This story is a bit different from the last two. In those two, Pharaoh was given an advance warning of what God was going to do. That warning was enough for the magicians to prepare their tricks to match what Moses and Aaron said would happen. In this story, because there was no advance warning, the magicians were unable to turn dust to lice.

Scholars tell us the word lice should be mosquitoes or gnats, for they are abundant in Egypt. Because they attack man and beast suggests that mosquitoes or gnats is the likely interpretation, and swarms of them often look like clouds of dust. It is a far reach to believe that "all the dust of the land became lice throughout all the land of Egypt." As dusty as Egypt is, this is an exaggeration that defies all understanding and reason. While the Nile was in flood, mosquitoes and gnats rose in swarms from the flooded rice fields and the air was darkened by them. Their sting would have caused swelling and irritation, and in this story there is no mention of the removal of the pests.

The story of the lice is the *P* version, and the following story of the flies is the *J* version. The main differences were in the way the stories were introduced and the way they ended. There was no warning of the lice and they were not removed. There was warning of the flies and they were later removed. The results of this story are common to the others, "and Pharaoh's heart was hardened."

In either case we are looking at a natural occurrence—nothing supernatural was needed to aid nature.

21   *The Flies*

◆ Exodus 8:20-32

> And there came a grievous swarm of flies into the house of Pharaoh, and into his servant's houses, and into all the Land of Egypt: the land was corrupted by reason of the swarm of flies.

This story is simply the *J* version of the last story from the *P* source. It is important to notice that all seven times the swarm of flies is mentioned, the word *flies* is in italics. Use of italics in the Bible means the word was not in the original text, or at least not the one being translated. No one knows what was intended when it was written. The authors of the King James Version (KJV) in 1611 put in the word *flies,* so that is what we have today. Some scholars think it refers to some type of beetle, but that is only a guess. The swarms of insects were limited in such a way to infest only the houses of the Egyptians. None were found in the land of Goshen where the Israelites lived.

The land of Goshen was given to the Israelites as a place to live because it was separated from the Egyptian cities. The Israelites were herdsmen, and the Egyptians didn't want to live near them. According to Genesis 46:34 the reason given was "for every shepherd is an abomination unto the Egyptians." This was the first time the plague was not visited upon the Israelites, and we shall see this same division in some later plagues, too.

Now it was not unusual for swarms of flies, mosquitoes, gnats or sand flies to be seen in Egypt—especially from all the dead and decaying frogs. This seemed even more overwhelming than usual as they even destroyed crops in the fields. As mentioned in the last story, this plague was announced in advance and removed when Pharaoh agreed to let the people go. One other major difference was the absence of flies in Goshen. Pharaoh was now willing to let Israel sacrifice in Egypt even though it would offend the Egyptians. Moses refused the offer and said, "We will go three days' journey into the wilderness, and sacrifice to the LORD our God, as he shall command us." Pharaoh said the people could go into the wilderness and sacrifice to their God if he would call off the flies. When God did, "Pharaoh hardened his heart at this time also; neither would he let the people go."

No one really expected Pharaoh to let the people go because it was only a game that was being played. Remember, God had already told Moses he would harden Pharaoh's heart so he would not let the people go. It would be sheer folly to think it would be different now.

Again the same natural events were taking place so no miracle was happening here.

22   The Murrain of Beasts

◆ Exodus 9:1-7

> Behold, the hand of the LORD is upon thy cattle which is in the field,
> upon the horses, upon the asses, upon the camels, upon the oxen, and
> upon the sheep: there shall be a very grievous murrain. And the LORD
> shall sever between the cattle of Israel and the cattle of Egypt: and there
> shall nothing die of all that is the children's of Israel.

This is a *J* story and is very brief. While there was a warning of the
plague, there was no mention of it ending. This plague only affected the
Egyptian cattle, which included horses, asses, camels, oxen and sheep;
the Israelites were not subject to this plague.

There was a warning given so the Egyptians could get their flocks out
of the fields and into their stables. Only those "in the field" were to be
killed. Though the plague was fatal we have no idea what it was that
killed "all the cattle of Egypt." One scholar says "all the cattle" meant
cattle of all kinds: horses, asses, oxen, camels and sheep, but not
necessarily all of all types. As for camels, it is doubtful whether Egyptians had camels in the 15th century B.C. Most scholars don't think
camels were domesticated until about the 11th century B.C. While we
are not given a description of what killed the cattle, it was more than
likely anthrax. Livestock have fallen victim to plagues throughout
history. Why this plague should be a miracle and all the rest natural
makes no sense.

When death strikes one part of a country and adjacent areas are
unaffected, why call this a miracle? It is possible that Moses sent men
to poison the cattle of Egypt. We have seen Moses using trickery before
and we shall see more. Notice again how the theme of the stories
continues: "and the heart of Pharaoh was hardened, and he did not let
the people go."

Natural or man-made causes were able to account for this story—nothing supernatural is needed.

23   The Boils

◆ Exodus 9:8-12

> And the LORD said unto Moses and unto Aaron, "Take to you handfuls
> of ashes of the furnace, and let Moses sprinkle it towards the heaven
> in the sight of Pharaoh. And it shall become small dust in all the land
> of Egypt, and shall be a boil breaking forth with blains upon man, and
> upon beast, throughout all the Land of Egypt."

Unless we correctly understand this to be but another version of the
last story, we won't know what beasts could be alive. In the last story

we read "all the cattle of Egypt died." This *P* story does not give the Egyptians any warning.

Moses was simply told what to do and he did it. No rod was used in this plague because Moses took ashes and threw them into the air in the presence of Pharaoh. No opportunity was allowed for escape and for the first time, people were smitten with a disease, not just animals. Apparently these boils were a type of burning carbuncle or skin disease with pustules or ulcers. Skin diseases such as this were not uncommon in Egypt—or other countries for that matter. These plagues were not only severe but affected animals as well. Even the magicians were unable to avoid these boils. Apparently the Israelites also suffered under this plague because no mention was made of a division between them and the Egyptians. We find no mention of this plague being fatal, only extremely painful and annoying. There was no indication of an end to the plague in this story.

Because such skin diseases were natural occurrences in Egypt, there would be times when they were more severe than others. No supernatural means were necessary to cause something as ordinary as we see here.

24   *The Hail*

◆ Exodus 9:13-35

> "Behold, tomorrow about this time I will cause it to rain a very grievous hail, such as hath not been in Egypt since the foundation thereof even until now. Send therefore now, and gather thy cattle, and all that thou hast in the field; for upon every man and beast which shall be found in the field, and shall not be brought home, the hail shall come down upon them, and they shall die."

This warning was longer than usual because it could mean death for man and beast if they didn't come in from the fields. Storms such as this were rare in Egypt, but they did occur. This storm was a combination of hail, lightning, and thunder. The hailstones were large enough to beat down the crops, break twigs from the trees, kill both man and beast, and generally destroy anything not protected. "And the flax and the barley was smitten: for the barley was in the ear, and the flax was bolled. But the wheat and the rie were not smitten: for they were not grown up."

Lightning was very abundant: "and the fire ran along upon the ground," electrocuting and burning anything in it's path. "Only in the land of Goshen, where the children of Israel were, was there no hail." Again, in the midst of great destruction, the land of Goshen was protected and preserved. Such a storm would not last very long, and since they came up suddenly, they stopped just as suddenly. Thunderstorms were accompanied by large electrical disturbances but were localized by cloud drift. The storm did not affect the land of Goshen as it went by.

In most years there are about 16,000,000 thunderstorms or about 45,000 a day. At any time there are about 2,000 thunderstorms in progress somewhere in the world. There are over 8,000,000 lightning strikes a day, or about 100 per second. By sheer weight of numbers, there will be a thunderstorm in some unusual area and this one in Egypt could have been just such a natural phenomenon. To assume one storm out of the 16,000,000 is supernatural and all the rest are natural is a stretch of the imagination.

This story contains an explanation of why these plague stories were written and why Pharaoh was the object of the devastation:

> "For I will at this time send all my plagues upon thine heart, and upon thy servants, and upon thy people; that thou mayest know that there is none like me in all the earth. For now I will stretch out my hand, that I may smite thee and thy people with pestilence; and thou shalt be cut off from the earth. And in very deed for this cause have I raised thee up, for to show in thee my power; and that my name may be declared throughout all the earth."

Again the LORD hardened Pharaoh's heart. Again Pharaoh admitted his error, asked that the storm cease and promised to let the people go. When the storm was over, the remorse was over. "And the heart of Pharaoh was hardened, neither would he let the children of Israel go."

This storm was either one of many natural storms or it could have been caused by a volcanic eruption. As was mentioned before, such winds and electrical storms are often generated by massive eruptions. When Santorini blew its top, this was exactly what could be expected.

Why look for a supernatural cause when such reasonable natural causes were available?

25 The Locusts

◆ Exodus 10:1-20

> And the LORD said unto Moses, "Stretch out thine hand over the land of Egypt for the locusts, that they may come up upon the land of Egypt, and eat every herb of the land, even all that the hail hath left." And Moses stretched forth his rod over the land of Egypt, and the LORD brought an east wind upon the land all that day, and all that night; and when it was morning, the east wind brought the locusts.

This was another plague about which Pharaoh was forewarned if the Israelites were not allowed to leave Egypt. Pharaoh refused, but he did try to negotiate. He would allow the men to go but the children would have to stay behind. God would not negotiate, so the locusts came.

This was neither the first time nor the last time locusts came to Egypt and destroyed the crops. The sirocco wind often brought swarms of locusts from the Arabian Desert. In 1889, a swarm of locusts covering about 2,000 square miles crossed the Red Sea. Swarms have been reported 1,200 miles from land as they were blown out over the Mediterranean Sea. Even today swarms of locusts darken the sky for hours at a time as they pass overhead. Purely natural in scope from beginning to end, there was no supernatural element in the story. Why would one swarm of locusts be a miracle and all the others natural?

Again the priests were using a common event in an attempt to make their God the controller of nature. They felt if they could show their God superior to the gods the Egyptians worshiped, they would gain followers. If the priests could show they had sway over their God by sacrifices and offerings, their power was assured. It can be understood why people in that day would feel there might be something to that line of reasoning. Today we see it as a power tactic designed to control believers.

The result of the locust plague was the same as the others, and Pharaoh begged Moses and Aaron to turn back the locusts. When the plague ended we have the characteristic phrase, "But the LORD hardened Pharaoh's heart, so that he would not let the children of Israel go." Obviously Pharaoh had no free will. He could not let the people go or he would have done so. How could anyone ignore all those outstanding events done by Moses and Aaron and not let the people go? The answer is simply that the stories are fiction. Based on factual or natural events they are nothing more than scare tactics to instill fear in the hearts of men and to cause them to follow God's commands as made up and mediated by the priests.

The wind that carried the locusts may have been a regular sirocco, or could have resulted from the Santorini eruption. Natural swarms of locusts don't require supernatural origins.

26   *The Darkness*

◆ Exodus 10:21-29

> And the LORD said unto Moses, "Stretch out thine hand toward heaven, that there may be darkness over the land of Egypt, even darkness which may be felt." And Moses stretched forth his hand toward heaven; and there was a thick darkness in all the land of Egypt three days.

Here is another plague without warning. This one did no damage nor did it cause death. Again only Egyptians were affected and "all the children of Israel had light in their dwellings."

How could darkness that could be felt have such a sharp dividing line that some people right next to others had light and the rest were in darkness? The answer again is a natural phenomenon—and one that was somewhat common to the area. A wind of the desert, called Khamsin, blows fine sand and dust in great clouds that darken the sun for two or three days at a time. That darkness could be felt because it is physical rather than mere lack of light. When the Khamsin blows the sand and dust, there are sometimes only narrow zones darkened and other areas are free of the dust. This may account for the story that the children of Israel had "light in their dwellings."

This story ends with the familiar refrain, "But the LORD hardened Pharaoh's heart, and he would not let them go." But here we have a little more, "And Pharaoh said unto him, Get thee from me, take heed to thyself, see my face no more; for in that day thou seest my face thou shalt die." One might still wonder why Pharaoh put up with Moses for so long before he threatened him with death. Why would a Pharaoh allow a Moses to come into his court time and time again, making threats and demands, and still be as gracious as he was? Finally Pharaoh seems to have had enough, and he told Moses that if he ever came back, he would die. This is possibly the priestly writer's idea of a buildup to the next and final plague where many will die. At any rate, the preliminaries are over and now we get into the main event.

Dust blown by the Khamsin, or the dust cloud from Santorini, could have accounted for the three days of darkness.

When you have such adequate natural causes, why would you look for supernatural causes?

27 *The Death of Firstborn*

◆ Exodus 11; 12:29-36

> And it came to pass, that at midnight the LORD smote all the firstborn in the land of Egypt, from the firstborn of Pharaoh that sat on his throne unto the firstborn of the captive that was in the dungeon; and all the firstborn of cattle. And Pharaoh rose up in the night, he, and all his servants, and all the Egyptians; and there was a great cry in Egypt; for there was not a house where there was not one dead.

What a night that must have been. In every house there was at least one dead person. Animals died that night, too. What a terrible thing for a loving God to do to innocent children just because God had a quarrel with Pharaoh. It just doesn't seem fair to punish those who had nothing to do with the decisions of Pharaoh.

It would seem that in Egypt plagues and pestilences went through now and then. People should realize it was not a judgment from God but only a natural occurrence. These people had to have a supernatural explanation for everything, so they blamed the God of the Israelites. Moses and Aaron were happy to take the blame—they saw it as praise favoring their God. Again the children of Israel were spared. This time they had to put blood from a sacrificed lamb on their lintel or they too would have suffered loss. This time the Egyptians were not warned, and some think it was because of Pharaoh's order to kill the sons born to the Israelites back in Exodus 1. No one knows what form of epidemic took its toll on the people and animals, but suddenly they were dead. While the Egyptians were dying, the Israelites were having a midnight meal of lamb, bitter herbs and unleavened bread. They packed their goods and got ready to leave.

Finally Pharaoh

> called for Moses and Aaron by night, and said, "Rise up, and get you forth from among my people, both ye and the children of Israel; and go, serve the LORD, as ye have said. Also take your flocks and your herds, as ye have said, and be gone; and bless me also." And the children of Israel did according to the word of Moses; and they borrowed of the Egyptians jewels of silver, and jewels of gold, and raiment: And the LORD gave the people favour in the sight of the Egyptians, so that they lent unto them such things as they required. And they spoiled the Egyptians.

Here we have the greatest jewel theft in the history of the world. The Israelites asked to borrow the jewelry from the Egyptians telling them they would bring it back while knowing they would be gone for good. There was no doubt it was thievery for the Bible says "and they spoiled the Egyptians." What a strange turn of events. One minute the Egyptians were angry with the Israelites because of the plagues and death of the firstborn, and now "the LORD gave the people favour in the sight of the Egyptians." At this point Pharoah wanted Israel to leave Egypt. With this in mind Moses sent the Israelites to get all they could from the Egyptians. Notice they didn't just give them their jewelry, but "they lent them such things as they required." They expected to get them back, but of course they never did. Because only the Egyptians died, it could have something to do with the food or water supply. It could have been something they ate that differed from the Israelites diet and caused food poisoning. It should not be taken literally that all who died were firstborn. The impression was that many died, and as the lamb sacrificed was to be for the firstborn, the story used the same wording for those Egyptians who died. Now at last the Israelites were free to leave Egypt.

The cause of death in Egypt could have been from natural or man-made food poisoning. Moses may have sent men to kill some Egyptians so Pharaoh would set the Hebrews free.

28 *The Pillars of Cloud and Fire*

◆ Exodus 13:20-22; 40:34-38

> And the LORD went before them by day in a pillar of cloud, to lead them the way; and by night in a pillar of fire, to give them light; to go by day and night.

The idea of the LORD was an interesting idea in those days. At the time of the wilderness journey the people were told God was in the pillar of fire by night and in a cloud by day. This may have started when Moses believed God was a fire within the bush. Later we will discover that God lived in a box called the Ark of the Covenant. Still later he moved into the Holy of Holies in the Temple. In this story a pillar of fire and smoke represented the presence of God and led to some speculation about just what this pillar was. Some believe the description was an accurate picture of Mt. Sinai. As Jehovah was a volcano God, according to some scholars, the theme of fire and smoke was correct. Smoke billowed out during the day and fire spewed forth at night. Hans Goedicke thinks it was a volcano image but he favored the one that erupted on the island of Santorini. Seen by the Israelites, they might have taken the eruption as a sign of the presence of their God.

"Dust devils" swirled through desert areas when wind stirred them up and they appeared as pillars or miniature tornadoes. They tended to wander as the winds blew, but it would have been difficult to follow one. Jets of fire in desert areas were not as common, but in antiquity sun worshipers found them and told fables about them. Moses found one on Mt. Sinai and it was then he felt he had met his God, Jehovah. The jets of flame might have been formed when earthquakes fractured the rock, opening a small hole to the surface through which natural gas escaped. When it was ignited by lightning, spark or fire it could have burned for years. Moses, who spent many years in this area, would have known about gas jets and used them to his advantage.

These explanations deal with natural phenomena and no supernatural element need be posited in the guise of a miracle.

When you read that Moses spent forty years tending Jethro's flocks and that the children of Israel spent forty years in the same wilderness, you need not take it literally. The number forty was used to show an indefinite number, so we see it often in the Bible. Moses was forty when he left Egypt, spent forty years before coming back for the Israelites, then wandered with them for another forty years. Moses and Jesus each fasted for forty days and David reigned for forty years. These are not to be construed as actual. With so many natural clouds and fires available, it is unnecessary to look for supernatural sources for them.

29   *Crossing the Red Sea*

◆ Exodus 14:1-31

> And Moses stretched out his hand over the sea; and the LORD caused the sea to go back by a strong east wind all that night, and made the sea dry land, and the waters were divided. And the children of Israel went into the midst of the sea upon the dry ground: and the waters were a wall unto then on their right hand, and on their left.

Although the KJV has translated the Hebrew *Yam Suph* as *Red Sea*, most scholars now agree it should be translated as *Sea of Reeds*. Several bodies of water would meet the conditions in the area between Egypt and Sinai. Lake Timsah, Lake Sirbonis, freshwater swamps east of Ramses, an isthmus of Suez, a sea canal, the Bitter lakes and several other bodies of water with papyrus reeds match the description the Bible gives. The actual route traveled is unknown. Scholars cannot even agree upon whether a northern, central or southern route was used. It will probably never be known.

Now we have the Israelites on the edge of an uncertain body of water and the Egyptian army with their horses and chariots approaching from behind. A strong east wind blowing all night would have driven back the shallow water leaving a pathway for the Israelites. When the wind stopped, the shallow water would have returned, and the narrow wheels of the chariots would have bogged down in the mud and they couldn't have crossed over the wet area. Portraying walls of water on either side is a Hebrew rhetorical flourish, not to be taken literally. The metaphor was intended as a place to ford a stream, river, or even small shallow lake, not to be understood as actual walls. We must remember that this took place in the middle of the night. The Egyptians did not realize until the morning watch that they were getting stuck in the mud.

Here we have enough natural to disallow any supernatural. Whenever there is a natural explanation for events it is dangerous to posit a supernatural explanation, and in this story the natural is more than adequate.

30   *The Wilderness Journey*

◆ Deuteronomy 8:4; 29:5

> "And I have led you forty years in the wilderness: your clothes are not waxen old upon you, and thy shoe is not waxen old upon thy foot."

How could people wander for forty years in the wilderness and their clothes and shoes not wear out? That is a difficult question, until we consider several circumstances often overlooked. Remember that the number forty simply means an indefinite amount. It was possible to travel from Egypt to Canaan in just a few weeks, but with families and flocks it may have taken the Israelites a full year. If they entered Canaan then, there would have been no problem at all for clothes and shoes to last a year. If that still seems like a long time for clothes and shoes to last we can look back and see what they did just before they left Egypt. First they took all their possessions and extra clothing, which probably wasn't much. Then they "borrowed of the Egyptians jewels of silver, and jewels of gold, and raiment" (Exodus 12:35). The clothes they were wearing when they left, their extra clothing and the clothing they got from the Egyptians would have been adequate to last them for a year.

Here again the natural can suffice. When people decide to include miracle stories in their literature it is only to impress their readers. After they told their stories each new teller embellished until the stories got out of hand. In the story of the journey, many years were added, and it seems to have been done so the people could stop at Mt. Sinai to get the Law. When the Deuteronomist wrote the Law about 600 B.C., he had to have Moses receive it from God, so he added this episode to the Exodus journey. Because the priests wanted power they made the story tell of the people's sin, and the extra time for the trek was punishment.

When this story was written the priests told what would happen to people who disobeyed God and his priests. It put fear in the people and brought power to the priests. In oral tradition it was easy to change stories. In early hand-written stories it was still easy to change them. When the printing press was invented it finally put an end to easy changes, and finally the story became formalized and standardized.

In the time of the Exodus the Israelites lacked a written language. The Egyptians, Babylonians, Akkadians and Sumerians had written languages, but Hebrew was not committed to writing until about 1000 B.C. There were no written records of the Pentateuch until 400 to 500 years after the time of Moses. In *Halley's Bible Handbook* we read, "The Modern Critical View is that it [the Pentateuch] is a composite work of various schools of priests, made about the 8th century B.C. for partisan purposes, based on oral traditions, the principal redactors of which are called *J, E,* and *P.*" Though Halley disagrees with this he is in a minority.

Here we have a natural event of a one-year journey changed to a miraculous journey of forty years. When we get to the story of the giving of the Law, it will be obvious that the Ten Commandments could not have been given during the journey. When we deal with Joshua's entry to Canaan we will see why only one year was spent on the journey. Now let's look at some things that the Israelites encountered on their trip from Egypt to Canaan.

31   The Waters of Marah

◆ Exodus 15:22-27; Numbers 33:8

> And when they came to Marah, they could not drink of the waters of Marah, for they were bitter: therefore the name of it was called Marah. And the people murmured against Moses, saying, "What shall we drink?" And he cried unto the LORD; and the LORD shewed him a tree, which when he had cast into the waters, the waters were made sweet.

About three days and fifty miles into their journey, they came to some undrinkable water. Moses was able to find a solution to the problem by throwing a tree into the water and the bitter water became sweet. Moses knew all about these tricks to make water drinkable because he had spent many years in the area tending the flocks of his father-in-law, Jethro. There are all kinds of cures people must find if they are to survive, and this was just one of many.

According to *The Interpreter's Bible*, "Various plants are used in different parts of the world for this purpose. E.F.K. Rosenmuller mentions Nellimaran in Coromandel, Sassafras in Florida and Yerva Caniani in Peru. Ferdinand de Lesseps was told by Arab Chiefs that they used in this way a certain bitter thorn, growing in the desert, but nothing is known of it." Other sources say it was a species of barberry growing in the desert. In any event, there was a natural cure for the problem—no supernatural means were needed.

Moses had learned to survive in the wilderness because he talked to and learned from those he met when he was there before. It was essential for people who spent their lives in these areas to learn what they needed to know for survival. Moses was a good student. Had he not understood the wilderness conditions he would never have undertaken such a journey. This story is from *J*; it deals with a natural solution to a water problem. A little later we will see *E* and *P* have Moses get water from a rock by means of a miracle.

When the Israelites had satisfied themselves with this water, they traveled on. "And they came to Elim, where were twelve wells of water and seventy palm trees: and they encamped there by the waters." Here is a pretty picture of what was also in the wilderness. A beautiful oasis in the desert where they could rest and be refreshed. The trip was not all bad, as we shall see as we go on to other enjoyable times the people had on their way to Canaan.

Isn't it obvious that because other people could make water potable, Moses could have done the same? This is a story of natural solutions to a problem and nothing supernatural was involved.

32   *The Manna*

◆ Exodus 16:1-36; Numbers 11:1-9

> And the whole congregation of the children of Israel murmured against Moses and Aaron in the wilderness. . . . Then said the LORD unto Moses, "Behold, I will rain bread from heaven for you; and the people shall go out and gather a certain rate every day."

This story is familiar because it is even referenced in the New Testament. The people were only a few days out of Egypt and they were hungry. As they remembered the flesh pots of Egypt, they felt they would starve to death in the wilderness. Here again Moses uses what he learned from his sojourn in the desert. He claimed God would give them bread from heaven—but he knew it was not from heaven: it came from an earthly tree. Keep in mind that Moses knew this desert and the Israelites had never been out of city life in Egypt. If you were born and reared in New York City and were taken to a wilderness area there to live off the land you would understand.

Moses was familiar with the Tamarisk or Tarfa tree and several others that grew in the desert. These trees exuded sweet juice from their trunks and branches in the form of small round white grains each evening in May, June and July. This juice has the flavor of honey but is somewhat waxy, and in warm sunshine it melts. Even today Arabs gather and use it, still calling it manna. The command to take enough on the sixth day so none would have to be taken on the Sabbath was added later. During the time of Moses there was no idea of a seven-day week, so we know that idea was added in centuries later. They had not even received the Ten Commandments at this stage of the journey so we may be certain there were many interpolations.

Another problem appears in Exodus 16:28: "And the LORD said unto Moses, 'How long refuse ye to keep my commandments and my laws?'" We won't see these commandments and laws until they appear in Exodus 20. In Exodus 16:33-34, "Moses said unto Aaron, 'Take a pot, and put an omer full of manna therein, and lay it up before the LORD, to be kept for your generations.' As the LORD commanded Moses, so Aaron laid it up before the Testimony, to be kept." This Testimony is the Ark of the Covenant and it wouldn't even be built until after the visit to Mt. Sinai. These anachronisms occur because as the priests inserted the *P* version into the *E* stories, they put them in the wrong places. The *P* material is from about 500 B.C. so one can see why it was so different from the *E* of several centuries earlier. Numbers 11 retells the story without *P* insertions and it makes more sense. This is another clue to the manner in which the Bible was assembled.

Our present Bible was written, rewritten, edited, added to, subtracted from, redacted and finally, after many centuries, it became fixed. About 400 B.C. the Torah, or first five books, became canon. In about 200 B.C., the books of the Prophets were agreed upon. About A.D. 90 the Writings including Psalms, Proverbs, Ester, Ruth, etc., also became scripture. The New Testament was put into its present form about A.D. 350. From these dates one can see much time passed before the Bible was voted to be what it is today. Every time a new translation or version is made, the Bible changes again and that is the main reason I stay with the KJV of 1611.

As far as the manna was concerned, it was—is—a natural product of the area.

33 *The Quail*

◆ Exodus 16:8-13; Numbers 11:1-34

> And it came to pass, that at even the quails came up, and covered the camp: and in the morning the dew lay round about the host.

It just doesn't get any better than that; quail and manna in the wilderness. How did so many quail just happen to be in the area at that particular time? The Bible says it was a miracle, but there had been that many quail there every year for thousands of years. They are very common on the Sinai peninsula. In the spring of each year they migrate north, and as they fly and become exhausted they are easy to catch. Moses was well aware of the abundance of quail and it was just a matter of timing. He could promise meat to the people knowing the quail were on their way.

With knowledge of the area, Moses was really king of the hill. He could pretend that each new item on the menu was a result of his asking it of God. He was a hero to the people because they knew nothing about the wilderness while Moses knew it like the back of his hand. In Exodus 16, quail were a treat but in Numbers 11 the quail appeared to cause a plague. When the people asked for meat, God told them they would have quail to eat. In Numbers 11, however, God said,

> Ye shall not eat one day, nor two days, nor five days, neither ten days, nor twenty days; But even a whole month, until it come out at your nostrils, and it be loathsome unto you: because that ye have despised the LORD which is among you, and have wept before him, saying, "Why came we forth out of Egypt."

The reason for the thirty-day period was that the migration of quail lasted only about thirty days.

Apparently as the first group arrived, they were stacked up three feet deep on the ground. Because of the time it took to clean them, coupled with the desert heat, some of the meat spoiled. The plague probably resulted from salmonella bacteria, which multiplied very quickly under the favorable conditions. "And while the flesh was yet between their teeth, ere it was chewed, the wrath of the LORD was kindled against the people and the LORD smote the people with a very great plague." Many people died because they simply didn't cook the quail thoroughly. Even now in the United States, 2,000 people die each year from salmonella. This was not a plague from God; it was simply a natural hazard of eating improperly cooked fowl. The priestly writers were not aware of the actual cause so they condemned the people for murmuring and said the plague was a punishment from God. The object of Numbers 11 is to cause people to believe and follow everything the priests tell them or they too could be punished by God.

This is a story of power and control over people. When seen as a natural disaster rather than a supernatural curse, we understand the motive of the writers and no longer consider it a miracle.

34 Water From the Rock

◆ Exodus 17:1-7; Numbers 20:1-13

> And the LORD said unto Moses, "Go on before the people, and take with thee of the elders of Israel; and thy rod, wherewith thou smotest the river, take in thine hand, and go. Behold, I will stand before thee there upon the rock in Horeb; and thou shalt smite the rock, and there shall come water out of it, that the people may drink." . . . And Moses lifted up his hand, and with his rod he smote the rock twice: and the water came out abundantly, and the congregation drank, and their beasts also.

These two stories are about the same event but the results are of consequence. In the *E* version in Exodus 17, it was proper for Moses to strike the rock with his rod. In the *P* version in Numbers 20, Moses was only to speak to the rock and water would come out. Moses struck the rock twice and as a result he and Aaron were not allowed to enter Canaan with the rest of the people. No matter how much good Moses had done for God, this one little mistake cost him his reward. The priests showed that even Moses lost his blessing from God, so everyone else better watch their step and obey everything the priests told them to do.

In this story we see the Israelites complaining again. Only a few days earlier they had manna and quail, and now they were on the verge of death from thirst. This story is typical of miracle stories in that there was hardly any impression from a recent miracle. It just goes to prove my point that they were not miracles, but only natural events. If one witnessed a real miracle, one would remember it for the rest of one's life. Because there never were any miracles, we can easily understand the people's attitude.

For Moses to hit a rock with his rod and have water come out may seem like a miracle. When you understand the circumstances it will be clear why it was only a mundane event. There is a huge aquifer under the Negev desert and the Sinai peninsula. When a layer of porous rock is sandwiched between two layers of impervious rock, water remains in the porous rock. Unless the water is pumped out, or the impervious rock is fractured, allowing the water to escape, it can remain for thousands of years. Because many aquifers are bowl-shaped with the ends in some hills or mountains, the water runs into the porous rock. When the aquifer is filled, the water is under pressure because the water in the higher areas exerts pressure on the lower areas. When a well is dug or an earthquake fractures the impervious rock, the water is forced to the surface and becomes an artesian well or spring.

Shepherds found these springs and, after watering their flocks, plugged the opening with rocks to keep the water from running out and evaporating. Now when Moses was pretending to follow God's directions, he simply hit the rock plugs so the water could flow out. In the first story he hit the rock once and dislodged it. In the second story he had to hit it twice because he probably missed the first time. This was just another of the tricks Moses learned from his fellow shepherds. It was only when this survival knowledge was converted by the priestly writers into supernatural events that there was talk of miracles. Moses knew that by doing tricks like this the people would follow him anywhere.

35   *Victory over Amalek*

◆ Exodus 17:8-16

> Then came Amalek, and fought with Israel in Rephidim. And Moses said unto Joshua, "Choose us out men, and go out, fight with Amalek: to morrow I will stand on the top of the hill with the rod of God in mind hand." And it came to pass, when Moses held up his hand, that Israel prevailed: and when he let down his hand, Amalek prevailed. And Joshua discomfited Amalek and his people with the edge of the sword.

If food and water problems were not enough, the people had to fight a war. Joshua was a general of the army of Israel, even though we have never heard of him before, and Israel won its first war. Moses just held up his hands and Israel prevailed, but when he lowered his hands, Israel lost the edge. This was nothing short of magic. The soldiers had nothing to do with the battle—only the position of Moses' hands meant anything. Moses, Aaron and Hur were up on a hill watching the battle below. As these three eighty-year-old men looked on, Moses raised his arms and Israel seemed to fight better. Maybe they saw him as a cheerleader. When Moses was too tired to hold up his arms. Aaron and Hur raised Moses' arms, and Israel won.

After the battle we find a peculiar utterance of God: "I will utterly put out the remembrance of Amalek from under heaven." This was just one more of God's promises that never came true because even now we remember Amalek. The very next verse says "And Moses built an altar, and called it Jehovah-nissi. For he said, 'Because the LORD hath sworn that the LORD will have war with Amalek from generation to generation.'" Isn't it odd that God was going to put away all remembrance of Amalek, and then he said they were going to be at war "from generation to generation?"

In this story we meet two new characters. Joshua, who would become the successor to Moses, and Hur, who was husband to Miriam (according to Josephus). The writers used this battle with Amalek to show the power Moses had with God. By simply having his arms up in the air, God gave a military victory to Israel. Perhaps that was the origin of our thumbs-up victory sign today as we simply abbreviated the arms up to thumbs up. I am afraid the roles were reversed in this story, and the army led by Joshua was of more importance than Moses on the mountain.

Magic is not what saved the day for Israel; it was the strategy and military might of Joshua and the army. This wasn't the story of Moses and the rod winning a supernatural victory, but Joshua and the sword winning a natural victory.

36 *Moses at Mt. Sinai*

◆ Exodus 19, 20, 34; Deuteronomy 4 & 5

> In the third month, when the children of Israel were gone forth out of the land of Egypt, the same day came they into the wilderness of Sinai. And Moses went up unto God, and the LORD called unto him out of the mountain, saying, "Thus shalt thou say to the house of Jacob, and tell the children of Israel; Ye have seen what I did unto the Egyptians, and how I bare you on eagle's wings, and brought you unto myself. Now therefore, if ye will obey my voice indeed, and keep my covenant, then ye shall be a peculiar treasure unto me above all people: for all the earth is mine: And ye shall be unto me a kingdom of priests, and an holy nation."

We still don't know where Mt. Sinai, or Horeb, is after all these years. All we know is that *J* and *P* called it Sinai and *E* called it Horeb. It was, no doubt, on this same mountain that Moses saw the burning bush, and that was the first time Moses met his God. In this story he brought the people of Israel out of Egypt to introduce them to his God. At this point in history God lived on a mountain. Later we will see that God lived in the Ark of the Covenant, then the Holy of Holies in the Temple. It wasn't until the Temple and Jerusalem were destroyed and the Ark of the Covenant lost that God lived anywhere but in a small box or room in the midst of Israel.

When Moses lived in Egypt he must have been unhappy with something so he left and went to Midian. While in Midian he married the daughter of the priest and started a family. Jethro, the priest of Midian and father-in-law of Moses, probably taught Moses about the God of Mt. Sinai. It was this God whom Moses was about to introduce to the children of Israel. Moses said Jehovah was the God of Abraham, Isaac and Jacob. This was only to cover up the fact that the Israelites never really had a God of their own. All the stories about Abraham were made up centuries later just to fill in gaps and make a continuous story. Once Moses had his God, he decided to get the children of Israel out of Egypt so they would follow his God and he would be their leader.

When he went back to Egypt, he recruited Aaron to be his spokesman, or translator, because Moses was Egyptian and didn't speak much Hebrew. He was successful in getting the Israelites out of Egypt and into the area of Mt. Sinai. Since Moses was the only one in the whole group who knew about this God, Moses was truly "king of the mountain." Moses was familiar with the mountain with its noises and other phenomena, and the people with him had never been near a volcano. Lightning, thunder, thick clouds of smoke, the whole mountain shook with earthquakes and "the voice of the trumpet exceeding loud," all added to the mystery. Moses even put the threat of death on anyone who went near the mountain, so he was in complete control.

There is a possibility that Jethro was in league with Moses, for we read in Exodus 18:1-27 that Jethro came out and met with Moses. Jethro told Moses exactly what to do so the people would have to follow in fear and trembling. "So Moses hearkened to the voice of his father-in-law, and did all that he had said." Jethro taught Moses all he knew and now Moses was about to teach the people. This was a family religion now opened to the children of Israel. If Jethro was also on the mountain with Moses, it would explain how Moses could spend forty days without food from the camp. Jethro had all they needed on the mountain. Some scholars say there was a shrine built on the mountain and it was there that Moses and Jethro made all the plans to impress the people and set up the new religion of Israel.

One of the more interesting stories about this trip to Mt. Sinai has to do with the two tables of stone on which were written the Ten Commandments. Do you know who cut the stones, who wrote on them and what was written? There seems to be some misunderstanding, so let's try to clear up the story. The oldest story was from *J*: (Exodus 34:1, 27)

And the LORD said unto Moses, "Hew thee two tables of stone." . . . And the LORD said unto Moses, "Write thou these words: for after the tenor of these words I have made a covenant with thee and with Israel."

Here it was Moses who cut the stone and wrote the commandments. *E* was written later and says: (Exodus 24:12)

And the LORD said unto Moses, "Come up to me into the mount, and be there: and I will give thee tables of stone, and a law, and commandments which I have written; that thou mayest teach them."

P agrees with *E* and says: (Exodus 31:18)

And he gave unto Moses, when he had made an end of communing with him upon Mount Sinai, two tables of testimony, tables of stone, written with the finger of God.

The Deuteronomist *(D)* says: (Deuteronomy 10:1-2)

At that time the LORD said unto me, "Hew thee two tables of stone like unto the first, and come up unto me into the mount, and make thee an ark of wood. And I will write on the tables the words that were in the first tables which thou brakest, and thou shalt put them in the ark."

From four sources we have three stories: Moses cut the stones and wrote on them, Moses cut the stones and God wrote on them, and God cut the stones and wrote on them. Notice what the *D* says about putting them into the ark. No one was allowed to even look into the Ark of the Covenant so I don't believe anyone ever saw the stones.

Now we come to the Ten Commandments themselves. We have three versions of them, so how can we decide which version was correct? The earliest is *J* and it appears in Exodus 34:1-28. You may not recognize these ten, but they were the only ones that were called the Ten Commandments by the Bible itself. Here Moses cut the stones and wrote on them these commandments. (1) "Thou shalt worship no other god: for the LORD, whose name is Jealous, is a jealous God. (2) Thou shalt make thee no molten gods. (3) The feast of unleavened bread shalt thou keep. (4) Six days thou shalt work, but on the seventh day thou shalt rest: in earing time and in harvest thou shalt rest. (5) Thou shalt observe the feast of weeks, of the first fruits of wheat harvest, and the feast of ingathering at the year's end. (6) Thrice in the year shall all your men children appear before the LORD God, the God of Israel. (7) Thou shalt not offer the blood of my sacrifice with leaven. (8) Neither shall the sacrifice of the Passover be left unto the morning. (9) The first of the first fruits of thy land thou shalt bring unto the house of the LORD thy God. (10) Thou shalt not seethe a kid in his mother's milk. And the Lord said unto Moses, 'Write thou these words.' And he wrote upon the tables the words of the covenant, the ten commandments."

The other lists you are more familiar with and they are *P*, Exodus 20 and *D*, Deuteronomy 5. "(1) Thou shalt have no other gods before me. (2) Thou shalt not make unto thee any graven image. (3) Thou shalt not take the name of the LORD thy God in vain. (4) Remember the Sabbath day to keep it holy. (5) Honor thy father and thy mother. (6) Thou shalt not kill. (7) Thou shalt not commit adultery. (8) Thou shalt not steal. (9) Thou shalt not bear false witness against thy neighbor. (10) Thou shalt not covet." The difference between Exodus 20 and Deuteronomy 5 was the reason given for keeping the seventh day holy. *P* says in Exodus 20 it was because the earth was created in six days and God rested on the seventh day. The *D* version didn't yet have a creation story so it says for the people, and their families, their flocks, and their servants to rest because God brought them out of Egypt.

These three groups of commandments show how the writers at different times reflected the prevailing teaching. The *J* is from the early days when agriculture was most important to the people. *D* and *P* are from later times when the priests were setting up a code of laws so they could govern and control the people. The priests put all these new laws into the mouth of Moses for a purpose. When they were in power they could say, "You better be good and do what Moses commanded and what we tell you or God will punish you." Probably the strongest evidence of origin for the religion of Israel is found in the final message of Moses: "And this is the blessing wherewith Moses the man of God blessed the children of Israel before his death. And he said, The LORD came from Sinai" (Deuteronomy 33:1-2).

We need also to be reminded that the Persian Book of Law was given to Zoroaster on a mountain amidst thunder and lightning. King Minos of Crete was given the law from his god on Mt. Dicta. Dionysius, the Greek law giver, was shown holding two tablets of stone with the laws chiseled into them. Even the Koran was written in heaven and given to Mohammed by an angel. In 1827 the angel Moroni appeared to Joseph Smith in New York state on a hill called Cumorah. The angel gave Smith some golden plates which he translated into what is known today as the *Book of Mormon*. While all the books are different, the source is always the same.

In all the stories we considered about Sinai, the natural explanations are very adequate to cover all that occurred. No supernatural activities need be added to confuse the issue.

37   The Deaths of Nadab and Abihu

◆ Leviticus 10:1-7; Numbers 3:1-4

> And Nadab and Abihu, the sons of Aaron, took either of them his censer, and put fire therein, and put incense thereon, and offered strange fire before the LORD, which he commanded them not. And there went out fire from the LORD, and devoured them, and they died before the LORD.

Nadab and Abihu were the eldest sons of Aaron and were consecrated to be priests. One day, as they offered incense, something happened and they were killed. We don't really know what they did that was worthy of death, but many have made speculations. Some say the fire they brought was not from the altar. There was no law at that time specifically that only fire from the altar could be used. Some think they were in violation for using their personal censers when they should have used the sacred utensils of the Temple. There was no basis for this charge in any law of that time. Another charge was that they entered the most holy place and encroached on the function of the high priest. There is no indication that this happened.

One other charge was that they brought and offered incense on their own initiative and without authority of Moses or Jethro. This has some merit because they may have seen something that they shouldn't have. Perhaps Moses or Jethro was responsible for their deaths because Nadab and Abihu discovered that it wasn't God who spoke, but Moses or Jethro. What could be worse for a new religion than to be exposed? More than likely Nadab and Abihu were not in the inner circle and were not aware that the whole program was written, produced and directed by Moses and Jethro. It was very important that no one violate the sacred trust by letting others know what went on in the "service of the LORD." The priesthood needed to maintain a secrecy so that they alone knew the mysteries of God. If the people became aware, the priests lost control. According to F.N. Morley, "All religions die of one disease, that of being found out."

Another case of priests dying for challenging higher priestly authority was the story of Dathan, Abiram and Korah. Apparently they too thought Moses was taking on too much himself and they wanted some of the action. They probably knew it was not the LORD that spoke but Moses himself. They too had to die, but we will look at their story later. These deaths were said to be due to "fire from the LORD," but no further explanation was given. Was this lightning or only figurative language to cover what happened? As their deaths took place at the altar or in the Tabernacle, Moses could have done it himself and blamed it on God.

There is no limit to how far some people would go to protect themselves and their jobs. This seems to be the case here and Nadab and Abihu had to be silenced. Supernatural? Miraculous?

38   Fire at Taberah

◆ Numbers 11:1-3; Deuteronomy 9:22

> And when the people complained, it displeased the LORD: and the LORD heard it; and his anger was kindled; and the fire of the LORD burnt among them, and consumed them that were in the uttermost parts of the camp. And the people cried unto Moses; and when Moses prayed unto the LORD, the fire was quenched. And he called the name of the place Taberah: because the fire of the LORD burnt among them.

Here is another short story the priests threw in to show what happened when people complained about God. How many times did people have to be told they must not challenge God's judgment? This was only one of dozens of stories in the Old Testament that were meant to instill fear into the people so they would obey God and his priests. We are not even told what the complaint was in this case, and it was only the outer edges of the camp that were punished. Fire broke out and it was blamed on "fire from the LORD." This could be the same "fire from the LORD" that killed Nadab and Abihu from the last story.

There are certain phrases and terms we need to recognize as catch-phrases and buzz-words. They have no basis in fact and are used only when supernatural events are being described. What possibly happened was a bolt of lightning hit the camp and started a fire. It could have been a lamp was knocked over and started a fire. Children may have been playing with a campfire and ignited a tent. There were many plausible causes that are valid so it is needless to posit a supernatural cause.

Many scholars agree that place names are sometimes much older than the time described. Each group that occupied the place made up a story to explain the origin of the name. As the Israelites needed to establish claim to as many places as possible, they made up stories to show a God-given title to each place at which they stopped. As they named it, they felt they had title to it and especially when they believed God had led them to the place. Of course, Moses was leading the people and he knew each of the places, the names, and possibly the actual history. Much history of the day was folklore. The Israelites simply added to the tales of the day, and the priests made the most of it by claiming these places for God.

Why should we look for a supernatural cause for a fire when so many natural events could have been responsible?

39   Miriam's Leprosy

◆ Numbers 12

> And Miriam and Aaron spake against Moses because of the Ethiopian
> woman who he had married: for he had married an Ethiopian woman.
> And they said, "Hath the LORD indeed spoken only by Moses? hath
> he not spoken also by us?" And the LORD heard it. . . . And the cloud
> departed from off the tabernacle; and, behold, Miriam became leprous,
> white as snow: and Aaron looked upon Miriam, and, behold, she was
> leprous.

Miriam and Aaron had a complaint about Moses' wife, but it was only
mentioned and forgotten. The second complaint, about Moses' authority, was the one that got them in real trouble. Miriam and Aaron thought
Moses was getting too much of the spotlight and they wanted some
recognition too. As a result of their complaint, Miriam was immediately
stricken with leprosy. Aaron was not punished so he pleaded with Moses
to ask God to heal Miriam: "Alas, my lord, I beseech thee, lay not the
sin upon us, wherein we have done foolishly, and wherein we have
sinned.' And Moses cried unto the LORD, saying, 'Heal her now, O
God, I beseech thee.'" As a result of Moses' prayer, Miriam was healed
of the leprosy immediately, but she had to stay out of the camp for seven
days.

What happened here is the same as what happened to Nadab and
Abihu. As Miriam and Aaron challenged Moses for the limelight, some
punishment had to be given. Only Moses had face-to-face meetings with
God; only Moses got to talk personally with God; only Moses got to deal
with God. All others must come to Moses who would then talk with God.
The reason, of course, was that Moses and Jethro were the ones who
made up the religion and they must maintain that secret. Moses was not
willing to kill Miriam and Aaron because they only challenged him and
still didn't know his secret. A warning had to be given that Moses was
the leader and the only spokesman for God, so the story of Miriam's
leprosy was concocted.

Part of the leprosy incident could be based on natural events. It is
possible for Miriam to have been so anxious and fearful that she felt
guilty and had a hysteric reaction. One symptom of hysteria is a skin
disorder that resembles leprosy and, because such symptoms can appear
and disappear quickly, this could describe the incident adequately. When
Moses talked with Miriam and calmed her down he suggested she be
cured of the skin disorder and she was cured. This type of hysteric
reaction was common then and still occurs today. We will be seeing more
of the symptoms of hysteria as we continue.

One possibility about why Aaron was not afflicted as Miriam was could be that because Aaron was a priest he must be kept from disgrace. This story is from the *E* tradition which favors Moses because the authors were priests from Shiloh and Moses was their hero. Because priests must stick together they must be careful not to speak ill of other priests, so they make Aaron refer to Moses as "my lord." To redress Aaron too severely would reflect on the priesthood so they let him off easy. The story of Aaron and the Golden calf is also an *E* story in which Aaron called Moses "my lord." The object is to show Moses superior to Aaron and Miriam so they are allowed to live and honor Moses.

The story is all natural in scope and there was no reason to invoke the supernatural to account for any part of it.

40 *Judgment against Rebellion*

◆ Numbers 16

Numbers 16 is two stories run together by the priestly editor. Until the stories are separated they make no sense. The story of Korah and his 250 followers is distinct from that of Dathan and Abiram. We shall look at the story of Korah first.

> Now Korah, the son of Izhar, the son of Kohath, the son of Levi . . . rose up before Moses, with certain of the children of Israel, two hundred and fifty princes of the assembly, famous in the congregation, men of renown: And they gathered themselves together against Moses and against Aaron, and said unto them, "Ye take too much upon you, seeing all the congregation are holy, every one of them, and the LORD is among them: wherefore then lift ye up yourselves above the congregation of the LORD?" And when Moses heard it he fell upon his face.

Korah and his 250 followers attempted to claim their rights as priests because Israel was to be a kingdom of priests. Korah's first complaint denied the ritualistic superiority of the Levites. The second complaint was that even among the Levites, Aaron's family had the exclusive right to serve. Notice that even then there were those who saw through the smokescreen put up by Moses and Aaron. Other people wanted a piece of the action—they wanted a part in upper-level management.

At that time Aaron's family got the choice of the offerings and sacrifices and Korah didn't think that was fair. Of course, Moses and Aaron could not allow this kind of rebellion, so they put out a challenge: "This do; Take your censers, Korah, and all his company; And put fire therein, and put incense in them before the LORD to-morrow: and it shall be that the man whom the LORD doth chose, he shall be holy. And there came out a fire from the LORD, and consumed the two hundred and fifty men that offered incense." Here "fire from the LORD" killed

Korah and the 250 followers. They wanted to become part of Moses' and Aaron's private program and as a result they all died. "But on the morrow all the congregation of the children of Israel murmured against Moses and against Aaron, saying, 'Ye have killed the people of the LORD.'" Somehow the word got out that it was Moses and Aaron who had killed Korah and his 250 men.

"And the LORD spake unto Moses, saying, 'Get you up from among this congregation, that I may consume them in a moment.'" Now they were in the midst of a real battle and when it was all over, 14,700 people, besides Korah and his 250, died. Apparently the entire Aaronic priesthood was embroiled in the action to put down the rebellion. Things almost got out of hand and many people died. It started with Korah, spread to 250, and finally thousands fought as Moses and Aaron defended their self-appointed positions. Almost 15,000 people died, but Moses and Aaron won the right to lead.

Murder rather than miracles seemed to be the order.

The other story deals with Dathan and Abiram and their complaint against Moses.

> And Dathan and Abiram, sons of Eliab, and On, son of Peleth, sons of Reuben, rose up before Moses. . . . And Moses sent to call Dathan and Abiram, the sons of Eliab: which said, "We will not come up: Is it a small thing that thou has brought us up out of a land that floweth with milk and honey, to kill us in the wilderness, except thou make thyself altogether a prince over us? Moreover thou hast not brought us into a land that floweth with milk and honey, or given us inheritance of fields and vineyards: wilt thou put out the eyes of these men? We will not come up."

This charge is entirely different from that of Korah, because this was against only Moses. Here, too, Moses did not take kindly to accusation, so he challenged Dathan and Abiram. Moses says:

> "Hereby ye shall know that the LORD hath sent me to do all these works; for I have not done them of mine own mind. If these men die the common death of all men, or if they be visited after the visitation of all men; then the LORD hath not sent me. But if the LORD make a new thing, and the earth open her mouth, and swallow them up, with all that appertain unto them, and they go down quick into the pit, then ye shall understand that these men have provoked the LORD." And it came to pass, as he made an end of speaking all these words, that the ground clave asunder that was under them: And the earth opened her mouth, and swallowed them up, and their houses.

The story of Dathan and Abiram deals with tribal primacy. Reuben was the first-born son of Israel and Levi was third-born. Dathan and Abiram, descendants of Reuben, felt superior to Moses, a descendant of Levi. All Dathan and Abiram wanted was a chance to be in on decision making and governing Israel. Moses was not about to share his power with anyone, as this story shows.

How the "earth opened her mouth and swallowed them up, and their houses," only the writer could tell. There may have been an earthquake at some time that caused the earth to crack open; someone fell in and this inspired the story. More likely it is only a fiction showing what would happen to anyone who would challenge Moses, Aaron, or any other priest. Three rebellions are mentioned in this chapter. It seems strange that if these events occurred, with the miracles and wonders described, that anyone would still challenge Moses and Aaron. If fire destroyed 250 men, if the earth opened and swallowed people, if 14,700 people died because they challenged Moses and Aaron, how could anyone be so foolish to try again? This is evidence that there were no supernatural activities going on. There were enough natural means to accomplish the events, or at least make-up stories that told of natural disasters, to cover all the situations. Even the stories that tell of supernatural happenings show that the people took it in stride with hardly a second thought. Throughout the Bible we see similar reactions to miracle stories as the characters showed little awe and wonder.

One conclusion seems obvious: there were no miracles.

41   Aaron's Rod

◆ Numbers 17&18

> And Moses spake unto the children of Israel, and every one of their princes gave him a rod apiece, for each prince one, according to their fathers' houses, even twelve rods: and the rod of Aaron was among their rods. And Moses laid up the rods before the LORD in the tabernacle of witness. And it came to pass, that on the morrow Moses went into the tabernacle of witness; and, behold, the rod of Aaron for the house of Levi was budded, and brought forth buds, and bloomed blossoms, and yielded almonds. And Moses brought out all the rods from before the LORD unto all the children of Israel: and they looked, and took every man his rod.

Notice the awe and disbelief the people showed when such an outstanding miracle occurred. A dead stick budded, bloomed and bore almonds overnight and the amazed response of the people is "they looked." Can one rationally accept as miraculous something that inspired no more awe than "they looked"?

This story is simply a necessary reinforcement of the last chapter. There were a lot of questions about who was to lead Israel and who were to be its priests. This story is by the *P* author, so Moses was to be the leader, and the family of Aaron were to be the priests.

And the LORD said unto Aaron, "Thou and thy sons and thy father's house with thee shall bear the iniquity of the sanctuary: and thou and thy sons with thee shall bear the iniquity of your priesthood."

The matter was now settled: Moses and Aaron would run the whole operation. They controlled the sanctuary, the offerings, the sacrifices, the major decisions, the minor decisions—everything was now under their control. Read all of Numbers 18 and see what privileges and power the priesthood granted to themselves as religious leaders. From that time on they did nothing but take care of the religious edifices and services and they received 10% of all that the other tribes had. This was a plum job, and now one can understand why the priests wrote what they wrote. No one was going to take their jobs away because death was the penalty for anyone who even came *near* the sanctuary or the altar. Moses made up the religion and Aaron ran it; no wonder they would get the best of everything.

How could Aaron have been so lucky that it was his rod that was selected? It's easy. Look carefully. Moses made the rules of the game. He already had a rod that had almonds on it, it had Aaron's name on it, and it was in the tabernacle. It was Moses who made up the rules, put the twelve rods in the tabernacle and took them out of the tabernacle. He left nothing to chance. How could it have been any different?

The whole story is natural in its planning and execution. The only miracle is that people still believe such stories in an age of enlightenment.

42 Moses and the Brazen Serpent

◆ Numbers 21:4-9; II Kings 18:4

And the people spake against God, and against Moses, "Wherefore have ye brought us up out of Egypt to die in the wilderness? for there is no bread, neither is there any water; and our soul loatheth this light bread." And the LORD sent fiery serpents among the people, and they bit the people; and much people of Israel died. . . . And the LORD said to Moses, "Make thee a fiery serpent, and set it upon a pole: and it shall come to pass, that everyone that is bitten, when he looketh upon it, shall live." And Moses made a serpent of brass, and put it upon a pole, and it came to pass, that if a serpent had bitten any man, when he beheld the serpent of brass, he lived.

Again the people murmured, complained and were punished. This time God sent "fiery serpents" to bite them and many died.

The word for serpents here is *seraphim* or *the burning ones*. Did you ever hear of seraphim before? Of course. Remember Isaiah 6:1-6. The seraphim were above the throne of God crying to each other, "Holy, holy,

holy, is the LORD of hosts: the whole earth is full of his glory." These seraphim had six wings and could fly. When people speak of seraphim they make them to be of human shape and countenance and like six-winged angels. Why don't they tell us seraphim were really snakes?

Another interesting character in Bible stories is the cherub. Artists usually depict them as baby-faced, winged angels, but the Bible shows them as none other than winged bulls like those shown in Assyrian art. Three stories, Ezekiel 1:1-14; 10:8-22 and Revelations 4 clearly show cherubs to be oxen. Three faces are described as lions, eagles and man, and the fourth, ox, cherub or calf. Certainly cherubs are not angels.

The serpent was the fertility symbol of the northern Kingdom of Israel, and, as Moses was associated with Israel, he made the brazen serpent. Here is proof the Ten Commandments were not given at that time in Israel's history. All we have to do is look at this brazen serpent and the commandment not to make any graven image. This was a graven image, and to go one step further, Israel worshiped this brazen serpent for about 750 years. In about 726 B.C. when Hezekiah became king of Judah, "He removed the high places, and brake the images, and cut down the groves, and brake in pieces the brazen serpent that Moses had made: for unto those days the children of Israel did burn incense to it: and he called it Nehushtan" (2 Kings 18:4). Did your minister tell you that Moses himself broke a commandment and that for 750 years the Israelites worshiped a brass snake? The story is in your Bible so maybe you should tell your minister and see if he has ever heard the story.

The reason the story is in scripture is a common one: when the people complained, they were punished. This time there was a little different twist, and an idol was made to serve as the magic charm. Sympathetic magic was a common practice in that time, or as we might say, spiritual homeopathy. More simply stated, "like cures like." To make an image of the pest, or whatever afflicted the people, and present that image to their God would banish the problem. The same magic was done by the Philistines in 1 Samuel 6 when they returned the Ark of the Covenant that they kept had for seven months.

I offer a natural explanation for the story of the fiery serpents sent by God to punish the people. When Moses lived in the wilderness, he found a spot where there were many snakes. When the people complained, he led them into this area and many were bitten. The story of the brazen serpent healing people was undoubtedly made up much later to justify having and worshiped an idol. If the snakes were not poisonous, their bite would only cause inflammation, so were called fiery serpents.

We have no need for the supernatural in this story.

43 A Well in the Desert

◆ Numbers 21:13-18

> The princes digged the well, the nobles of the people digged it, by the direction of the lawgiver, with their staves.

Water on the desert surface may have been scarce, but it was not far from the surface. Under the Negev desert and the Sinai peninsula, there is a huge aquifer. Because it is bowl-shaped, water can be artesian in some areas. To dig a well and find water was not miraculous because there were many wells all over the area traveled by the Israelites. Some were already there when Moses was in the area previously, and some were dug by the Israelites. In that area water was available for the effort it took to dig for it. Some of those wells are there today and are still used.

Even though water was near the surface, they needed to look for trees and bushes so they could know their roots were feeding on the water. It would be senseless to dig where there was nothing but sand and rock. Moses spent many years in this very country tending flocks that needed a lot of water. He was well aware of what signs to look for when preparing to dig a well. He used his knowledge gained from those who taught him to live in the desert.

Only natural means were used to find water and there was no reason to suggest supernatural means were necessary.

44 Balaam's Ass Talks Back

◆ Numbers 22:1-35

> And Balaam rose up in the morning, and saddled his ass, and went with the princes of Moab. . . . But the angel of the LORD stood in a path of the vineyard, a wall being on this side, and a wall on that side. . . . And when the ass saw the angel of the LORD, she fell down under Balaam: and Balaam's anger was kindled, and he smote the ass with a staff. And the LORD opened the mouth of the ass, and she spoke unto Balaam, "What have I done unto thee, that thou has smitten me these three times?"

Now one would think Balaam would have been amazed that an ass could speak, but he wasn't. He simply answered the ass and they had a short conversation. It seems to be very common in the Bible that when something extraordinary happens the people are impressed to yawn. Even when the dead were raised to life no one seems to get really excited.

Balaam was a soothsayer from the East and was neither Hebrew nor Moabite. Balak was king of the Moabites and felt threatened by the Israelites. It was common in those days to hire people to curse your enemies, and Balaam was approached by elders sent from Balak in this vein. When Balaam talked it over with God, he was told he could go, but only to bless Israel. Balaam went according to God's instructions, but God got angry even though Balaam was following his orders. The problem in this story is that part is *J* and part *E*. As they were poorly edited, there are several contradictions.

Balaam was under a certain amount of stress and anxiety, and when his ass refused to go between two walls that were very close together, Balaam got upset. He beat the ass and that made him feel guilty and he experienced a hysteric hallucination. He heard his ass speak and saw a vision of an angel with a sword. These circumstances fit the conditions of the story and satisfied the needs of those who require that all stories in the Bible be literal events. The only difference was that the natural realm satisfied all the requirements and no supernatural interference was needed. Because the story is in the Bible people believe it literally. The explanation of hysteric hallucination allows us to accept what happened, but does not require us to see it as a miracle.

We will be seeing much more that was due to hysteria, so be prepared to consider this as a valid explanation. Many events that seem to be out of the ordinary are products of a mind under the control of hysteria. As in other stories, look for the natural rather than the supernatural.

45   *Israel Defeats the Midianites*

◆ Numbers 25 & 31

> And Israel abode in Shittim, and the people began to commit whore-dom with the daughters of Moab. . . . And, behold, one of the children of Israel came and brought unto his brethren a Midianitish woman in the sight of Moses, and in the sight of all the congregation of the children of Israel. . . . [W]hen Phinehas, the son of Eliazer, the son of Aaron the priest saw it, he rose up from among the congregation, and took a javelin in his hand; And he went after the man of Israel into the tent, and thrust both of them through, the man of Israel and the woman through her belly. So the plague was stayed from the children of Israel. And those that died in the plague were twenty and four thousand.

The story begins with the men of Israel and the daughters of Moab. The LORD got angry with them and told Moses to execute the chiefs of the people. No killings are reported and all of a sudden the story ends at Numbers 25:5. A new story opens at Numbers 25:6 but it has no beginning. It simply tells of the deaths of an Israelite man named Zimri and his Midianite wife, Cozbi. Why the story about the Moabite women ended and the one about the Midianite woman began is not explained.

The first part is from *J* and the Midianite story is from *P*. Somehow a plague had come on Israel, and when Phinehas killed the man and his wife the plague ended and we were told 24,000 people died. As a result of these deaths, ". . . the LORD spake unto Moses saying, 'Vex the Midianites, and smite them.'" In Numbers 31, God tells Moses to get the people ready for war:

> Of every tribe a thousand, throughout all the tribes of Israel, shall ye send to the war. . . . And they warred against the Midianites, as the LORD commanded Moses; and they slew all the males. And they slew the kings of Midian. And the children of Israel took all the women of Midian captives, and their little ones, and took the spoil of all their cattle, and all of their flocks, and all their goods. And they burnt all their cities wherein they dwelt, and all their goodly castles, with fire.

That looked like the end of the Midianites because all the men were killed and all women taken captive. Two hundred years later however, Midian held Israel captive for seven years according to Judges 6:1.

This was truly an amazing battle and no Israelites were killed. We don't know how many Midianite men were killed but let's look at what they captured. The 12,000 Israelites rounded up 675,000 sheep, 72,000 cattle and 61,000 asses; 808,000 animals all herded by 12,000 men. Also taken by the 12,000 men were "all the women of Midian . . . and their little ones," and 600 lbs. of gold. Moses was angry because they took the women and children. He said, "Now therefore kill every male among the little ones, and kill every woman that hath known man by lying with him. But all the women children, that have not known a man by lying with him, keep alive for yourselves. . . . And thirty and two thousand persons in all, of women that had not known man by lying with him" remained. All these animals and virgins were divided among the 12,000 warriors, the men who didn't go to war, the officers, the Levites and the priests. Since there were 600,000 men in Israel, some got virgins and some didn't because only 32,000 were shared. Think of it: 12,000 men killed tens of thousands of men, women and children. It is interesting to note that Balaam was killed in the battle, and probably his talking ass died with him. They then shared with all Israel 808,000 animals, 32,000 virgins and 600 lbs. of gold, and not a single Israelite died in battle.

Getting back to the plague that started the whole episode, it was probably just one of the common plagues that went around. It may have started with the Midianites. It was possibly a venereal disease the Israelites contracted from the Midianite women. It may have been a disease to which the local people were immune but the Israelites were not. We are not told what the plague was, but it was certainly a natural disease. Most Bible scholars admit the numbers in the story are pure fiction made up to illustrate a point. The victory in battle belonged to God so the spoils were his, too. The spoils were to be divided according to his will and his laws. Because killing in war defiled men, they had to spend seven days in purification before they could return to camp.

Many people have the idea that God ordered these wars and so they were justified. That is not the real meaning of the story. The keeping of the laws of division and purification were the lessons to be learned. The division of the spoils was very clearly explained and followed. The implication was made that if the Israelites had not committed whoredom with other people, the plague would have been averted. Finally, the soldiers were allowed to take only what could be purified by fire or water.

No miracle was performed except by the pen of the priest who wrote the story.

46   *The Death of Moses*

◆ Deuteronomy 34

> And the LORD said unto him, "This is the land which I sware unto Abraham, unto Isaac, and unto Jacob, saying, I will give it unto thy seed: I have caused thee to see it with thine eyes, but thou shalt not go over thither." So Moses the servant of the LORD died there in the land of Moab, according to the word of the LORD. And he buried him in a valley in the land of Moab, over against Beth-peor: but no man knoweth of his sepulchre unto this day.

What a sad ending for a great man. No consideration for all he had done for his God and his people but to die alone, and not even in the promised land. Many lesser men got all kinds of tribute, acknowledgment, graves and monuments when they died, but not Moses. Thousands of people who did nothing *but* murmur and complain got to go into Canaan, but not Moses. Thousands got to share the milk and honey, but not Moses. Thousands got to have their grape vine and fig tree, but not Moses. What kind of God would use a man until he was worn out and then discard him?

We are told that Moses wrote the first five books of the Bible, and in this one he wrote about his death—after he was dead and buried. We aren't told how Moses died. We are told that God buried him, but the location of the grave was not given. I wonder why we have stories of Enoch and Elijah going to heaven but Moses just died and was buried. If there were any justice, Moses should have crossed the Jordan and lived awhile in Canaan before he died. God said the land had been promised to Abraham, but he never received it. The land was then promised to Isaac, but he never received it. The land was then promised to Jacob, and he never received it. The land was later claimed to be a Christian inheritance, but let me make a guess that Christians won't receive it either.

When Moses was about to die there are two descriptions given of the man: "And Moses went and spake these words unto all Israel. And he said unto them, I am an hundred and twenty years old this day; I can no more go out and come in" (Deuteronomy 31:1-2). This was written by the Deuteronomist. "And Moses was an hundred and twenty years old when he died: his eye was not dim, nor his natural force abated" (Deuteronomy 34:7). This account is by the *P* writer who said Moses was in excellent physical condition until he died. They couldn't dispute the fact that Moses hadn't entered Canaan, but they could make him strong to the end.

As far as how Moses died, there is no miracle needed. He may have been murdered by his enemies. He may have been killed and eaten by wild beasts. He may have fallen into a deep canyon and died of injuries. We just don't know what became of Moses. If Moses' death had been by a miracle it would have been to his benefit and well publicized. This was not a happy supernatural story, but a sad natural story of a great leader's death.

Chapter 4

Joshua and Judges

47 *Israel Crosses Jordan*

◆ Joshua 3:7-17; 4

> And as they that bare the ark were come unto Jordan, and the feet of the priests that bare the ark were dipped in the brim of the water, (for Jordan overfloweth all his banks all the time of harvest,) That the waters which came down from above stood and rose up upon a heap very far from the city of Adam, that is beside Zaretan: and those that came down toward the sea of the plain, even the salt sea, failed, and were cut off: and the people passed over right against Jericho. And the priests that bare the ark of the covenant of the LORD stood firm on dry ground in the midst of Jordan, and all the Israelites passed over on dry ground, until all the people were passed clean over Jordan.

This is quite a story as the river dried up long enough for thousands of people to cross on dry ground. It is especially impressive because it happened during flood season. The river was usually about sixty feet wide and about five feet deep but, in April, the spring rains and melting snows in Lebanon caused the river to flood.

There are several natural ways the river could have stopped flowing so let's look at them now. At the city of Adam, sixteen miles upstream, there are clay banks on the sides of the river. These banks are about forty feet high and are subject to landslides. During flood season, the water was known to undercut the banks, and they would collapse into the river and block the flow. Earthquakes have also caused these banks to collapse and dam the river. In 1927 an earthquake dammed the river for twenty-one hours. Another way was suggested by the story itself. "Then Joshua commanded the officers of the people, saying, 'Pass through the host, and command the people, saying, Prepare you victuals; for within three days ye shall pass over this Jordan, to go in to possess the land, which the LORD your God giveth you to possess it'" (Joshua 1:10-11). I see here a plan to send men upstream, undercut the clay banks, and block the river long enough for the people to cross to Jericho.

The story goes on to say, "That the waters which came down from above stood and rose up upon a heap very far from the city of Adam, that is beside Zaretan." This makes it clear that the water backed up behind the dam at Adam all the way to Zaretan twelve miles upstream from Adam. I think the river was blocked on purpose so the people could cross, and they were probably unaware that Joshua had planned the whole thing. Joshua was a good leader, so he prepared the people, and when the flow stopped, the people made their move. Moses and Joshua sent spies into Canaan, and they learned about the clay banks at Adam. Joshua used this information to impress and inspire his people. Perfect timing was necessary and Joshua was well prepared to handle the job.

This story is a natural, man-caused event—nothing supernatural took place. I want to point out one more verse before we go on. "And Joshua set up twelve stones in the midst of Jordan, in the place where the feet of the priests which bore the ark of the covenant stood: and they are there unto this day." Remember these twelve stones. We will say more about them later.

48 *Joshua and the Angel*

◆ Joshua 5:13-15

> And it came to pass, when Joshua was by Jericho, that he lifted up his eyes and looked, and, behold, there stood a man over against him with his sword drawn in his hand: and Joshua went unto him, and said unto him, "Art thou for us, or for our adversaries?" And the man said, "Nay; but as captain of the host of the LORD am I now come." And Joshua fell on his face to the earth, and did worship, and said unto him, "What saith my lord unto his servant?" And the captain of the LORD's host said unto Joshua, "Loose thy shoe from off thy foot; for the place whereon thou standeth is holy." And Joshua did so.

This story was written to make Joshua equal to Moses as leader of the Israelites. Because Moses was not allowed into Canaan, a new leader had to be chosen, and with this announcement, Joshua took the job.

Notice how this story matched Exodus 3:1-6 in which the angel told Moses he was to take off his shoes and become leader of the Israelites. Both occasions found the individuals alone. If Joshua saw anyone, it was the result of hysteric hallucination due to anxiety and pressure as a result of leading a rebellious people. Many of the more important Bible stories recount the experiences of people who were alone. What evidence is there to show that these stories have any validity except for the word of the one who told the tale?

Two events precede this story and they need to be mentioned. "At that time the LORD said unto Joshua, 'Make thee sharp knives, and circumcise again the children of Israel the second time.'" This is peculiar because God told Abraham that circumcision was part of an everlasting covenant. The facts are that as new followers joined the Israelites some of them were not circumcised, and in order to celebrate Passover, they needed to have it done. Of Passover it had been said, "And this day shall be unto you for a memorial; and ye shall keep it for a feast to the LORD throughout your generations; ye shall keep it a feast by an ordinance for ever" (Exodus 12:14). There is no way the people would not keep the Passover after such an impressive deliverance from Egypt. Therefore it is my contention that the Passover Joshua convened was exactly one year from the day the Israelites left Egypt. There were no forty years of aimless wanderings during which the Passover was not observed. Moses would never have allowed such a thing to happen and God would not have allowed it either.

There were at least two groups that came from Egypt to Canaan: One about 1400 B.C. and another about 1200 B.C. These different dates allow for the fact that some cities were destroyed in each period, and one group was led by Moses and the other by Joshua. So here we have a one-year journey from Egypt to Canaan, and now things begin to make sense. Clothes and shoes last the whole trip. Food and water were not so great a problem for one year as they would have been for forty years. Circumcision and Passover were not neglected. Laws given centuries later weren't made during the trip, so they, too, are now more believable. The whole program of a one-year journey with natural events is much more acceptable than a forty-year journey with unbelievable, supernatural fables.

49 *Joshua at Jericho*

◆ Joshua 6

> And it came to pass on the seventh day, that they rose early about the dawning of the day, and compassed the city after the same manner seven times: only on that day they compassed the city seven times. And it came to pass the seventh time, when the priests blew with their trumpets, Joshua said unto the people, "Shout; for LORD hath given you the city." . . . So the people shouted when the priests blew with the trumpets: and it came to pass, when the people heard the sound of

the trumpet, and the people shouted with a great shout, that the wall fell down flat, so that the people went up into the city, every man straight before him, and they took the city. And they utterly destroyed all that was in the city, both man and woman, young and old, and ox, and sheep, and ass, with the edge of the sword.

That is a pretty good story of destruction. The first thing they did when they entered the promised land was to raze an entire city and its inhabitants. There probably weren't too many people though because the city only covered six or seven acres; that would be a square with about 550 foot sides.

Jericho is one of the oldest cities in the world. It was first built about 8000 B.C. It was built of sun-dried mud brick and has been destroyed and rebuilt many times. Evidence shows it was totally destroyed and burned about 1400 B.C. There was a double wall around the city about 12–15 feet apart. Planks were put up spanning the tops of the walls, and houses were built over the space between the walls. Hagar and her family lived in one of these houses on the walls. Hagar had sheltered two spies Joshua sent to look over the city. As a reward, she and her family were promised safety when the city was destroyed. Even though we are told both walls completely collapsed, "Joshua saved Rahab the harlot alive, and her father's household, and all that she had." The promise of safety was fulfilled, and Rahab became a member of the family line that produced Jesus. You can read that in the genealogy in the book of Matthew.

Just what caused the destruction of the city is not known. The city of Jericho was on a fault known as the Jericho fault; it had suffered from earthquakes in the past. If the city was destroyed by an earthquake some time before Joshua got to the area, its destruction would still have been credited to Joshua and his God. There is a theory that the low-frequency sound of the trumpets and the people's shouts set up harmonic vibrations that caused the walls to fall. Some scholars think there was an earthquake and some aftershocks that blocked the Jordan and also destroyed the city of Jericho a few days later. We must remember that events did not have to have occurred as the Bible records them. Events which were separated by years or even by decades are recorded as consecutive events. Even stories separated by centuries and recorded centuries later would appear to be happening one right after the other.

To destroy a small city like Jericho, surrounded by mud bricks stacked up on a faulty foundation, wouldn't have taken much of an earthquake. Evidence shows the outer wall fell outward and the inner wall was dragged along with it. Since Jericho had been rebuilt many times—the old bricks became the foundations for the new buildings—the city seemed to be on a hill. As old mud bricks built up the ground level each time the city was destroyed, the city was thirty or forty feet higher than the surrounding area. As the outer and inner walls fell away from the city they left everything flat and "the people went up into the city, every man straight before him." They didn't have to climb over a pile of rubble because it was laid down flat. Mud bricks put together with mud mortar can stand for centuries, but when earthquakes shake them they lose their integrity and they crumble. This story differs from the Midianite story in that no people or flocks were taken as spoils. "And they burnt the city with fire, and all that was therein: only the silver and the gold, and vessels of brass and of iron, they put into the treasury of the house of the LORD." Just how much silver and gold they had we shall see when Solomon builds the Temple.

This story is built upon natural events. They are enough to account for the destruction of the city, so no supernatural means are necessary.

50   *Joshua at Ai*

◆   Joshua 7 & 8

> So there went up thither of the people about three thousand men: and they fled before the men of Ai. And the men of Ai smote of them about thirty and six men.

Here we see that Israel failed against the men of Ai. Joshua was devastated and he blamed God. But God said, "Israel hath sinned, and they have also transgressed my covenant which I commanded them: for they have even taken of the accursed thing, and have also stolen, and dissembled also, and they have put it even among their stuff." God wouldn't take the blame, because someone stole something from him and that someone must be punished. To find out who it was, Joshua started by finding the tribe, then the family and household and finally the man himself. The method of finding the guilty man was not complicated because they used spies. Once they knew who was guilty they played it up and said God told them. Achan was the man who stole a robe, some silver and some gold. When he confessed, he was not forgiven, but he, his family and his livestock were stoned, and then all their belongings and bodies were burned and covered with stones.

There was a belief that sin was inherited and passed down to future generations, so when someone was guilty of such a sin, he, and all he had were destroyed. There was a lesson to be learned, and this served as a deterrent as each one looked out for the other. To protect themselves, they watched each other, for they knew the sins of one could result in the destruction of all. Certainly no supernatural means were used to discover Achan's guilt when natural spies were adequate.

When the matter of Achan was resolved, Joshua sent the men out against Ai once more. This time they planned an ambush. With enough men this time, they destroyed the city of Ai. "And so it was, that all that fell that day, both of men and women, were twelve thousand, even all the men of Ai." Joshua had over thirty thousand men this time so there was no question that they would win. This proved to the people that God was right, and that Achan's sin had caused the defeat the first time. The real reason they lost the first battle was that they only sent three thousand men instead of the thirty thousand they sent for the second battle. The story of casting lots to find the guilty party was a priestly game to show the people they could not get away with anything. This was designed not only to help the people to be better people, but also to make the priest's job easier.

One problem with this story concerns the cities of Ai and Bethel. Ai was destroyed about 2200 B.C., and for about nine hundred years no one had lived there. There was a city called Bethel about one-and-a-half miles away that was built by the people of Ai after their city was destroyed. There is evidence that Bethel was destroyed about 1250 B.C., so if a city was destroyed by Joshua, it was probably Bethel, not Ai. Jericho was destroyed about 1400 B.C., and so we see evidence that there were two separate invasions about two hundred years apart. Again we see that the cities were not very large—about twelve thousand people. For such a small city to stand against an army of thirty thousand fighting men was simply out of the question.

With odds like this, don't you think it is unnecessary to posit a miracle?

51   *The Battle at Gibeon*

◆ Joshua 10:1-11

> And the LORD discomfited them before Israel, and slew them with a great slaughter at Gibeon, and chased them along the way that goeth to Beth-horon, and smote them to Azekah, and unto Makkedah. And it came to pass, as they fled from before Israel, and were in the going down to Beth-horon, that the LORD cast down great stones from heaven upon them unto Azekah, and they died: they were more which died with hailstones than they whom the children of Israel slew with the sword.

Gibeon had a treaty with Israel, and even though it was made as a result of Gibeonite deception, Israel honored the treaty. A league of five kings had attacked Gibeon, so Israel joined the battle and fought for Gibeon. Joshua and his men killed many of the enemy, and as they were pursuing the remaining, a storm came up and huge hailstones killed more of the enemy.

Gibeon was a great royal city with strong men of war, so when they made a treaty with Israel they became mighty. Because of the large combined army and Joshua's good strategy, it was obvious that the attackers were losing, so they fled. The fact that a storm came up was coincidental. It was a natural phenomenon, not a supernatural occurrence. This was but one of 16,000,000 thunderstorms that occur on earth each year. Because storms come up frequently, there is no reason to call one a miracle and not the rest.

52   The Sun & Moon Stand Still

◆ Joshua 10:12-14

> Then spake Joshua to the LORD in the day when the LORD delivered up the Amorites before the children of Israel, and he said in the sight of Israel, "Sun, stand thou still upon Gibeon; and thou, Moon, in the valley of Ajalon." And the sun stood still, and the moon stayed, until the people had avenged themselves upon their enemies. Is not this written in the book of Jasher? So the sun stood still in the midst of heaven, and hasted not to go down about a whole day. And there was no day like that before it or after it, that the LORD hearkened unto the voice of a man: for the LORD fought for Israel.

Joshua and God just couldn't get enough killing done that day so they conspired to lengthen it so they could do more. This account is from the Book of Jasher—which no longer exists. It was evidently a collection of ancient hero songs and poems compiled about 1000 B.C. The KJV has the story in prose, but the RSV uses the original poetic form.

This story was never meant to be taken literally—it was only the wishful thinking of Joshua, wanting enough time to defeat his enemy. I am sure you have been in a situation where you were enjoying yourself so much you wished time would stand still. That was the way Joshua might have felt. I am sure you have been in a situation where you were miserable and wished time would speed up so the unpleasantness would pass more quickly. It is not uncommon for us to wish our lives away by wanting a birthday, holiday or vacation to hurry and arrive. We can look at a watch or clock and see time does pass. It still seems to go so slowly in times of trouble and so fast in times of enjoyment. Joshua had no timepiece, so he could only guess the time by the position of the sun. There is no way a person can tell how much time passes without some measuring device, and they just didn't have one. Anyone would be sympathetic with Joshua wanting to finish the battle before dark. What allows one to presume God would work a miracle such as this?

For the sun to stand still it must first move. We must remember that in those days, the earth was flat and both sun and moon went around the earth. Just because one may believe that the Bible is God's book and that God knows everything, it is a mistake to believe the writers knew as much as we. Even as late as 1632 the Catholic Church would not accept Galileo's view that the earth circled the sun, so he was accused of heresy. Religion saw the sun and the moon and said they revolved around the earth. Science saw them and said the moon revolves around the earth, while the earth revolves around the sun. It took centuries for the Church to accept reality. If we refuse to accept facts today, continuing to believe Bible fictions, we are no better off than people thousands of years ago.

This story about Joshua was written about 500 B.C., during the Babylonian Exile. Because the Israelites believed they were God's chosen people, the priests made up these stories to boost their sagging spirits. The Israelites never believed the sun and moon actually stood still. They understood the reason the story was written. The Babylonians worshiped the sun and moon and Israel had their God. What the story said was simple: Our God is greater than your gods, as our God made your gods stand still. This story makes sense only in this setting. The problem Christians make is taking a Jewish book, by Jewish writers, and trying to tell the Jews what their book means. This is sheer folly. Earth is spinning about 1,000 mph at a point on the equator. The rotational inertia for the mass of Earth is so prodigious that bringing it to a halt would be like putting an apartment building in front of an express freight train. The laws of physics require that there would have been cataclysmic earthquakes and upheavals the likes of which have never been visited before or since upon this mote in space we call home. If Earth had stopped in its orbit, those same laws of physics would have required that it fall into the sun. There is no way the story could be literally true. It could only happen in poetry—that is the way it was written.

No miracle took place. To suppose that the sun and moon stood still is as fantastic as it is impossible.

53   *The Book of Judges*

◆ Judges 2:16-19

> And when the LORD raised them up judges, then the LORD was with the judge, and delivered them out of the hand of their enemies all the days of the judge: for it repented the LORD because of their groanings by reason of them that oppressed them and vexed them.

Some look on this as a miracle that when there was a judge, the LORD blessed them and when there was no judge, the people returned to sinful living. There is nothing strange about this when you consider that only good things are mentioned in most stories. We must also consider that the stories were written by priests to increase their influence over the people. During the time between Moses and Solomon—about 400 years—judges ruled Israel. The priesthood was at a low ebb because they didn't have much authority until they wrote their versions of the earlier stories between 1000 B.C. and 500 B.C.

One very important factor in the Bible is that most stories were written, or rewritten, much later than the time in which they were set. If we think of them as having been written as newspapers or diaries, we will never understand what happened. The priestly editors or redactors revised all of the stories to make current heroes the leading characters in the old stories. For priests to have power in 500 B.C., they had to make up stories that gave them that power in the time of Moses, 1400 B.C. For people to accept laws nobody ever heard of in 500 B.C., the priests had to manufacture the antiquity of the laws given to Moses. When the children of Israel left Egypt, they knew nothing of a God. One had to be minted and Moses did it by saying his God was also the God of Abraham, Isaac and Jacob. Even the story of Moses was not fully written until about 500 B.C.

In the time of Josiah, about 622 B.C., the Deuteronomic law was written, and the author also wrote the stories of the people's early years in Canaan. In these stories the judges were said to have led Israel: the stories of Deborah, Gideon and Samson became the book of Judges. The people of Josiah's time were told the laws they would have to obey bore the authenticity of hundreds of years. They had been lost and just newly found. Many times we see this in the Old Testament stories. People didn't know about things that allegedly started centuries earlier. How could the people know Moses made the brazen serpent that they worshiped for 700 years and not know it violated one of the Ten Commandments given to Moses? The story of the law did not exist then.

When we look at the New Testament, we will see the same thing. Mark and Paul didn't write about the virgin birth of Jesus because that story was not extant when they wrote.

54   *Othniel Judges Israel*

◆ Judges 1:12-15; 3:7-11

And the children of Israel did evil in the sight of the LORD, and forgot the LORD their God, and served Baalim and the groves. Therefore the anger of the LORD was hot against Israel, and he sold them into the hand of Chushan-rishathaim king of Mesopotamia: and the children of Israel served Chushan-rishathaim eight years. And when the children of Israel cried unto the LORD, the LORD raised up a deliverer to the children of Israel, who delivered them, even Othniel the son of Kenaz, Caleb's younger brother. And the land had rest forty years.

Othniel was called to judge Israel and he was able to lead them to victory and freedom, and they lived in peace for forty years. This was but the first of many times Israel was to flip-flop from serving God to worshiping idols. How a nation of people who were supposed to be so close to their God could turn from him and return so quickly is difficult to understand.

When the book of Judges was written, the priests were attempting to put together a story to bridge the gap from Moses to their time. After Joshua died, the people lived among the Canaanites and never seemed to be able to decide who they would worship. They vacillated for years, and when they turned away from God and were oppressed by other nations, God raised a judge and delivered them. In most of the stories of judges, the people would serve God for forty years. When the judge died, they would forget God again. This went on until Eli and Samuel came into power and they were judges, priests, and prophets.

These stories are not dependable history. Only brief glimpses of names, episodes, invasions, battles, and victories are given without any actual verification or evidence in historical records. When there are shreds of validity in one story, the next one disproves what seemed to be factual in the preceding one. We are left in the dark about what we can safely believe. We probably do best to read the stories, recognize the nature of their origin behind them, and enjoy the mood-swings of God's chosen people.

In these stories the "spirit of the LORD" is about equivalent to the New Testament "Holy Spirit," except there was no idea of a separate personality. There was nothing supernatural in this story. It was only the natural high and low points in a nation's morality. Leaders come and go in all nations, and Israel was no exception.

55   *Gideon and Fire from the rock*

◆   Judges 6:11-24

> Gideon was with his father Joash when the angel of the LORD appeared unto him, and said unto him, "The LORD is with thee, thou mighty man of valour. . . . Go in this thy might, and thou shalt save Israel from the hand of the Midianites."

The Midianites had been coming into the cities of Israel and stealing their crops for about seven years and Israel was "greatly impoverished." They called on the LORD for help, "And there came an angel of the LORD" and told Gideon he was chosen to deliver Israel from the enemy. Of course we read the standard response, "my family is poor in Manasseh, and I am the least in my father's house." The hero figures usually plead humility; we saw this same characterization in Moses, Isaiah, Jeremiah, David, and many others.

Gideon asked for a sign, and when he offered meat and bread to the angel, he was told to put the offering on a rock. When Gideon did as ordered, the angel touched the offering with his staff. Then "there rose up fire out of the rock, and consumed the flesh and the unleavened cakes. Then the angel of the LORD departed out of his sight." Now this would likely overwhelm anyone, but Gideon hardly seems more surprised than to just guess it was the LORD's doing, so he built an altar. An altar in that time was but a stack of rocks, and there were rocks everywhere. Whether anything such as fire issued from the rock or whether it was only a hysteric hallucination is anybody's guess. Gideon was alone when it happened, so believe what you will. My feeling is it was a hysteric hallucination of sight and sound induced by the fear of Midianite persecution. Gideon wanted to do whatever he could for his people, and his anxiety may have triggered the hysteria.

That same night

> the LORD said unto him, "Take thy father's young bullock, even the second bullock of seven years old, and throw down the altar of Baal that thy father hath, and cut down the grove that is by it: and build an altar unto the LORD thy God upon the top of this rock, in the ordered place, and take the second bullock, and offer a burnt sacrifice with the wood of the grove which thou shalt cut down."

There was guilt in Gideon's mind when he thought he had heard from God while realizing that his father worshiped other gods. This guilt, along with his anxiety, may have triggered another hallucination to make him believe he must sacrifice his father's bull and destroy his father's altar and grove as well. When Gideon did these things, his father stood by him and made him a kind of hero. Gideon was still not persuaded by Divine proof. He asked for another sign.

56 *Gideon and the Fleece*

◆ Judges 6:36-40

> And Gideon said unto God, "If thou wilt save Israel by mine hand, as thou hast said, Behold I will put a fleece of wool in the floor; and if the dew be on the fleece only, and it be dry upon all the earth beside, then shall I know that thou wilt save Israel by mine hand, as thou hast said."

When it happened just as he asked, he still wasn't sure, so he demanded that the conditions be reversed: wet ground and dry fleece. When this was accomplished he was finally satisfied. Since he was alone we have only the writers word; but I see him having hallucinations to ease a troubled mind. Even today there are people so troubled by other people's actions that they work themselves into great anxiety. These people often have hysteric hallucinations in which they see and hear someone ordering them to kill sinners. When they do as they are told, they claim it was God who gave the instructions.

These may not have been supernatural events—only hallucinations brought on by hysteria.

57 *Gideon and Midian*

◆ Judges 7

> And the LORD said unto Gideon, "The people that are with thee are too many for me to give the Midianites into their hands, lest Israel vaunt themselves against me, saying, 'Mine own hand hath saved me.'"

Once Gideon was satisfied he was doing God's work, he was able to persuade thirty-two thousand men to follow him to battle. God said it was too many, so twenty-two thousand turned back, afraid. God said there were still too many until Gideon finally had only three hundred men to go with him. With three hundred men, each with a trumpet, a lighted lamp and a pitcher, Gideon set up a strategy. At a certain time, each man was to blow his trumpet, break the pitcher, hold the lamp and shout, "The sword of the LORD, and of Gideon." When they did this, the Midianites became so frightened that they killed each other until only fifteen thousand of the one hundred thirty-five thousand remained. Gideon and his three hundred chased and finally killed all these fifteen thousand, too, and the battle ended. The number of Midianites was probably much smaller than one hundred thirty-five thousand. In their frightened condition they may have killed so many that only a hundred or so remained, and the three hundred with Gideon could have easily killed them.

With a story like this we must realize it is an exaggerated account. Parts of any story can be factual, so we need to try to understand how one could do what Gideon did. Gideon, like most who desire to serve their country, was under a great deal of strain, stress, and anxiety. This would have been enough to cause hysteria and the resulting hallucinations of sight and sound.

If you think this story is far-fetched, continue. In 1425 Joan of Arc, then thirteen years old, head voices and saw visions urging her to go to the aid of her country, France. Joan had been in the midst of national turmoil and conflict. She had observed combat and when the siege of Orléans came, the voices grew more insistent. She made a believer of the captain who gave her a small group of soldiers and, dressed as a male page, she convinced Charles VII that she was sent by God. Dressed in white armor, she led a garrison of troops to victory on May 8, 1429. The tide turned against Joan, and in 1431 she was tried by a Bishop and a court of French clergy on charges of witchcraft. She was burned at the stake May 31, 1431 as a witch and a heretic. Gideon was a hero in his day because people welcomed visions and voices. In Joan's day, the Christian Church rejected them. What a difference a day makes.

Gideon's story is one of the best in Judges, and he was remembered for his good deeds. Indeed, they were *his* deeds; no supernatural intervention is required. His hysteric hallucinations, coupled with his battlefield strategy caused him to become a hero of Israel.

58   The Birth of Samson

◆ Judges 13

> And the angel of the LORD appeared unto the woman, and said unto her, "Behold now, thou art barren, and bearest not: but thou shalt conceive, and bear a son. . . . And no razor shall come on his head: for the child shall be a Nazarite unto God from the womb: and he shall begin to deliver Israel out of the hand of the Philistines."

This is the common story preceding an uncommon man. An angel told a barren woman that she would bear a special son. This son was to be a Nazarite, which meant he was not to drink wine, vinegar or any strong drink, not to eat grapes, fresh or dried, not to cut his hair, and not to touch any dead body. "And Manoah said unto the angel of the LORD, 'What is thy name, that when thy sayings come to pass we may do thee honour?'" It was important for people to know the name of other people, or of angels, because they believed that knowing someone's name gave power over them. The angel said his name was a secret.

> So Manoah took a kid with a meat offering, and offered it upon a rock unto the LORD: and the angel did wondrously; and Manoah and his wife looked on. For it came to pass, when the flame went up towards heaven from off the altar, the angel of the LORD ascended in the flame of the altar. And Manoah and his wife looked on it, and fell on their faces to the ground.

This angel was special in that he went up in flames as no other was said to have done. The woman was stressed and anxious because she was barren, which probably brought on a hysteric hallucination in which she saw and conversed with an angel. When she suggested that Manoah also come see the angel, he confirmed what she had described to him.

The power of suggestion is able to cause others to experience the same visions, as we shall see in other Bible stories. Modern psychology calls it mass hysteria. Occasionally we find a group of people who experience the same vision. We also find a few who are not in the same frame of mind and don't see the vision. In the New Testament, some saw Jesus, "but some doubted." This symptom of hysteria may be the basis of many miracle stories in the Bible.

In this story, the child was born and they named him Samson, which meant Sun-man. Sun worship was widespread then, and there was a temple named *Beth-shemesh*, or "house of the sun," near where Manoah lived. Many stories, legends, myths and tales from folklore are woven into the fabric of these stories. We will find sources in many ancient stories that the Israelites heard and appropriated as their own. Since the Philistines were in control of the land, the Israelites were again crying out to their God for deliverance. Samson was to be the one to "begin to deliver Israel out of the hand of the Philistines."

This story of the angel announcing the birth of Samson may have been a hallucination and not a supernatural event.

59   *Samson Kills a Lion*

◆   Judges 14:5-10

> Then went Samson down, and his father and his mother, to Timnath, and came to the vineyards of Timnath: and, behold, a young lion roared against him. And the spirit of the LORD came mightily upon him, and he rent him as he would have rent a kid, and he had nothing in his hand: but he told not his father or his mother what he had done.

This chapter deals with Samson choosing a Philistine wife, blatantly contrary to Israelite practice. The parents were the ones who chose the brides for their sons.

This story has Samson and his parents on the road together, but when he killed the lion he was alone. How his parents could be with him and not know he killed a lion is the result of poor editing. The early story has Samson making the arrangements himself. The later story had to get the parents there before the arrangements could be made, so there was some confusion.

In the killing of the lion, we saw Samson doing what other heroes had done for years. Engidu tore a lion apart; Hercules killed the Nemean lion barehanded; Polydames killed a lion; David killed a lion; Beniah slew a lion, and Beniah's father "slew two lion-like men of Moab" (2 Samuel 23:20). The story of bees producing honey in the carcass of the lion is not to be taken literally because bees don't make hives in decaying matter. This was part of the solar myth "that the midsummer constellation with its warm sunny weather favors the work of bees. When the sun is in Leo, honey is plentiful," according to A. Smythe Palmer. For a man to kill a young lion barehanded is not out of the question, but in this story it is not to be considered as fact.

The story is only a means of showing Samson with the "strength of the sun."

60   Samson and the Foxes

◆ Judges 15:1-6

> And Samson went and caught three hundred foxes, and took fire-brands, and turned tail to tail, and put a firebrand in the midst between two tails. And when he had set the brands on fire, he let them go into the standing corn of the Philistines, and burnt up both the shocks, and also the standing corn, with the vineyards and olives.

This story is the result of Samson's father-in-law not respecting the marriage and giving his daughter to someone else. Samson was very angry, so he decided to get even and burn their crops. How Samson could capture three hundred foxes by himself is not to be understood as fact—it was only part of a solar myth. The destruction of the crops was somehow balanced by the Philistines who burned his wife and her father to death.

Here again there was no miracle. It is only a myth.

61   Samson Kills Some Philistines

◆ Judges 15:7-8

> And Samson said unto them, "Though ye have done this, yet will I be avenged of you, and after that I will cease." And he smote them hip and thigh with a great slaughter: and he went down and dwelt in the top of the rock Etam.

There is nothing here but more retaliation. We don't understand the term "hip and thigh" today. It is probably a proverbial expression of the time. This was not a product of supernatural power. It was only part of a story to magnify Samson's strength.

62   Samson Escapes From Bonds

◆ Judges 15:9-14

> And they bound him with two new cords.

The men of Judah found Samson, bound him, brought him to Lehi, and delivered him to the Philistines. "And the spirit of the LORD came mightily upon him, and the cords that were upon his arms became as flax that was burnt with fire, and his bands loosed from off his hands." This could have been a trick played on the Philistines by the men of Judah.

They may have used weakened bonds so Samson could escape to kill more Philistines.

Natural means are all that were in evidence here, and no miracle was needed to break weak ropes.

63   Samson and the Jawbone of the Ass

◆ Judges 15:15-20

> And he found a new jawbone of an ass, and put forth his hand, and took it, and slew a thousand men therewith.

This sounds like a phenomenal accomplishment, but the Bible clearly says one man killed one thousand men with the jawbone of an ass. This is really nothing new in the book of Judges. There is the story of "Shamgar the son of Anath, which slew of the Philistines six hundred men with an ox goad: and he also delivered Israel" (Judges 3:31). It was great sport killing Philistines, hundreds at a time. Shamgar killed six hundred and now Samson killed one thousand. When one makes up a story, one might as well make up a good one.

We are told this took place at Lehi, a word that means *jawbone*. It is no coincidence that there was a fresh jawbone of an ass that Samson found very conveniently. One of the keys to understanding Bible stories is names. Here it is the name of a location that betrays a fabrication. The name of the place tells the story as well as the narrative does. In other examples, the name of the person gives a clue to what we might expect from him or her. Most of the names of prophets, kings and heroes were "God names": they are compounds of *El, Iah,* or *Jah,* names of the Hebrew God. Elijah is such a combination. It means "Jehovah is God." Solomon combines the names of three sun gods, *Sol, Om* and *On.* Israel also has three god names; *Is* for Isis, *Ra,* and *El.* I could go on but I think the device is clear.

There is no need for super-human strength or supernatural power when the author had a good pen and enough paper to give rein to his imagination.

64   Samson at Gaza

◆ Judges 16:1-3

> Then went Samson to Gaza, and saw there an harlot, and went in unto her. . . . And Samson lay till midnight, and arose at midnight, and took the doors of the gate of the city, and the two posts, and went away with them, bar and all, and put them upon his shoulders, and carried them up to the top of a hill that is before Hebron.

Samson went all the way to Gaza, a principal Philistine city, and consorted with a harlot. He stayed with her until midnight, and then stole the gates of the city and carried them to Hebron, thirty miles away. This could hardly have been an actual event—it is part of a solar myth. The gates and posts were the same as the pillars of Dagon's temple. Again we are dealing in myth, not miracle.

65   *Samson's Haircut*

◆ Judges 16:4-22

> "There hath not come a razor upon mine head; for I have been a Nazarite unto God from my mother's womb: if I be shaven, then my strength will go from me, and I shall become weak, and be like any other man."

Samson took up with another woman and this time he met his match. Some say the third time is a charm, and Delilah was the third woman for Samson. Delilah was promised 5,500 pieces of silver if she could learn the secret of Samson's strength. After some trial and error, she finally learned it was his hair that gave him his strength.

The seven strands of Samson's hair signified the sun's rays with their seven colors of the rainbow. When the sun lost its rays, its power was gone, and when Samson lost the "seven locks of his head" his power was likewise gone. Delilah means "darkness," and now the story nears its climax and Samson is in for a fall. In Greek myth, Apollo was the sun and Homer called him "he of the unshaven hair." Now Sampson's secret was out and as his locks fall his strength evaporates. When "the Philistines took him, and put out his eyes," they put out his lights, continuing the simile. So the strength of the sun became darkness as Delilah overcame Samson. There is one verse that still left hope, "Howbeit the hair of his head began to grow after he was shaven." He was now blind and made to grind wheat in prison. His hair grew and with it his strength returned, but his story is almost at an end.

Can a person today expect great strength by letting his hair grow long? Of course not! That only worked in myth, fairy tales, and Bible stories. There was no power in the hair of Samson, not natural or supernatural. The story is only a solar myth and the power was only in the telling.

66   *Samson at Dagon's Temple*

◆ Judges 16:23-31

> And Samson took hold of the two middle pillars upon which the house stood, and on which it was borne up, of the one with his right hand, and of the other with his left. And Samson said, "Let me die with the

Philistines." And he bowed himself with all his might; and the house fell upon the lords, and upon all the people that were therein. So the dead which he slew at his death were more than they which he slew in his life.

Even though he was blind, Samson still had the ability to bring down the house. His strength returned as his hair grew. When he was between the two main supports of the temple, he was able to dislodge them. The temple collapsed and about three thousand people were killed.

This episode needs no supernatural help because it never actually happened. The story is a hero tale based on a solar myth, and the priests put it in to teach a lesson. The story shows that self-indulgence can lead to self-destruction. If people don't follow all the rules God lays down, they will die a terrible death. The story ends with the body of Samson being taken back to his homeland and buried in the tomb of his father, Manoah. What a powerful story for the Israelites to have had Samson be their judge for twenty years.

In this story of Samson, intertwined with solar myth, we need not look for a miracle, but for a moral. Unless God controlled the strength of a man or a nation there was great peril for civilization.

67   *The Birth of Samuel*

◆ 1 Samuel 1

Elkanah and his wife, Hannah, were good people and served God well. Elkanah also had a wife named Peninnah who bore him children, and she lorded it over Hannah who was childless "because the LORD had shut up her womb." Hannah had prayed about this "and the LORD remembered her. Wherefore it came to pass, when the time was come about after Hannah had conceived, that she bare a son, and called his name Samuel." Here is the regular formula for having a successful son. A woman, usually old, was barren, and after praying to God, she was granted a son. This was the case for Sarah, Hannah, Elisabeth, the wife of Manoah and many others. The child born was almost always a son of exceptional value to God. Many times the child was not only dedicated to God, but given to God. The boys were raised by the priests in the service of God all the days of their lives. Samson and Samuel were Nazarites and John the Baptist was possibly a Nazarite too.

The key phrase here as elsewhere is, "the LORD had shut up her womb." This is a sad commentary because it caused people great agony and personal pain. In this story Peninnah despised Hannah because she, Hannah, was childless. In many instances, when other wives or servants bore children to the husband, inevitable antagonism arose to spread misery and dissension. There would be a time of prayer, a visit by an angel, and nine months later a son. In obligatory archetypal fashion, the child would be given to God to serve him, and the mother would only have the child for two or three years. In Samuel's case, when he was weaned he was given to Eli to be raised in the house of the LORD.

These stories are literary formulas for the story Luke wrote about the birth of John the Baptist and Jesus. Even the song of Hannah became the basis for the *Magnificat* in Luke. Another verse rings familiar: "And the child Samuel grew on, and was in favour both with the LORD, and also with men." The more we look at the Old Testament, the more we begin to see it is the literary pattern for the New Testament.

The reason the women were barren may be traced to hysteric origins. Jewish culture placed high priority on children, and if the wives were slow in conceiving, they became anxious and fearful of displeasing their husbands. In this story, Hannah was provoked by Peninnah to the point that she developed hysteric barrenness. When the barren woman was calmed and comforted the hysteria was relieved. After a suggestion given by someone, usually an angel in a hysteric hallucination, the woman would finally conceive and bear a son.

This story is one with natural explanations for barrenness, visions of an angelic messenger and natural conception and birth. No miracle was necessary for the birth of a child.

68   *The Call of Samuel*

◆   1 Samuel 3

> And the child Samuel ministered unto the LORD before Eli. And the word of the LORD was precious in those days; there was no open vision.

Samuel lived with Eli the priest in the tabernacle at Shiloh. He had been there about nine years when he heard a voice while he slept. "The LORD called Samuel: and he answered, 'Here am I.'" The third time he heard the voice "Eli perceived that the LORD had called the child. Therefore Eli said unto Samuel, 'Go, lie down: and it shall be, if he call thee, that thou shalt say, Speak, LORD; for thy servant heareth.'" God again spoke to Samuel and told him Eli and his household would be purged because of the wickedness of Eli's two sons, Hophni and Phinehas. When morning came, Eli made Samuel tell him what God had said and Eli simply said, "It is the LORD: let him do what seemeth him good."

Until this time, when Samuel was about twelve years old, "Samuel did not know the LORD, neither was the word of the LORD yet revealed unto him." That seems peculiar after having lived with the priest in the tabernacle and not having known God—but that was the story. It may be that after all this time Samuel was becoming anxious and needed to know God. This could have triggered a hysteric hallucination in which he heard a voice—the voice of God. The fact that Samuel knew about the wickedness of Eli's sons became part of his revelation.

Nothing supernatural was involved, just a natural episode of hysteria, and behold a new hero for God was born.

69 *The Fall of Dagon*

◆ 1 Samuel 5:1-5

> And the Philistines took the ark of God, and, brought it from Eben-ezer unto Ashdod. When the Philistines took the ark of God, they brought it into the house of Dagon, and set it by Dagon. And when they of Ashdod arose early on the morrow, behold, Dagon was fallen upon his face to the earth before the ark of the LORD. And they took Dagon, and set him in his place again.

Dagon was the god of the Philistines, and his statue was in the temple at Ashdod. The Philistines had been victorious in battle with Israel after Sampson destroyed Dagon's temple in Gaza. With the victory, the Philistines took the Ark of the Covenant and set it in Dagon's temple. It appears that the two Gods couldn't get along with each other and this story bears that out.

The Ark of the Covenant was the dwelling place of the God of Israel. The statue of Dagon was Dagon himself, and when the two were in the same room something was going to happen. In this story the statue of Dagon fell on its face two days in a row. On the second day, "the head of Dagon and both the palms of his hands were cut off upon the threshold; only the stump of Dagon was left to him." Evidently the power of the God of Israel was so great that the statue could not stand before him.

There are many ways this could have occurred naturally, a couple of which make more sense to me. An earthquake and aftershock could have tipped the statue over or some clever Israelites could have slipped into the temple and pushed it over. There is no reason to think a supernatural event was needed when natural or human causes are adequate.

70 *The Emerods of the Philistines*

◆ 1 Samuel 5:6-12; 6:1-17

> And it was so, that, after they had carried it about, the hand of the LORD was against the city with a very great destruction: and he smote the men of the city, both small and great, and they had emerods in their secret parts.

The Philistines had the Ark of the Covenant for about seven months when the trouble began. The Philistines were afflicted with emerods or hemorrhoids. Some scholars think the plague was boils or tumors resulting from bubonic plague. The Septuagint told the story of a plague of mice occurring simultaneously, and they may have spread the bubonic plague. As a result of these two plagues, the Philistines decided to return the ark along with five golden hemorrhoids and five golden mice. These golden objects were not put into the ark itself, but were put into "a coffer by the side thereof." In the next story you will see how it was returned. The offering was a kind of homeopathic magic, offering symbols of plagues to cure plagues. We saw the same thing when Moses made the brazen serpent.

There is nothing miraculous about these plagues. They were as natural as the bubonic and pneumonic plagues known as the Black Death in 14th Century Europe.

71 Two Cows and a Cart

◆ 1 Samuel 6:6-17

> "Now therefore make a new cart, and take two milch kine, on which there hath come no yoke, and tie the kine to the cart, and bring their calves home from them: And take the ark of the LORD, and lay it upon the cart; and put the jewels of gold, which ye return him for a trespass offering, in the coffer by the side thereof; and send it away, that it may go."

To return the ark, the Philistines made a new cart and took two milk cows to pull the cart. They loaded the Ark of the Covenant and the coffer with the golden emerods and mice and sent them on their way to Beth-shemesh.

The Philistines decided to wait "And see, if it goeth up the way of his own coast to Beth-shemesh, then he hath done us this great evil: but if not, then we shall know that it is not his hand that smote us; it was chance that happened to us." As the cows pulled the cart to Bethshemesh, they followed it to the border to make sure the ark was safely received.

When the people of Bethshemesh saw the ark they rejoiced. In their exuberance they broke up the cart, cut up the wood and offered the two cows as a burnt offering to the LORD. That seemed like a good thing to do, but wait until you see how God rewarded them in the next story. For cows to pull a cart along the road to the next city hardly seems a difficult task.

No supernatural means are necessary to account for natural events.

72 *Death at Bethshemesh*

◆ 1 Samuel 6:12-21

> And he smote the men of Beth-shemesh, because they had looked into
> the ark of the LORD, even he smote of the people fifty thousand and
> threescore and ten men: and the people lamented, because the LORD
> had smitten many of the people with a great slaughter. And the men
> of Beth-shemesh said, "Who is able to stand before this holy LORD
> God? And to whom shall he go up from us?"

What a strange way to reward the people who rescued the ark and
offered up sacrifices to God for its return.

The village of Bethshemesh was very small—about 1,400 souls. How
could 50,070 men be killed from a population of 1,400 one might ask?
The only answer, according to scholars, is that the text was corrupted at
this point. Josephus says the number killed was 70, the RSV says 70,
and the KJV said 50,070. Who to believe? The reason they were killed
was stated as "they had looked into the ark." Again there is disagreement
among the scholars. Some say it should read, "looked at the ark of the
LORD." Often people tell us not what the Bible says, but rather what
they wish it said to justify their belief. In any event, people died for trying
to pay homage to God. For a God who can see into the hearts of man
rather than just outward acts, it makes one wonder.

Whether 70 or 50,070 died, I think the writer is justified in asking,
"Who is able to stand before this holy LORD God?" How can anyone
expect to be able to satisfy God if he may at any time kill those who try?
I see this story as a power play by the priests who wanted to keep people
at a distance. Only *they* could approach God. There need be nothing
supernatural here, and if anyone died it was probably from the plague
that was carried on the cart or the infected cows.

73 *Samuel at Ebenezer*

◆ 1 Samuel 7:1-17

> And when the Philistines heard that the children of Israel were gathered
> together to Mizpeh, the lords of the Philistines went up against Israel.
> And when the children of Israel heard it, they were afraid of the
> Philistines. . . . And as Samuel was offering up the burnt offering, the
> Philistines drew near to battle against Israel: but the LORD thundered
> with a great thunder on that day upon the Philistines, and discomfited
> them; and they were smitten before Israel. . . . Then Samuel took a
> stone, and set it between Mizpeh and Shen, and called the name of it
> Eben-ezer, saying, "Hitherto hath the LORD helped us."

Samuel had persuaded the people to "put away the strange gods," tear down the altars, cut down the groves, and turn back to the God of Israel. When they finally made their move and Samuel was offering sacrifices, the Philistines attacked.

Without any military battle, God sent a "great thunder" and smote the Philistines "and they came no more into the coasts of Israel." While this sounds great, it is not in accord with later chapters, where more battles with the Philistines took place. The problem is again due to text editing by the Deuteronomist and the stories from the *J* and *E* traditions. As for the battle being called off because of a thunderstorm, there is nothing difficult to understand about that. In ancient times when there was thunder and lightning, the combatants left the battlefield. Superstitious people thought the gods spoke in thunder so they called off the battle.

Purely natural events such as these need no supernatural assistance.

74   *Saul and the Lost Asses*

◆   1 Samuel 9; 10:1-2

> And the asses of Kish, Saul's father were lost. And Kish said to Saul his son, "Take now one of the servants with thee, and arise, go seek the asses."

As background information to this story, it is important to understand that the Israelites were dissatisfied because they had no real leader. The other nations had kings to lead and rule them and Israel felt left out. They called on Samuel to, "Give us a king to judge us." Even though Samuel told them how a king would treat them, they still wanted a king. When Saul was out looking for his father's lost asses, Samuel met him and made him King of Israel.

Saul was a large man "head and shoulders above" any of the others and this was probably what impressed Samuel. This part of the Saul story was like the Samson story: a solar myth. Saul was one with Sol the sun god, "head and shoulders above" the other cosmic bodies. As the sun is sovereign to the moon and planets, so Saul was to be king of his people. The asses Saul sought were symbolic and part of many creation and solar myths. Bacchus and Vulcan rode asses against the Titans. Moses and his family returned to Egypt riding asses. Mary and Jesus rode on an ass into Egypt and Jesus rode an ass into Jerusalem. Here the first king of Israel and the future king of Israel found the asses they sought. Finding lost asses wasn't the problem in need of supernatural help. The story is a fiction to bring Samuel and Saul together. The reason for the whole story was to tell why the nation of Israel changed from a theocracy to a monarchy.

75   *Samuel at Gilgal*

◆ 1 Samuel 12:16-25

> "Now therefore stand and see this great thing, which the LORD will
> do before your eyes. Is it not wheat harvest today? I will call unto the
> LORD, and he shall send thunder and rain: that ye may perceive and
> see that your wickedness is great, which ye have done in the sight of
> the LORD, in asking for a king." So Samuel called unto the LORD;
> and the LORD sent thunder and rain that day: and all the people greatly
> feared the LORD and Samuel.

The theme of this story is the theme of most Old Testament stories:
Fear God and his priests. These fears must always be seen to follow, the
latter from the former. Most of the time the priest said he had no
power—but he could call upon God to do his bidding. Here Samuel tells
the people what he was about to have God do, and it happened.

The idea of a thunderstorm at harvest time was unusual. That was why
it was called a miracle. Such a storm could, and on occasion, did occur,
and we know it was not a supernatural event. Just because something in
nature occurs once in 10, 20 or 100 years doesn't make it a miracle. The
purpose was to tell a story, that, when the people heard it, they "greatly
feared the LORD and Samuel." I challenge the people of God to go to
the middle of the Sahara Desert and ask God for a six inch rainfall when
the temperature is one hundred degrees. There have probably been days
when six inches of rain fell in this area but only under natural conditions.
To request and receive a six-inch rainfall under supernatural conditions
is totally out of the question.

76   *The Witch of Endor*

◆ 1 Samuel 28

> And when Saul enquired of the LORD, the LORD answered him not,
> neither by dreams, nor by Urim, nor by prophets. Then said Saul unto
> his servants, "Seek me a woman that hath a familiar spirit, that I may
> go to her, and enquire of her." And his servants said to him, "Behold,
> there is a woman that hath a familiar spirit at Endor." And Saul
> disguised himself, and put on other raiment, and he went, and two men
> with him, and they came to the woman by night: and he said, "I pray
> thee, divine unto me by the familiar spirit, and bring me him up, whom
> I shall name unto thee." Then said the woman, "Whom shall I bring
> up unto thee?" And he said, "Bring me up Samuel." And when the
> woman saw Samuel, she cried with a loud voice; and the woman spake
> to Saul, saying, "Why hast thou deceived me? for thou art Saul." And
> Samuel said to Saul, "Why hast thou disquieted me, to bring me up?"

Samuel had died; the Philistines were ready to attack Israel; Saul was scared. He tried to get information from God using dreams, Urim and prophets, but nothing worked for him. As a last resort he tried a woman with a familiar spirit, or, as we would call her, a medium. Saul had ordered all such women killed, but somehow this woman escaped. When she recognized Saul she was afraid he would kill her, but after he assured her she would be safe she went on with the seance. Lo and behold, Samuel appeared—or did he?

What may have happened was a hysteric hallucination by Saul in which he saw and heard Samuel. Saul was anxious, stressed, fearful, guilty and defensive—the kinds of conditions that may lead to a state of hysteria. One more condition in the story was important. "And there was no strength in him; for he had eaten no bread all the day, nor all the night." We will see Peter going into the same type of hysteria in the New Testament book of Acts. In Saul's vision, he saw Samuel and spoke with him. He already knew he would be condemned so that was what he heard Samuel say. The whole seance was a natural event, not requiring anything supernatural. Even today, people have seances and the same thing can happen. In most cases, however, people don't become hysteric and the medium or psychic is only deluding the paying customer with deception or trickery.

In this story the woman didn't see Samuel because he didn't appear. When the Bible says the woman saw Samuel, scholars say it should read, she saw Saul (1 Samuel 28:12). She would have recognized Saul because of his height, and not because she saw Samuel. Stories like this were written to show that people who violated God's laws—as made up by the priests—were not looked upon kindly. This is yet another scare story put together by the priests to augment their power and prestige.

Chapter 5

Stories of the Kings

77   *David Kills a Lion and a Bear*

◆ 1 Samuel 17:31-37

> And David said unto Saul, "Thy servant kept his father's sheep, and there came a lion, and a bear, and took a lamb out of the flock: And I went after him, and smote him, and delivered it out of his mouth: and when he arose against me, I caught him by his beard, and smote him, and slew him. Thy servant slew both the lion and the bear."

This little story told by David has no confirmation in any other Bible passage. It was probably written to equate David with Samson in slaying a lion, and the part about the bear was just added for good measure. David tended his father's flocks just as Moses tended Jethro's flocks and Saul tended his father's herd of asses. Perhaps David made up this story so Saul would be convinced that even though he was young, he was brave. With such a background, David was certainly qualified to fight against Goliath and lead Israel. The story of the lion and the bear were a symbol to signify physical strength and qualify David among the ranks of the heroes. This story is just a little fluff to build a background for the following episode with Goliath. It is more likely that if David killed these beasts he would have used his sling. This story would have had an important place in telling of his early days if it were literally true.

There is no reason to look for anything supernatural here when the whole story is symbolic.

107

78　*David and Goliath*

◆　1 Samuel 17

> And it came to pass, when the Philistine arose, and came and drew nigh to meet David, that David hasted, and ran toward the army to meet the Philistine. And David put his hand in his bag, and took thence a stone, and slang it, and smote the Philistine in his forehead, that the stone sunk into his forehead; and he fell upon his face to the earth.

Goliath, the Philistine, was the champion of the Philistine army, and for forty days he challenged Saul's army to send out someone to fight him. The story said Goliath stood about nine-and-a-half feet tall. He had a brass helmet, a coat of mail, leg protection of brass, brass body armor, a huge spear, a shield and a sword.

Anyone going up to fight against him hand-to-hand was decidedly outmatched in size and strength. David knew he couldn't fight Goliath on equal terms, but he was confident in his ability with a sling. With that as his equalizer, he knew he could win the battle. He took five smooth stones in his bag and ran toward Goliath who was so shocked to see such a young man—a boy—that he must have just stood amazed. With the element of surprise to his advantage, David took a stone and hurled it at Goliath's forehead. Goliath's forehead had no protection, and in a split second, the battle was over. David took Goliath's sword, cut off the giant's head and walked away.

When David was brought to the king, Saul said to him "Whose son art thou, thou young man?" How peculiar that David had to be introduced to Saul. Earlier we were told "Wherefore Saul sent messengers unto Jesse, and said, 'Send me David thy son, which is with thy sheep.' And David came to Saul, and stood before him: and he loved him greatly; and he became his armourbearer" (1 Samuel 16:19-21). Saul should have known David—if that story is correct. Again we find the editors have mixed up two versions of the narrative so they don't harmonize.

Also at odds are the two stories of Goliath's death. In this story in 1 Samuel 17 we read of David killing Goliath, but in 2 Samuel we have another story. "And there was again a battle in Gob with the Philistines, where Elhanan the son of Jaare-oregim, a Bethlehemite, slew the brother of Goliath the Gittite, the staff of whose spear was like a weaver's beam" (2 Samuel 21:19). Even though this text said "the brother of Goliath," the words "the brother of" are in italics, which means they were not in the original. The text should actually read, "Elhanan . . . slew . . . Goliath." Such stories as these were attributed, at a later time, to a current hero. When David became king, he also became the slayer of Goliath.

This is a good example of the way most Old Testament stories were made up. Special events were collected from stories from many countries and attributed to the hero the writer wanted to glorify. This story concerns natural ability, and if David was as good with a sling as the story says, he needed no supernatural aid to kill Goliath. David could well have been a marksman with a sling and even killed a man in battle. This could have been the basis for the story and the victim was changed to Goliath.

79   *The Death of Uzzah*

◆ 2 Samuel 6

> And they set the ark of God upon a new cart, and brought it out of the house of Abinadab that was in Gibeah; and Uzzah and Ahio, the sons of Abinadab, drave the new cart. . . . And when they came to Nachon's threshingfloor, Uzzah put forth his hand to the ark of God, and took hold of it; for the oxen shook it. And the anger of the LORD was kindled against Uzzah; and God smote him there for his error; and there he died by the ark of God.

This is another story of a man being executed for trying to keep the Ark of the Covenant from suffering damage. Uzzah seems to have reached out his hand to steady the ark and was killed instantly.

There are some major problems with the translations of these verses. Some of the earliest versions do not have the words "his hand." Some translators have made the story say the oxen were dunging rather than stumbling, and Uzzah's *error,* was made to read Uzzah's *slip.* In other words, instead of Uzzah putting forth his hand, he slipped on the dung and hit his head on the stone floor and died. This is more palatable to those who can't have God kill the man because he tried to help. All we can be sure of is that Uzzah died and there had to be some reason for his death. It appears that the object of the story was to show the ark was too holy for a common person to touch. Remember, God lived in the ark during this part of Israel's history.

Why did David use a new cart instead of having the priests carry the Ark according to the rules? Probably because the rules hadn't been made up yet. Remember, the priests made up rules about 750 B.C., and they said Moses was given them seven hundred years earlier. During the time of David (1000 B.C.) no such rules existed. To prove this we saw David ask "How shall the ark of the LORD come to me?" If Uzzah actually slipped, fell, hit his head on the floor and died, there is no supernatural cause involved. The story as it now reads doesn't make much sense, so maybe an alternate translation does clarify the problem.

80   *Famine and Pestilence Strike Israel*

◆ 2 Samuel 21:1-14; 24:1-17; 1 Chronicles 21:1

> Then there was a famine in the days of David three years, year after year; and David inquired of the LORD. And the LORD answered, "It is for Saul, and for his bloody house, because he slew the Gibeonites."

It seems odd that because Saul killed some Gibeonites years before, now there was a famine. There is no record of Saul having killed any Gibeonites, but that doesn't seem to matter. Gibeonites were not Israelites, but Amorites or Canaanites. When David asked how he could satisfy them, they asked for seven of Saul's sons that they might kill them. David gave the Gibeonites seven of Saul's sons and they "hanged them in the hill before the LORD: and they fell all seven together, and were put to death in the days of the harvest." After this killing and the burial of the seven with Saul and Jonathon, the famine ended.

> And again the anger of the LORD was kindled against Israel, and he moved David against them to say, "Go, number Israel and Judah. . . ." And Satan stood up against Israel and provoked David to number Israel.

These two contradictory verses tell of a single event: the numbering of Israel by David. As a result of this census, God was angry, and as a punishment, he gave David three choices.

> Go and say unto David, "Thus saith the LORD, I offer thee three things; choose thee one of them, that I may do it unto thee." So Gad came to David, and told him, and said unto him, "Shall seven years of famine come unto thee in thy land? or wilt thou flee three months before thine enemies, while they pursue thee? or that there be three days' pestilence in thy land? now advise, and see what answer I shall return to him that sent me."

David chose the third one and as a result of the pestilence, seventy thousand men died.

This seems pretty harsh to kill seventy thousand men just because David called for a census as ordered by God. We also have a verse that says Satan caused David to count the people, so which one are we to believe? In the Old Testament, Satan is not the same entity as in the New Testament. Satan appeared before God in the book of Job only as an adversary. After the Babylonian Exile and in New Testament times, Satan became a personification of evil or the Devil. In Jesus' time, some Jews believed in angels, devils, heaven and hell, but many did not. The Pharisees believed, but the Sadducees didn't.

In Old Testament times, Jews didn't believe in a personal Devil or a literal hell—and most still don't. Obviously Satan was, in this story, an angelic representative of God, not opposed to, but rather furthering, the will of God. Seeing Satan in this manner removes the seeming contradiction in the two stories. This leaves only God to cause David to take the census for which he was then condemned and seventy thousand men died. Such evidently was the nature of a kind and loving God. This was the same God who hardened the heart of Pharaoh. God also ordered the children of Israel to destroy thirty-one nations of people in Canaan so they could "inherit" the land.

It is as if there is a God in the Old Testament different from the one Jesus speaks of in the New Testament. The difference was actually only in the minds of the writers of the stories. In the minds of the Old Testament priests, God was to be feared so people would obey the priests. In the New Testament, Jesus taught that fear was replaced by love. These stories of famine and pestilence were to show how God dealt with those who disobeyed him. When the priests gained power over the people, they took it in the name of God. This is but another instance of scare tactics that the priestly writers used to maintain their position of power.

Only natural greed for power and not supernatural power is shown here.

81   *The Story of Solomon*

◆ 1 Kings 3:1-15; 4:29-30; 8 & 9

> In Gibeon the LORD appeared to Solomon in a dream by night: and God said, "Ask what I shall give thee. . . . Give therefore thy servant an understanding heart to judge thy people, that I may discern between good and bad: for who is able to judge this thy so great a people?"

Solomon was the son of David and Bathsheba. After David died, Solomon became king. Because Solomon did what was right in the sight of God, he had a dream and God promised him anything he wanted; the story says he chose wisdom. He became not only the wisest but the most wealthy, magnificent and last king of the united kingdoms of Israel and Judah.

> And God gave Solomon wisdom and understanding exceeding much, and largeness of heart, even as the sand that is on the sea shore. And Solomon's wisdom exceeded the wisdom of all the children of the east country, and all the wisdom of Egypt. For he was wiser than all men.

This man was so great one or two wives were not sufficient, so we are told. "And he had seven hundred wives, princesses, and three hundred concubines: and his wives turned away his heart" (1 Kings 11:3). This could hardly be construed as a product of godly wisdom: it led him to idolatry and downfall. His father, David, lusted after Solomon's mother, and, after an adulterous affair, David had Bathsheba's husband killed.

Solomon must have heard this story over and over, but he was no better than David, and he too lusted after women.

To say the wisdom of Solomon was supernatural, and a "gift of God," is sheer nonsense. When we look at the whole story we see it ended in the destruction of Solomon. If he were intelligent, discerning, and wise, it was natural because he was the son of a king and would have had good tutoring and training. There is no need for anything more than this to explain his wisdom.

The other event in Solomon's story that seems tinged with the supernatural was at the dedication of the Temple. Solomon spent years having the Temple built, and most people think it was a huge building. The dimensions were only 90 feet long, 30 feet wide and 45 feet high—about 2,700 square feet of outside dimension. Almost 30,000 Israelites and 150,000 Canaanites were cutting stones, felling trees, making pillars and doing the work needed to prepare, transport and assemble the building. In today's money, it would have cost about ten billion dollars, and all that for just a small church building.

Remember all the gold and silver the Israelites stole from the Egyptians? This is where they used it. "Now, behold, in my trouble I have prepared for the house of the LORD an hundred thousand talents of gold, and a thousand thousand talents of silver" (1 Chronicles 22:14). This verse David spoke and the word *trouble* has a margin note saying it could read "in my poverty." That is about 7,500,000 pounds of gold, and 75,000,000 pounds of silver. Let's see what happened at the dedication of this Temple: "And Solomon offered a sacrifice of peace offerings, which he offered unto the LORD, two and twenty thousand oxen, and an hundred and twenty thousand sheep. So the king and all the children of Israel dedicated the house of the LORD" (1 Kings 8:63). It must be noted that at the dedication, the

> brasen altar that was before the LORD was too little to receive the burnt offerings, and meat offerings, and the fat of the peace offerings. And at that time Solomon held a feast, and all Israel with him, a great congregation, from the entering in of Hamath unto the river of Egypt, before the LORD our God, seven days and seven days, even fourteen days.

No mention is made in these chapters of 1 Kings of any priestly participation at the Temple. The priests only carried the Ark of the Covenant: all the offering was done by Solomon. In the companion book of 2 Chronicles, the priests and Levites did the work of the Temple and made the offerings. I found this very strange until I remembered that Kings was compiled by a prophet while Chronicles was compiled by a priest. "Now when Solomon had made an end of praying, the fire came down from heaven, and consumed the burnt offering and the sacrifices; and the glory of the LORD filled the house" (2 Chronicles 7:1). 1 Kings didn't have fire from heaven but, "it came to pass, when the priests were come up out of the holy place, that the cloud filled the house of the LORD, So that the priests could not stand to minister because of the cloud: for the glory of the LORD had filled the house of the LORD" (1 Kings 8:10-11). Whether it was fire or a cloud, there could have been something rigged to produce the effect. With such a sumptuous Temple there needed to be a spectacular show, and fire or cloud would impress the people. One writer may have tried to outdo the other by producing fire, while the first writer only needed a cloud. Since both are fabricated stories, it hardly matters anyway.

As elegant as the Temple was, no secular history gives any evidence that it even existed. No one outside of the Biblical writers ever mention the most magnificent and lavish building ever constructed up to that time. It was said to have been built about 970 B.C., and destroyed by the Babylonians in 586 B.C. when Judah was captured and the people exiled. Even the Babylonians didn't mention the Temple in their records. As for Solomon, no evidence has been found to suggest he ever lived. "Solomon" is an interesting name. It is a combination of three names of sun-gods. Sol was the Roman sun god. Om was the Hindu sun-god. On was the Chaldean or Egyptian sun-god.

There is hardly anything supernatural in this story. The natural poetic license of the writers may account for such lavish tales of excess.

82   Jeroboam and the Withered Hand

◆   1 Kings 13:1-10

> And, behold, there came a man of God out of Judah by the word of the LORD unto Bethel: and Jeroboam stood by the altar to burn incense. . . . And it came to pass, when king Jeroboam heard the saying of the man of God, which had cried against the altar in Bethel, that he put forth his hand from the altar, saying, "Lay hold on him." And his hand, which he put forth against him, dried up, so that he could not pull it in again to him. . . And the king answered and said unto the man of God, "Intreat now the face of the LORD thy God, and pray for me, that my hand be restored me again." And the man of God besought the LORD, and the king's hand was restored him again, and became as it was before.

Here again, a man, king Jeroboam, was offering burnt incense to God at an altar. This showed a time when priests were not the only ones who could burn incense and do sacred things.

The man of God was an unnamed prophet and he intimidated Jeroboam. Due to fear of this "man of God," Jeroboam may have experienced an attack of hysteria, and his arm became paralyzed. Hysteric paralysis was common in Bible times, and we shall see more of it in New Testament stories later on. In this case of hysteria, the symptom was triggered as Jeroboam stretched out his hand toward the man. When Jeroboam asked for relief from the paralysis, the man prayed and his hand was cured. Hysteria was brought on and cured by Jeroboam's reaction to the man of God. Fear started the paralysis, and assurance relieved the problem. Even more simple yet, it may have been a muscle spasm and nothing more!

Nothing supernatural happened—as it was only a natural case of hysteria.

83   *The Devouring Lion*

◆ 1 Kings 13:7-32

> And the king said unto the man of God, "Come home with me and refresh thyself, and I will give thee a reward." And the man of God said unto the king, "If thou wilt give me half thine house, I will not go in with thee, neither will I eat bread nor drink water in this place: For so was it charged me by the word of the LORD, saying, 'Eat no bread, nor drink water, nor turn again by the same way that thou camest.'"

This was what the man of God was told to do and he did it. Soon another man met him and said,

> "I am a prophet also as thou art; and an angel spake unto me by the word of the LORD, saying, 'Bring him back with thee into thine house, that he may eat bread and drink water.'" But he lied unto him. So he went back with him, and did eat bread in his house and drank water. . . . And it came to pass, after he had eaten bread, and after he had drunk, that he saddled for him the ass, to wit, for the prophet whom he had brought back. And when he was gone, a lion met him by the way, and slew him: and his carcase was cast in the way, and the ass stood by it, the lion also stood by the carcase.

Because of disobedience, a lion killed the man of God, but the lion didn't harm the ass. This is supposed to be a miracle, but when a lion has had a big meal, it doesn't continue to kill for the sport of it. As it had eaten enough of the man to satisfy its hunger, it just laid down and went to sleep. The ass was no threat to the lion, and the well-fed lion was no threat to the ass.

This is not supernatural, but is probably only another priestly story to scare those who would disobey God or the priest.

84 *Ahijah's Revelation*

◆ 1 Kings 14:1-18

> At that time Abijah the son of Jeroboam fell sick. And Jeroboam said to his wife, "Arise, I pray thee, and disguise thyself, that thou be not known to be the wife of Jeroboam; and get thee to Shiloh: behold, there is Ahijah the prophet, which told me that I should be king over this people. And take with thee ten loaves, and cracknels, and a cruse of honey, and go to him: he shall tell thee what shall become of the child."

She disguised herself and went, but even though Ahijah was blind, he knew her and cursed the family of Jeroboam.

> "Therefore, behold, I will bring evil upon the house of Jeroboam, and will cut off from Jeroboam him that pisseth against the wall, and him that is shut up and left in Israel, and will take away the remnant of the house of Jeroboam, as a man taketh away dung, till it be all gone."

The reason Ahijah recognized Jeroboam's wife was simply because the prophet had confederates to keep him aware of what went on. Even a sighted prophet was clever enough to have agents to keep him posted on events in other places. So Ahijah was ready and waiting when she came in to see him. Ahijah was the priest of Shiloh, and Jeroboam followed the priests of Bethel. That was reason enough for Ahijah to pronounce doom on Jeroboam. The fact that this is a *D* story and the writer was a priest from Shiloh, shows why the story was written. Priests of Shiloh were not always on good terms with priests of Bethel. These priests were fighting for their jobs, and when someone threatened their livelihood, they got even. Abijah died when his mother returned, and the next story tells what became of Jeroboam.

85 *The Death of Jeroboam*

◆ 1 Kings 14:1-31; 2 Chronicles 13:20

> Neither did Jeroboam recover strength again in the days of Abijah: and the LORD struck him, and he died.

In 1 Kings he simply "slept with his fathers" but in 2 Chronicles "the LORD struck him." Just how Jeroboam died, we don't know. Because Jeroboam had "done evil above all that were before thee: for thou hast gone and made thee other gods, and molten images, to provoke me to anger, and hast cast me behind thy back: Therefore, behold, I will bring evil upon the house of Jeroboam." With such a reputation, how could anyone say anything good about his death. The term "the LORD struck him" is not literal, but a means used by the priestly writers to show the results of doing evil. It doesn't take a miracle to die. It was merely a way the writers used to keep people in line.

86   Uzziah's Leprosy

◆ 2 Kings 15:1-8; 2 Chronicles 26

> But when he was strong, his heart was lifted up to his destruction: for he transgressed against the LORD his God, and went into the temple of the LORD to burn incense upon the altar of incense. . . . Then Uzziah was wroth, and had a censer in his hand to burn incense: and while he was wroth with the priests, the leprosy even rose up in his forehead before the priests in the house of the LORD, from beside the incense altar. . . . And Uzziah the king was a leper unto the day of his death.

This is a sad story of one of Judah's better kings, for "he did that which was right in the sight of the LORD" until "he was strong." As Uzziah decided to burn incense to the LORD, the priests told him it was only they who could burn incense. Uzziah got mad at them, took a censer and went to the altar. As he was about to burn the incense, his forehead became leprous and he was taken from the temple. He lived the rest of his life in a separate house.

In Kings, he was called Azariah, and in Chronicles, Uzziah, but don't be confused, for they are one in the same. Also, don't be confused about the disease called leprosy. It wasn't Hansen's disease as we call leprosy today. In Bible times almost any skin disorder was called leprosy. The fact that the Bible says it came upon Uzziah immediately is an indication it was likely a symptom of hysteria. Uzziah was so angry with the priests and he probably had a guilty conscience, too. Together these problems triggered the hysteric reaction which caused the skin disorder. In other stories, Miriam and Naaman were cured of their hysteric leprosy, but Uzziah was not. More than likely, there was no one who understood the program at that time. It was "in the year that king Uzziah died" that Isaiah became a prophet of God. Maybe Isaiah could have helped Uzziah, but he came too late.

Although the use of incense on a special altar didn't start until two or three centuries after Uzziah, the story was interpolated into Chronicles by the author of *P*. In Kings, there is no reason given for Uzziah's leprosy because it was from an earlier source. The fact that Uzziah was offering incense poses no problems in the Kings story, but the *P* writer makes it the most important factor in the Chronicles account. The intent of the *P* author is to enhance the power of the priests. They were the only ones who could offer incense, and when even a king attempted to violate the priestly privilege he was stricken with leprosy. If the story were true, the hysteric leprosy would explain it as it was probably patterned after an actual event. The fact is that it is an interpolation in a manufactured story. In either case, the cause was only natural.

87   *Slaughter of the Assyrians*

◆ 2 Kings 18 & 19; 2 Chronicles 32:21; Isaiah 37:36

> Now in the fourteenth year of king Hezekiah did Sennacherib king of
> Assyria come up against all the fenced cities of Judah and took them.
> . . . Thus shall ye speak to Hezekiah king of Judah, saying, "Let not
> thy God in whom thou trusteth deceive thee, saying, Jerusalem shall
> not be delivered into the hand of the king of Assyria. . . ." Then Isaiah
> the son of Amoz sent to Hezekiah, saying, "Thus saith the LORD God
> of Israel, That which thou hast prayed to me against Sennacherib king
> of Assyria I have heard. . . ." And it came to pass that night, that the
> angel of the LORD went out, and smote in the camp of the Assyrians
> an hundred fourscore and five thousand: and when they arose early in
> the morning, behold, they were all dead corpses.

Sennacherib, king of Assyria was on a conquest. He had just taken
over after the death of Sargon and was out to prove himself. He had been
angered by a general insurrection of the tributary states of the west, and
Hezekiah, king of Judah.

In his zeal for God, Hezekiah destroyed Assyrian emblems of worship.
The Assyrians challenged Judah and took 146 cities, deported many
Israelites, and Hezekiah paid a large tribute to the king of Assyria after
he besieged Jerusalem. Hezekiah went to Isaiah and pled for God's help,
and God said "For I will defend this city, to save it, for mine own sake,
and for my servant David." That very night, 185,000 Assyrian soldiers
died in their camp, Sennacherib went home and Jerusalem was saved.
Hezekiah did "right in the sight of the LORD," by removing high places,
destroying images, cutting down groves and places of worship. He also
"brake in pieces the brasen serpent that Moses had made: for unto those
days the children of Israel did burn incense to it." Israelites had worshiped the bronze serpent for about 750 years according to this story.

Hezekiah decided that even though the Northern Kingdom of Israel
had fallen to the Assyrians, the Southern Kingdom of Judah would no
longer pay tribute. Other nations subject to Assyria also rebelled and
Sennacherib decided to teach them a lesson, so he went into Judah and
captured 146 cities. He wanted Jerusalem, but Hezekiah sent all the gold
and silver from the temple to bribe him. Sennacherib wouldn't surrender,
so he brought an army and was ready to attack Jerusalem when disaster
struck. In a single night, 185,000 Assyrian soldiers died of unknown
causes. The Bible account alone tells of this crushing defeat. No other
record of such an event is to be found in any nation's history. Scholars
believe the whole episode of the preparation for the attack to the
mysterious death of 185,000 men is fabrication. The *P* writers would

gain power and prestige if people believed God sent an angel and destroyed such an army, threatening Judah.

Because the story is pure fabrication, no supernatural events occurred and again we have only fantasy.

88   *Hezekiah's Healing*

◆ 2 Kings 20:1-11; 2 Chronicles 32:24; Isaiah 38

> In those days was Hezekiah sick unto death. And the prophet Isaiah the son of Amoz came to him, and said unto him, "Thus saith the LORD, Set thine house in order; for thou shalt die, and not live." Then he turned his face to the wall, and prayed unto the LORD. . . . Thus saith the LORD, the God of David thy father, "I have heard thy prayer, I have seen thy tears: behold, I will heal thee: on the third day thou shalt go up unto the house of the LORD. And I will add unto thy days fifteen years; and I will deliver thee and this city out of the hand of the king of Assyria; and I will defend this city for mine own sake, and for my servant David's sake." And Isaiah said, "Take a lump of figs." And they took and laid it on the boil, and he recovered. And Hezekiah said unto Isaiah, "What shall be the sign that the LORD will heal me, and that I shall go up into the house of the LORD the third day?" . . . And Isaiah the prophet cried unto the LORD: and he brought the shadow ten degrees backward, by which it had gone down in the dial of Ahaz.

Hezekiah had a sore boil and like many of us today he said, "It hurts so much I am going to die." That doesn't mean it would kill him, but idioms have a way of sounding like facts centuries later when stories are told and retold. A simple plaster of figs was used, the boil was cured and Hezekiah lived another fifteen years. Isaiah told the king he was going to die, but he was wrong. The story of imminent death was false and the story of the sundial was made up to cover the error. Isaiah said the LORD changed his mind and so Isaiah justified the failed prophesy. How many times have you heard, or even said, "I am so sick I know I am going to die?" We all get carried away when we don't feel well. Hezekiah and Isaiah had the same problem, but they went on record.

According to Deuteronomy

> When a prophet speaketh in the name of the LORD, if the thing follow not, nor come to pass, that is the thing which the LORD hath not spoken, but the prophet hath spoken presumptuously. . . . But the prophet, which shall presume to speak a word in my name, which I have not commanded him to speak, or that shall speak in the name of other gods, even that prophet shall die (Deuteronomy 18:20-22).

Why was it assumed that a prophet could prophesy something hundreds of years in the future? All prophesies had to come to pass shortly or the prophet would be killed. The Jews were never concerned with events in the distant future because only the present time was of any consequence to them. Anything more than two or three years away was out of the question. When you read of a prophesy coming true many years later, you are reading an interpolation added by a later writer after the event had occurred. The priests made up prophesies after the fact and put them into stories written many years before. This fulfillment of prophesy added to the power and prestige of the priesthood.

This story of a natural poultice of figs is adequate to cure a natural boil and no miracle is necessary in the story.

Chapter 6

Elijah and Elisha

89   Elijah Predicts a Long Drought

◆ 1 Kings 17:1; James 5:17

> And Elijah the Tishbite, who was of the inhabitants of Gilead, said
> unto Ahab, "As the LORD God of Israel liveth, before whom I stand,
> there shall not be dew or rain these years, but according to my word.
> . . ." Elias was a man subject to the same passions as we are, and he
> prayed earnestly that it might not rain: and it rained not on the earth
> by the space of three years and six months.

Here, as if out of nowhere, comes a man proclaiming himself to be the spokesman for God. Unannounced and unknown, Elijah went right to the king of Israel and told him there would be a drought and a famine. No preliminary discussion, no demands, no alternatives; just a drought and famine would come to Israel. Elijah is a "god-name" in that it is composed of *El* and *Jah,* which literally means *Yah,* or "Jehovah is God." We hear the name *Jehovah,* but it is not a Jewish word because the Jews have no letter "J" in their language. *Yahweh* may be closer, but strange to say, we do not know God's name. The Jews don't know it and neither do the Christians. Are you aware that nobody knows God's name? How presumptuous of Elijah to proclaim himself the spokesman for God. At that time there were apparently no priests in Israel to challenge him, and as we shall soon see, even the king followed Elijah's orders.

Droughts were not at all uncommon in Israel so there was no need of any supernatural means as natural means were adequate.

90   *Elijah Fed by Ravens*

◆   1 Kings 17:2-7

> And the word of the LORD came unto him, saying, "Get thee hence, and turn thee eastward, and hide thyself by the brook Cherith, that is before Jordan. And it shall be, that thou shalt drink of the brook; and I have commanded the ravens to feed thee there."

When Elijah announced the famine, he left town and went to the brook Cherith. I imagine Elijah set up a plan before he made such a threat to the king. He probably had food stashed by this brook to feed himself. The story teller also added a bit about ravens feeding Elijah and there was some sense in the story. Ravens carry things in their beaks and on occasion they drop them. Ravens carry nuts and drop them on rocks to crack them open. They carry small rodents to nesting sites. They steal food from people and other animals and carry it to their nests. There was probably a nesting site near the brook, and as a result, some food was inadvertently dropped and Elijah found it.

This story deals with natural occurrences so no supernatural means are necessary.

91   *Meal and Oil Multiplied*

◆   1 Kings 17:8-16

> And the word of the LORD came unto him, saying, "Arise, get thee to Zarephath, which belongeth to Zidon, and dwell there: behold, I have commanded a widow woman there to sustain thee."

Probably after a year or two the brook dried up and Elijah left it and went to Zarephath, a few miles from Sidon on the Mediterranean coast. There was a widow who took him in and fed him with her meal and oil. The story teller said she was just about out of food when he came. By some means the food lasted for some time and she was able to feed Elijah, herself and her son.

Several ideas come to mind about how the meal and oil lasted. She could have had other supplies that were not in the barrel and cruse. They may have been stored somewhere else. By bringing out her reserves, she could have replenished her kitchen. Elijah knew of the coming famine and could have hidden a large supply of meal and oil and added small amounts to her supply day by day. Her neighbors may have felt sorry for her and added to her supply every few days. This is entirely possible— people do such things today.

I once heard about a trick a new car salesman played on a customer. After he sold a new car to his neighbor, he went to the man's house every two or three nights and poured gas into the tank of the new car. The man who bought the car was very happy with it and especially with the gas mileage. The salesman continued adding gas to the car for about two months. The man was boasting about the fabulous mileage and then the salesman stopped putting gas in the man's car. Pretty soon the man ran low on gas and had to start buying it himself and his mileage was only average after that. The salesman never told the customer what he had done, and the neighbor was sure a miracle had occurred.

Many things happen of which we are unaware. Just because someone is playing a trick on us, we may see it as something supernatural, which it wasn't. The story of the meal and oil was of natural causes and not a miracle.

92 Elijah Raises the Widow's Son

◆ 1 Kings 17:17-24

> And it came to pass after these things, that the son of the woman, the mistress of the house, fell sick; and the sickness was so sore, that there was no breath left in him. . . . And he stretched himself upon the child three times, and cried unto the LORD, and said, "O LORD my God, I pray thee, let this child's soul come into him again." And the LORD heard the voice of Elijah; and the soul of the child came into him again, and he revived.

This is the first case in the Bible of a dead person coming back to life. The idea that the soul returned is not what Christians think of today. Jews never believed in an immortal soul, so that is not the intent of the story. When Elijah "stretched himself upon the child" he may have performed artificial respiration or even mouth-to-mouth resuscitation. The story says "there was no breath left in him" and this indicates all he did was get the boy to breathe again. This was only a natural action and no supernatural assistance was needed. As the child was not in the condition for very long, there were no complications or brain damage, and all was back to normal in just a few minutes.

93 Elijah at Carmel

◆ 1 Kings 18:1-39

Elijah said to Ahab, king of Israel

> "Now therefore send and gather to me all Israel unto Mount Carmel, and the prophets of Baal four hundred and fifty, and the prophets of the groves four hundred, which eat at Jezebel's table." So Ahab sent unto all the children of Israel, and gathered the prophets together unto Mount Carmel.

I am really amazed that this is so easily accepted as if it could actually happen. Look at the story carefully and you will see several key phrases which are clues to it having been made up. The first clue is when a self-proclaimed prophet presumes to tell the king of Israel what to do. Elijah told Ahab to get all the people of Israel and 850 prophets of Baal and Asherah and the king himself and travel to Mt. Carmel. The key here is that the king did as he was ordered. What we see here is similar to Moses, another self-proclaimed prophet from the desert, going to a national leader and giving him orders.

Imagine a preacher today going to the White House and telling the President of the United States to get Congress to meet him at Pikes Peak. The preacher would not get to see the President, let alone give him some silly order and have him respond favorably. Why people think a Pharaoh or a king would consider following orders of such people is utter folly. The story said they all went to Mt. Carmel and Elijah took charge. The 850 prophets built an altar, put on some wood, cut up the bull, and laid it on the wood. Then they called on their gods to send fire from heaven. Of course there was no way they could call down fire, but they tried just the same. They prayed, yelled, jumped around, cut themselves and after all this, they were unable to call fire from heaven.

Now it was Elijah's turn. He took twelve rocks and piled them up for an altar. A trench was dug around the altar. Wood was added, a bull was cut up and put on the wood, then twelve barrels of water were poured over the whole stack. Elijah said a short prayer and "Then the fire of the LORD fell and consumed the burnt sacrifice, and the wood, and the stones, and the dust, and licked up the water that was in the trench." How could such a thing happen? Several ideas have been proposed over the years. One was that lightning struck the altar. Some scholars say the altar was on the side of Mt. Carmel at about 1,600 feet elevation. If Elijah had driven a lightning rod into the altar, it would have attracted a bolt of lightning. The lightning would consume the sacrifice, wood, altar, and water quite nicely.

Another was that is wasn't water, but naphtha, a natural gasoline, that was poured on the altar. Because this was oil country, pools of natural distillates of petroleum could be found. Zarephath was not far from Mt. Carmel, and Elijah could have learned of such a pool of flammable liquid from people there. Once the altar and sacrifice were saturated with the flammable liquid, Elijah had only to make a spark and the whole thing would go up in flames.

Now we have another clue. "And Elijah said unto them, Take the prophets of Baal; let not one of them escape. And they took them: and Elijah brought them down to the brook Kishon, and slew them there." It was important for Elijah to kill the 850 prophets so they wouldn't figure out his trick and blow the whistle on him. Elijah couldn't afford to have any of them discover his lightning-rod or gasoline act. Prophets had to be just a cut above the regular people in order to be prophets. Elijah was afraid one of them would expose his trick, so they all had to die.

What Elijah did was purely natural and no supernatural assistance was needed. Because Elijah listened to people about geology and meteorology, he was aware when a storm was coming his way, and he used it all to his advantage.

94 Rain Ends the Drought

♦ I Kings 18:1-2,41-46

> And Elijah said to Ahab, Get thee up, eat and drink; for there is a sound of abundance of rain. . . . And it came to pass in the meanwhile, that the heaven was black with clouds, and wind, and there was a great rain. And Ahab rode and went to Jezreel.

Rain is a natural event following lightning, and thunder is the "sound of abundance of rain." After a long dry spell, the thunderstorms usually bring great amounts of rain and Elijah was aware of this. We hear stories of Native Americans doing rain dances and the rain that follows. Even Native Americans won't waste their time dancing when there aren't clouds in the sky. Just a little bit of meteorological training can tell an astute observer what is happening, and Elijah was ready for it when the rain came.

95 Elijah and Ahab Go to Jezreel

♦ 1 Kings 18:46

> And the hand of the LORD was upon Elijah; and he girded up his loins, and ran before Ahab to the entrance of Jezreel.

Some see in this verse a power coming over Elijah that enabled him to run faster than Ahab's chariot could carry him. They probably all came across the 10–15 mile plain together, and it may have been wet enough to slow down the narrow-wheeled chariot of Ahab. We need to be aware that Ahab and Elijah are on very good terms. They seem to get along well together, even after Elijah killed the 850 prophets. Ahab may even have let Elijah ride with him in his chariot until the wheels began to sink in too deep and then Elijah may have run on ahead.

There is no evidence of any supernatural happenings and no indication there was a race going on between Ahab and Elijah.

96   *An Angel Feeds Elijah*

◆   1 Kings 19:1-18

> And as he lay and slept under a juniper tree, behold, then an angel touched him, and said unto him, "Arise and eat." And he looked, and, behold, there was a cake baken on the coals, and a cruse of water at his head. And he did eat and drink, and laid him down again. And the angel of the LORD came again a second time, and touched him, and said, "Arise and eat; because the journey is too great for thee." And he arose, and did eat and drink, and went in the strength of that meat forty days and forty nights unto Horeb the mount of God.

After his return from Mt. Carmel, Elijah was threatened by a message from Jezebel. He traveled all the way to Beersheba, a hundred miles south. There he was visited by an angel and fed twice. On the strength of the meals he then traveled forty days and nights to the mount of God, Horeb or Sinai. Remember *E* calls it Horeb, and *J* calls it Sinai.

When we read of Elijah visited by an angel, we must realize the story was added after the Exile because that was when angels entered the picture. Most of the Old Testament was written or rewritten after the Exile and during the time of Ezra, about 444 B.C. It was during their stay in Babylon that the Israelites learned of heaven, hell, angels and devils. Not all believed in all these ideas and even in Jesus' time there was disagreement between the Pharisees and the Sadducees. More than likely, as Elijah slept, someone brought him food and drink and in his waking drowsiness, he didn't recognize his benefactor. The story was told and retold and gradually evolved until it is as we have it. Later editors added the angel and the forty days without food or water. The people of that area and time were very neighborly and did feed strangers. It would have been nothing extraordinary for Elijah to have been fed by someone he did not recognize.

Nothing in the story needs supernatural help—the hospitality and generosity of the people were enough to get Elijah fed.

97   *The Still Small Voice*

◆   1 Kings 19:9-18

> And he came thither unto a cave, and lodged there; and, behold, the word of the LORD came to him, and he said unto him, "What doest thou here, Elijah? . . ." And, behold, the LORD passed by and a great and strong wind rent the mountains, and brake in pieces the rocks before the LORD; but the LORD was not in the wind: and after the wind, an earthquake; but the LORD was not in the earthquake: And after the earthquake a fire; but the LORD was not in the fire: and after the fire a still small voice.

Elijah was on Mt. Horeb or Mt. Sinai, and he was hearing voices as did Moses. In fact much of what happened to Elijah also happened to Moses centuries before.

Both spent forty days and nights without food. While Moses was sheltered "in the clift of the rock," Elijah "stood in the entering in of the cave." God said to Moses he would "cover thee with my hand" and Elijah "wrapped his face in his mantle." Both got the Sinai sound-and-light show. From this it is easy to conclude that the Elijah story is but a copy of the Moses story, so Elijah, too, can be a true prophet of God. After a long fast, a trip across the desert, the anxiety and fear of God and the need to serve him, Elijah had a hysteric hallucination. Elijah saw and heard the same things Moses did because he knew the story and wanted the same things for himself.

There is nothing supernatural in the story as Elijah was only a copy-cat of Moses. Whether Elijah actually went to Mt. Sinai, or the writer only said he did, the result was the same.

98 *Elijah and the Fire from Heaven*

◆ 2 Kings 1:9-15

> "Thou man of God," the king hath said, "Come down." And Elijah answered and said to the captain of fifty, "If I be a man of God, then let fire come down from heaven and consume thee and thy fifty." And there came down fire from heaven, and consumed him and his fifty.

This story takes place when the king of Israel wanted Elijah to come to him. He sent a captain and fifty men and Elijah destroyed them by calling down fire from heaven. A second captain and fifty men were sent and Elijah destroyed them the same way. Now 102 men are dead and a third captain and fifty men came to Elijah from Ahaziah, son of Ahab and Jezebel and now king of Israel. This captain begged for his life and the lives of the fifty with him. Elijah heard an angel tell him to spare them and to go with him to the king.

I wonder whether it seems plausible to the average person that God would kill 102 men and then allow Elijah to do what was asked of him in the first place. I believe the stories were concocted by priests to demonstrate God's power and cause people to obey the priests as God's representatives. Even if you believe in the Devil, you won't find anything done by Satan in the whole Bible as terrible as this. The worst act attributed to Satan was causing Job to have boils, and that is only in a fable.

Nothing supernatural occurred here. The story is only made up and we can take it with a pound of salt and go on to the next story.

99   *Elijah Crosses The Jordan*

◆ 2 Kings 2:1-8

> And Elijah took his mantle, and wrapped it together, and smote the waters, and they were divided hither and thither, so that they two went over on dry ground.

Elijah was on his way to die and everybody knew it. All the sons of the prophets, Elisha and Elijah himself knew the end was near. This was the last time he was to cross the Jordon, so he decided to do it with a flair. As fifty sons of the prophets watched from a distance, Elijah used his mantle to do what Moses and Joshua were said to have done, and parted the water. This was not at flood season, so more than likely they simply walked through shallow water or stepped on rocks as stepping stones. Remember the twelve stones Joshua set up "in the midst of Jordan" (Joshua 4:9)? They were still there and these were the stepping stones Elijah and Elisha used. The fifty viewers from "afar off" thought they saw something marvelous, or Elisha later told them the water parted and they believed it. This was only a copy-cat story intended to give support to Elisha who was to replace Elijah as prophet. It has been said that anyone can walk on water if the temperature is right—about forty degrees below zero—or if he knows where the rocks are. Here Elijah knew where the rocks were.

Nothing supernatural here, just natural, shallow water and good stepping stones.

100   *What Happened to Elijah?*

◆ 2 Kings 2:9-18

> And it came to pass, as they still went on, and talked, that, behold, there appeared a chariot of fire, and horses of fire, and parted them both asunder; and Elijah went up by a whirlwind into heaven.

This story of Elijah going up in a whirlwind has been confusing because most people seem to think Elijah went up to heaven in a fiery chariot. The story of a chariot and horses was either made up or was a hysteric hallucination seen by Elisha as the result of anxiety about the death of Elijah. There is even a song of Elijah and a "sweet chariot." Earlier in the chapter it said, "And it came to pass, when the LORD would take up Elijah into heaven by a whirlwind, that Elijah went with Elisha from Gilgal."

We don't know happened to Elijah's body. All we know is that it was picked up by a whirlwind and no one ever saw him again. I can guess it was carried and dropped some distance away in a deserted place and eaten by wild animals. We know Elijah didn't really go to heaven, because Jesus said so, "And no man hath ascended up to heaven, but he that came down from heaven, even the Son of Man which is in heaven" (John 3:13). Let's read on and see what we can discover.

> And they said unto him, "Behold now, there be with thy servants fifty strong men; let them go, we pray thee, and seek thy master: lest peradventure the spirit of the LORD hath taken him up, and cast him upon some mountain, or into some valley." . . . They sent therefore fifty men; and they sought three days, but found him not.

Here is the idea that the "spirit of the LORD" was the same as the whirlwind, and by translation it was. *Spirit* in Hebrew and Greek means "air," "wind," "breath" or in this case spirit meant "whirlwind." One other theory was that Elisha wanted to be the boss and so he killed Elijah, buried the body, took his mantle and made up the whole story.

In any event, the natural always supersedes the supernatural and there is no reason to look for a miracle here.

101 Elisha Crosses the Jordan

◆ 2 Kings 2:12-14

> And he took the mantle of Elijah that fell from him, and smote the waters, and said, "Where is the LORD God of Elijah?" and when he also had smitten the waters, they parted hither and thither: and Elisha went over.

This story is identical with the previous one in which Elijah and Elisha cross in the other direction. Nothing is said of the waters coming back together again, so I believe they never really parted. Hitting water will always make it splash "hither and thither" and we only have the word of Elisha that they parted. The river was the same level, and he crossed where they crossed before. The story was only written to transfer authority from Elijah to Elisha.

No miracle here as he walked on the same stepping stones as before.

102 Elisha and the Spring of Water

◆ 2 Kings 2:19-22

> And the men of the city said unto Elisha, "Behold, I pray thee, the situation of this city is pleasant, as my lord seeth: but the water is naught, and the ground barren." And he said, "Bring me a new cruse, and put salt therein." And they brought it to him. And he went forth unto the spring of the waters, and cast the salt in there, and said, "Thus saith the LORD, I have healed these waters; there shall not be from thence any more death or barren land." So the waters were healed unto this day, according to the saying of Elisha which he spake.

There isn't much information in this story and its authenticity is questionable. It appears to be a copy-cat story of Exodus 15 where Moses healed the water at Marah.

If there is any truth to the story, it could have been a very natural situation in which an enemy put something into the spring to cause the problem. An animal may have fouled the water. An earthquake may have caused some shift under the spring and some soil fell into the spring causing the water to taste bad. These are natural and short-lived situations, so putting salt in the water could have done the same thing as waiting a day or so. The water had been good, turned bad and returned to good.

It is an example of a temporary situation that was cured by time, not supernatural means.

103   *Elisha Curses the Little Children*

◆ 2 Kings 2:23-25

> And he went up from thence unto Beth-el: and as he was going up by the way, there came forth little children out of the city, and mocked him, and said unto him, "Go up, thou bald head; go up, thou bald head." And he turned back and looked on them, and cursed them in the name of the LORD. And there came forth two she bears out of the wood, and tare forty and two children of them.

Elijah and Elisha were from Shiloh, and they considered Bethel to be a place of wickedness. It was common in those days for prophets and priests of Shiloh to be very antagonistic to those from Bethel. In this story, Elisha was responding to the young boys from Bethel by cursing them in the name of God. Elisha was not responsible for the two bears that came out of the woods and attacked the boys, but he didn't try to help them either. Even though baldness was somewhat of a disgrace, it seems unbelievable for a man of God to curse children because they pointed it out to him. This story must be viewed in the context of the morality of that day. Since Hebrews didn't believe in heaven or hell, they didn't see it as a problem to curse each other in God's name.

When one recognizes that the story was written by priests, one can see that the object was the promotion of their special brand of religion. Those of the rival camp were considered as enemies, and all was fair in the religious war. The morality of Jesus was to turn the other cheek when mocked, but for Elisha it was a matter of retribution, and even if the result was death it didn't matter.

The fact that bears attacked children is natural for bears, and not the result of a miracle.

104 Elisha and the Flooded Ditches

◆ 2 Kings 3:1-27

> And he said, "Thus saith the LORD, make this valley full of ditches."
> For thus saith the LORD, "Ye shall not see wind, neither shall ye see
> rain; yet that valley shall be filled with water, that ye may drink, both
> ye, and your cattle, and your beasts."

The people were in a dry valley and needed water, so Elisha told them
to dig ditches or pits and shallow wells. Because the valley was situated
over a large aquifer, the water, being under pressure, seeped into the pits
and they filled up. When the enemies looked at the valley and saw the
light reflect off the water, it looked red and they thought it was blood.
They assumed the blood meant the Israelites had lost a battle and they
went down to collect the spoils. The Israelites were waiting for them and
the Moabites were routed and fled.

The fact that there was artesian water in the valley is purely natural
and no miracle was necessary for water under pressure to come to the
surface. The story took place in the land of Edom, and Edom means
"red." The soil color could have added to the effect of coloring the water.

105 Elisha and the Widow's Oil

◆ 2 Kings 4:1-7

> Now there cried a certain woman of the wives of the sons of the
> prophets unto Elisha, saying, "Thy servant my husband is dead; and
> thou knowest that thy servant did fear the LORD: and the creditor is
> come to take unto him my two sons to be bondmen." And Elisha said
> unto her, "What shall I do for thee? tell me, What hast thou in the
> house?" And she said, "Thine handmaid hath not anything in the house,
> save a pot of oil." Then he said, "Go, borrow thee vessels abroad of
> all thy neighbors, even empty vessels; borrow not a few." . . . So she
> went from him and shut the door upon her and upon her sons, who
> brought the vessels to her; and she poured out. And it came to pass,
> when the vessels were full, that she said unto her son, "Bring me yet
> a vessel." And he said unto her, "There is not a vessel more." And the
> oil stayed. Then she came and told the man of God. And he said, "Go,
> sell the oil, and pay thy debt; and live thou and thy children of the rest."

This story can be viewed in several ways to discover its significance
for us. How large a pot of oil did the woman have? There may have been
enough to meet the need by selling it outright. The fact that the doors
were closed may indicate there was a hidden supply of oil under the floor
or in the walls. How much money did the woman owe to her creditor?
It may have been a small amount and easily satisfied with the value of
the oil she had. The neighbors who lent the vessels may have felt sorry

for her and paid more than the oil was worth so she could pay her debt. Elisha may have brought in extra oil and not told her. It may very well be that this story was just a copycat story of Elijah who did the same for the widow of Zarephath with both meal and oil.

All the methods mentioned are natural means of explaining the story, so no supernatural event need be considered.

106   *Shunammite's Son*

◆   2 Kings 4:8-37

> And when the child was grown, it fell on a day, that he went out to his father to the reapers. And he said unto his father, "My head, my head." And he said to a lad, "Carry him to his mother." And when he had taken him, and brought him to his mother, he sat on her knees till noon, and then died. . . . And when Elisha was come into the house, behold, the child was dead, and laid upon his bed. He went in therefore, and shut the door upon them twain, and prayed unto the LORD. And he went up, and lay upon the child, and put his mouth upon his mouth, and his eyes upon his eyes, and his hands upon his hands: and he stretched himself upon the child; and the flesh of the child waxed warm. Then he returned, and walked in the house to and fro; and went up, and stretched himself upon him: and the child sneezed seven times, and the child opened his eyes.

The Shunammite woman and her husband were wealthy. They built a small room for Elisha to rest himself when passing through the area. Elisha asked what he could do to repay them and when he found out she was childless, he told her she would have a son the next year. When the son was grown, he went into the fields with his father, and suffered sunstroke and died. Elisha had his servant Gehazi lay his staff on the boy's face to no avail. Elisha remembered Elijah telling him how he revived the son of the woman of Zarephath with mouth-to-mouth resuscitation. He tried but that didn't work either.

Elisha now realized that the boy was in a hysteric coma. Either from the excitement of being in the fields, or heat prostration, caused the boy to become hysterical and it resulted in a coma. Breathing would have become so shallow it couldn't even be noticed. Heartbeat would have slowed to almost nothing. The skin would even have taken on the waxy pallor of death. For all intents and purposes, the boy was dead. Fortunately, Elisha knew what was happening and when alone with the boy, he talked to him to give him assurance and suggested that he regain consciousness. The child revived and was presented to his mother alive and well.

Because the boy had not died, only natural means were used to revive him. No miracle was involved.

107 Poisoned Pottage Made Palatable

◆ 2 Kings 4:38-41

> And one went out into the field to gather herbs, and found a wild vine, and gathered thereof wild gourds his lap full, and came and shred them into the pot of pottage: for they knew them not. So they poured out for the men to eat. And it came to pass, as they were eating of the pottage, that they cried out, and said, "O thou man of God, there is death in the pot." And they could not eat thereof. But he said, "Then bring meal." And he cast it into the pot; and he said, "Pour out for the people, that they may eat." And there was no harm in the pot.

This story of a vegetable stew is typical of a meal served to a large group of people. The stew may have tasted strange or bitter, but there was no danger of any kind. There is always someone who will yell out "This stuff will kill you," or "This stuff is poison."

What we have here is a simple case of an idiom or figure of speech taken literally. By adding meal to the mix it certainly did not change anything unless it thickened it a little bit. They probably needed no more than satisfaction of the mind, and Elisha put them at ease. There was no report of sickness or death, because there was no poison.

No miracle was performed here as everything was purely natural and normal in the pot.

108 The Feeding of 100

◆ 2 Kings 4:42-44

> And there came a man from Baal-shalisha and brought the man of God bread of the firstfruits, twenty loaves of barley, and full ears of corn in the husk thereof. And he said, "Give unto the people, that they may eat." And his servitor said, "What, should I set this before an hundred men?" He said again, "Give the people, that they may eat: for thus saith the LORD, 'They shall eat, and shall leave thereof.'" So he set it before them, and they did eat, and left thereof, according to the word of the LORD.

A man brought twenty loaves of bread, and no one knows how many full ears of corn, and one hundred men ate. The story says they all ate and "left thereof." We don't know whether they had extra, or if they left some because they didn't like it.

This is a simple story, but some people got carried away and called it a miracle. Some see miracles in everything that happens. Miracles are supposed to be unusual events, outstanding occurrences. To some people, even childbirth is a miracle even though it happens 4,000,000 times a year in the United States alone. Here, food was served to a group of men, they ate, and some was left. Some people want to call it a miracle. The Bible doesn't even say it was a miracle.

Nothing but natural events were present in this story of one man's generosity.

109   *Naaman Cured of Leprosy*

◆   2 Kings 5:1-19

> Now Naaman, captain of the host of the king of Syria, was a great man with his master, and honourable, because by him the LORD had given deliverance unto Syria: he was also a mighty man in valour, but he was a leper. . . . And Elisha sent a messenger unto him, saying, "Go and wash in Jordan seven times, and thy flesh shall come again to thee, and thou shalt be clean." . . . Then went he down, and dipped himself seven times in Jordan, according to the saying of the man of God: and his flesh came again like the flesh of a little child, and he was clean.

Naaman was a proud man, and when Elisha's servant told him he should dip himself into the muddy Jordan, he rebelled. Syria had clean rivers and Naaman was angry because Elisha hadn't come himself to heal him. Finally he was persuaded that what was asked of him was not too difficult when he had so much to gain. He went to the Jordan, dipped seven times and was cured.

We need to know that when the Bible speaks of leprosy, it isn't a matter of Hansen's disease as we know leprosy today. Many skin disorders were called leprosy because of limited medical knowledge. Being a military man, Naaman was in many battles, and in time of conflict, anxiety or fear, he probably developed hysteric symptoms of a skin disorder. This was not uncommon in ancient times. We read of many in the Bible who were able to find relief and then present themselves to the priests who pronounced them clean. All that was needed was a suggestion of a cure and the symptoms could immediately disappear.

There was meaning in the story when Naaman, the Syrian, had to leave Syria and wash in the Jordan. Because the God of Israel was only in Israel at that time we see an interesting statement.

> "Behold, now I know that there is no God in all the earth, but in Israel." And Naaman said, "Shall there not then, I pray thee, be given to thy servant two mules' burden of earth? for thy servant will henceforth offer neither burnt offering nor sacrifice unto other gods, but unto the LORD."

Do you see what Naaman wanted here? Two mule-loads of earth to take back to Syria, so he could have a part of Israel on which to worship the God of Israel. That is the same as a bottle of water from Lourdes. The healing of Naaman came after Gehazi explained that Naaman needed to relax. Gehazi suggested the water of Jordan would cleanse him, and he accepted his cure. The story was meant to teach that there was but one God—the God of Israel.

The cure was by natural means and no supernatural event took place.

110 Gehazi Becomes Leprous

◆ 2 Kings 5:20-27

> But Gehazi, the servant of Elisha the man of God, said, "Behold, my master hath spared Naaman this Syrian, in not receiving at his hands that which he brought: but, as the LORD liveth, I will run after him, and take somewhat of him." So Gehazi followed after Naaman. And when Naaman saw him running after him, he lighted down from the chariot to meet him, and said, "Is all well?" And he said, "All is well. My master hath sent me, saying, 'Behold, even now there be come to me from mount Ephraim two young men of the sons of the prophets: give them, I pray thee, a talent of silver, and two changes of garments.'" And Naaman said, "Be content, take two talents. And he urged him, and bound two talents of silver in two bags, with two changes of garments, and laid them upon two of his servants; and they bare them before him. . . . But he went in, and stood before his master. And Elisha said unto him, "Whence comest thou, Gehazi?" And he said, "Thy servant went no whither. . . . The leprosy therefore of Naaman shall cleave unto thee, and unto thy seed for ever." And he went out from his presence a leper as white as snow.

This is a sad story of covetousness and lying on the part of Gehazi. There is no doubt that Elisha and Gehazi lived by less than simple means, but to covet and lie led debased Gehazi even deeper. As soon as Gehazi saw Elisha he knew he was in trouble. Elisha had informants in the area to keep him posted, so he knew what Gehazi had done. Stricken with guilt and fear, Gehazi became hysterical. When Elisha suggested Gehazi would take on Naaman's leprosy, he did show similar symptoms that Naaman had. Hysteria is the agent that makes voodoo work, and the same circumstances exist today among its practitioners. As long as the one who is cursed believes the one who pronounces the curse has power to do it, the curse is effective. If Gehazi had not believed Elisha was able to do what he said, he would not have been afflicted. There is also the element of power extended to all the prophets and priests of this God. With such fear instilled in the hearts of the people, they would not even consider doing such sinful acts. As was his faith, so was the punishment for his guilt and fear. This story may well have been the pattern for the story of Ananias and Sapphira in the book of Acts.

This is a story of natural events and no supernatural means were employed.

111   *The Floating Ax Head*

◆ 2 Kings 6:1-7

> But as one was felling a beam, the ax head fell into the water: and he cried, and said, "Alas, master! for it was borrowed." And the man of God said, "Where fell it?" And he showed him the place. And he cut down a stick, and cast it in thither; and the iron did swim. Therefore said he, "Take it up to thee." And he put out his hand, and took it.

Here we have the simple story of a man losing a borrowed ax head. The sons of the prophets felt crowded in their dwelling, so they decided to add to it and went out to cut some timbers. One man borrowed an ax and as he was cutting a tree, the head flew off into the Jordan. Elisha cut a stick, threw it into the water and the ax head apparently floated to the surface and the man retrieved it.

I have to tell you, this simple story has me stumped. I do not know how to explain it. One writer suggests Elisha pushed the stick into the hole in the ax head and lifted it to the surface so the man could take it. Another suggestion was the stick was thrown, as a spear, stuck in the hole in the ax head, and floated it to the surface. These seem so simple that no story would even have been written. I find nothing physical, spiritual or meaningful in the story and must simply say I don't know. Perhaps something was left out in the telling or translating. In any case, if you have the answer, please let me know.

112   *Open and Blinded Eyes*

◆ 2 Kings 6:8-23

> And Elisha prayed, and said, "LORD, I pray thee, open his eyes, that he may see." And the LORD opened the eyes of the young man; and he saw: and, behold, the mountain was full of horses and chariots of fire round about Elisha.

Because the servant of Elisha was overcome with stress and fear because of the forces of Syria, he had an attack of hysteria. By the power of suggestion, Elisha caused the servant to experience a hysteric hallucination of "horses and chariots of fire." This is the same thing Elisha said he saw when Elijah was taken from him. Now we realize Elisha understood how to control other people's minds.

> And when they came down to him, Elisha prayed unto the LORD, and said, "Smite this people, I pray thee, with blindness." And he smote them with blindness according to the word of Elisha. And Elisha said unto them, "this is not the way, neither is this the city: follow me, and I will bring you to the man whom ye seek." But he led them to Samaria. And it came to pass, when they were come into Samaria, that Elisha

said, "LORD, open the eyes of these men, that they may see." And the LORD opened their eyes, and they saw; and, behold, they were in the midst of Samaria.

The Syrian troops were looking for Elisha and probably didn't know what he looked like. When they saw him, they didn't recognize him and he convinced them that they were in the wrong city. The mention of blindness does not refer to eyesight, but to understanding. No mention is made of the Syrians not being able to see.

Elisha led them into Samaria where he finally told them who he was and where they were. When the king of Israel asked Elisha if they should kill the Syrians, Elisha said no. Instead they fed them and sent them home. The strategy worked, "So the bands of Syria came no more into the land of Israel." Earlier in the story, Elisha was said to have known what the king of Syria said, even in his bedroom, and the king asked which of his servants told Elisha. None confessed, but there is every reason to think that Elisha had his agents working to keep him informed. The story tells of the king's spies and you have to know that he was not the only one with spies.

In these stories of eyes being blinded and opened, there are no miracles or supernatural events that took place. In both stories, just plain, natural means of spies and deception serve the purposes.

113   *The Syrian Siege*

◆ 2 Kings 6:24-7:20

> And it came to pass after this, that Ben-hadad king of Syria gathered all his host, and went up, and besieged Samaria. And there was a great famine in Samaria.

The siege by Syria left Samaria in a famine, and people were eating their children to stay alive. The king of Israel blamed Elisha and threatened his life, but Elisha said by the next day, everything would be well. As the story went, everything did get better the next day. "For the LORD had made the host of the Syrians to hear a noise of chariots, and a noise of horses, even the noise of a great host: and they said one to another, 'Lo, the king of Israel hath hired against us the kings of the Hittites, and the kings of the Egyptians, to come upon us.' Wherefore they arose and fled in the twilight, and left their tents, and their horses, and their asses, even the camp as it was, and fled for their life."

Panic overtook the Syrians and they took off and left all their supplies. When the king of Israel learned what had happened he sent troops, got all the supplies and fed the people of Israel. Perhaps a Syrian guard was under such stress and fear that he had a hysteric hallucination. As he imagined there were chariots and soldiers, he told others about it. Without even checking, they too imagined they were in danger and in the panic that ensued, they all fled the camp.

There is nothing supernatural involved. Everything that happened was natural.

114   *Elisha's Bones and the Dead Man*

◆ 2 Kings 13:14-21

> And Elisha died, and they buried him. And the bands of the Moabites invaded the land at the coming in of the year. And it came to pass, as they were burying a man, that, behold, they spied a band of men; and they cast the man into the sepulchre of Elisha: and when the man was let down, and touched the bones of Elisha, he revived, and stood up on his feet.

This is a story of Elisha's power to raise the dead even after he himself was dead and buried. In ancient times people were not buried in graves and covered with dirt. They were put into tombs dug into the side of hills and closed with large stones. In this story a man was to be buried, but the funeral party saw a band of Moabites and got scared. They quickly opened a tomb, which was said to be the tomb of Elisha. As they put the corpse into the tomb, it landed on the bones of Elisha, which were on the floor of the tomb. The jolt caused the man to revive and he stood up and apparently left the tomb under his own power.

When a person is in a hysteric coma, there is such shallow breathing and faint heartbeat that it is difficult to tell whether he is dead or alive. Obviously the man was not dead, but merely in the throes of a hysteric coma. We are not told why the man died, but it was probably from fear or as a defense mechanism due to the bands of marauding Moabites. He succumbed to hysteria which resulted in a hysteric coma. He was presumed dead and so he was being buried. Many people have been buried alive. Graves have been opened and the evidence was clear: scratch marks in the caskets suggest the person woke from the coma and tried to get out. Other cases exist in which a casket was on a cart going to the graveyard and the body awakened when the cart wheel hit a bump.

The key to this story lies in the haste with which "they cast the man into the sepulchre of Elisha." The shock of landing on the bones awakened him. The same would have happened if he landed on anyone else's bones—or upon rocks. The story was undoubtedly written by disciples of Elisha, and because a similar event had happened, they simply put Elisha's name in the story. Had the man been gently laid in the tomb, he would have died of starvation after a few days. Under the same condition, Lazarus lay in his tomb and Jesus jolted him out of his coma by yelling, "Lazarus come forth."

Here we only need to look for natural means to see what took place; no supernatural means were needed.

Chapter 7

Daniel and Jonah

115 Daniel is Chosen

◆ Daniel 1:1-21

And the king spake unto Ashpenaz the master of his eunuchs, that he should bring certain of the children of Israel, and of the kings' seed, and of the princes. . . . Now among these were of the children of Judah, Daniel, Hananiah, Mishael, and Azariah: Unto whom the prince of the eunuchs gave names: for he gave unto Daniel the name of Belteshazzar; and to Hananiah, of Shadrach; and to Mishael, of Meshach; and to Azariah, of Abed-nego. Now God had brought Daniel into favour and tender love with the prince of the eunuchs. As for these four children, God gave them knowledge and skill in all learning and wisdom: and Daniel had understanding in all visions and dreams.

What a group these four made up. They wouldn't eat the fancy food of kings, but chose a vegetarian diet so they wouldn't break any dietary laws. They were schooled for three years with other Jews, children of the king, and princes. These four Jews were at the top of the class. I don't find it hard to believe these four, selected for their mental abilities, were more intelligent than the rest. The Jewish home has always been the place of learning from childhood. Even today the home of practicing Jews is equal to most schools in training of religion, morals, ethics and tradition. These four were apt students, and sometimes those of high birth didn't apply themselves as much as the young Jews.

In this story we see the benefit of keeping the dietary laws and not eating what the Gentiles ate. The object was to keep the laws and be holy so God could bless the nation. The superiority of the four Jewish men was symbolic of the nation: as they kept God's laws and overcame, so would Israel. The story said the Jews were healthier than the rest because they watched their diet, and that makes good sense.

These stories are set in the period of the Babylonian Exile so they dealt with the time between 586 to 536 B.C. The book of Daniel was written about 165 B.C. and this gives us a clue about why the stories were written. In 165 B.C. the Maccabees were just gaining their independence from the Selucids, the Greek kings of Syria. Antiochus IV Epiphanes was king. Mattathias and his sons rebelled and won freedom for the nation of Israel. There was still much to be done, and Daniel was written to inspire the Jews to action. The book of Daniel was written in Hebrew and Aramaic. There are Persian and Greek words in the book, so we know it was written much later than the Exile. I have a problem with names in this story because Daniel kept his Jewish name while the other three give up their Jewish names to take Babylonian ones. Many concepts and theological ideals are from second century B.C., verifying the late date of 165 B.C.

There is nothing supernatural in selecting four healthy men, who followed a healthful diet and applied themselves to their studies. It was perfectly natural that they should surpass those who failed to discipline themselves. Such was the meaning of the story to the Jews of 165 B.C.

116   *Daniel and the King's Dreams*

◆ Daniel 2 & 4

> And in the second year of the reign of Nebuchadnezzar Nebuchad-nezzar dreamed dreams, wherewith his spirit was troubled, and his sleep brake from him. Then the king commanded to call the magicians, and the astrologers, and the sorcerers, and the Chaldeans, for to shew the king his dreams. So they came and stood before the king. . . . The king answered and said to the Chaldeans, "The thing is gone from me: if ye will not make known unto me the dream, with the interpretation thereof, ye shall be cut in pieces, and your houses shall be made a dunghill."

This story of the dream Nebuchadnezzar forgot brought Daniel into the spotlight. No one knew what the dream was, so Daniel went before the king. Daniel said, "there is a God in heaven that revealeth secrets, and maketh known to the king Nebuchadnezzar what shall be in the latter days. Thy dream, and the visions of thy head upon thy bed, are these." Daniel then told Nebuchadnezzar the story of the great statue in human form. "Then the king made Daniel a great man, and gave him many great gifts, and made him ruler over the whole province of Babylon, and chief of the governors over all the wise men of Babylon. Then Daniel requested of the king, and he set Shadrach, Meshach, and Abed-nego, over the affairs of the province of Babylon: but Daniel sat in the gate of the king."

Daniel didn't know the king's dream, but unlike the astrologers, magicians, and Chaldeans, he was smart enough to get with his three friends and concoct one. Daniel related the dream to the king, who never said he remembered, but because it flattered him, he "made Daniel a great man." This story is twin to the story of Joseph interpreting Pharaoh's dream, except Pharaoh remembered the dream. Daniel and Joseph were both captured, unjustly persecuted, exalted to rulership, lived pure lives in impure courts and died in foreign lands.

The story Daniel told was of a great statue with a head of gold, breast and arms of silver, belly and thighs of brass, legs of iron and feet of iron and clay. Daniel said that a stone broke the image to pieces. Because Daniel said Nebuchadnezzar was the head of gold, the king was so vain he made Daniel a ruler of Babylon. The king also praised the Jewish God and called him the "God of gods." This story was written to show the Jews of 165 B.C. that as Nebuchadnezzar and his kingdom would collapse, so would Antiochus IV Epiphanes and his Syrian kingdom fall. If only the Jews would be as faithful as Daniel and his three friends the Jews would triumph again.

There is nothing supernatural in the story. It was only written to inspire the Jews.

The second vision is in Daniel 4:

> Thus were the visions of mine head in my bed; I saw, and behold a tree in the midst of the earth, and the height thereof was great. The leaves thereof were fair, and the fruit thereof much, and in it was meat for all: the beasts of the fields had shadow under it, and the fowls of the heaven dwelt in the boughs thereof, and all flesh was fed of it.

This great tree was to be cut down and only the stump left. When Daniel was called in to interpret the dream, he said that the tree was the king and that the story referred to banishment from Babylon. After seven years of exile, he would be out of his mind and then he would be restored to his power and his sanity. Again the king praised Daniel and his God for making the dream known to him.

The story of the king of Babylon portrayed as a tree is similar to the story in Ezekiel 31. There the story of Assyria's glory came just before its fall. This too was a made-up story to show how the Assyrian king repented of his pride and turned to the God of the Jews. As these stories were written during the battle against the Syrian rule of Antiochus IV Epiphanes, the object was to show how Israel could win. Since the Babylonians had been overthrown in the past, the nation of Judah could be victorious over Syria. If they would turn to God, he would give them the victory. If the Jews could unite in worship and military strength, they too could be restored to their former freedom and glory.

A character named Daniel was an ancient hero, either from the days of the Assyrian conquest of Israel or the Babylonian conquest of Judah. Ezekiel mentioned a Daniel in conjunction with Noah and Job as heroes of the Jew's past in Ezekiel 14:12-14 and 28:3. These are simply fabricated stories, so obviously no supernatural powers are needed to explain them.

117   The Fiery Furnace

◆ Daniel 3

> Nebuchadnezzar the king made an image of gold, whose height was threescore cubits, and the breadth thereof six cubits: he set it up in the plain of Dura, in the province of Babylon. . . . Then an herald cried aloud, "To you it is commanded, O people, nations, and languages, That at what time ye hear the sound of the cornet, flute, harp, sackbut, psaltery, dulcimer, and all kinds of musick, ye fall down and worship the golden image that Nebuchadnezzar the king hath set up: And whoso falleth not down and worshippeth shall the same hour be cast into the midst of a burning fiery furnace." Shadrach, Meshach, and Abed-nego, answered and said to the king, "O Nebuchadnezzar, we are not careful to answer thee in this matter. If it be so, our God whom we serve is able to deliver us from the burning fiery furnace, and he will deliver us out of thine hand, O king. But if not, be it known unto thee, O king, that we will not serve thy gods, nor worship the golden image which thou hast set up."

After they survived the furnace, "Then the king promoted Shadrach, Meshach, and Abed-nego, in the province of Babylon."

This is but another story to build the confidence of the Jews in their struggle against Antiochus IV Epiphanes, king of Syria in 165 B.C. The fact that the three Jews defied political power and triumphed would prove that the Jewish nation also could win against Syrian oppression in their day. Antiochus Epiphanes had set up a golden image of Apollo, so this story had Nebuchadnezzar set up an image of gold. God protected three Jewish men in the fiery furnace. In their time of persecution, God also would protect Judah as they struggled against Syria. It is peculiar that Daniel is not mentioned in this story because he would have been in the furnace too. When we realize it is only a make-believe story, we need not look for reason or logic: it is but an allegory of Judah fighting for freedom.

Nothing supernatural need be sought when all it took was the stroke of the pen to work wonders.

118 The Handwriting on the Wall

◆ Daniel 5

> Bel-shazzar the king made a great feast to a thousand of his lords, and
> drank wine before the thousand. Bel-shazzar, whiles he tasted the
> wine, commanded to bring the golden and silver vessels which his
> father Nebuchadnezzar had taken out of the temple which was in
> Jerusalem . . . and the king, and his princes, his wives, and his
> concubines, drank in them. They drank wine, and praised the gods of
> gold, and of silver, of brass, of iron, of wood, and of stone. In the same
> hour came forth fingers of a man's hand, and wrote over against the
> candlestick upon the plaister of the wall of the king's palace: and the
> king saw the part of the hand that wrote. . . . Then came in all the king's
> wise men: but they could not read the writing, nor make known to the
> king the interpretation thereof.

After Daniel was called in, he read the writing, interpreted it, and was
given gifts and a promotion. "In that night was Belshazzar the king of
the Chaldeans slain. And Darius the Median took the kingdom, being
about threescore and two years old." What a great story, but it is only a
story.

This story was written about 370 years after the event it described.
The Jews had no regular chronological system, so there is great confusion in the names and order of the rulers of Babylon. Nebuchadnezzar
had no son named Belshazzar. There was a Belshazzar who was the son
of Nabonidus, king of Babylon from 555–538 B.C., but he was not related
to Nebuchadnezzar, and this Belshazzar never became king. Nothing is
known of Darius the Mede, and the Medes never had a kingdom that
ruled Babylon between Nebuchadnezzar's rule and that of the Persians.
The rule of Babylon went directly from Nabonidus to Cyrus, king of
Persia. The poor chronology is an important piece of evidence that helps
us determine when the book of Daniel was written. The fact that this
story does not agree with actual history didn't matter then and it really
doesn't matter now. The real meaning is in the religious lessons from
which the reader is to draw encouragement.

The story deals with the desecration of the golden vessels from the
Temple and how God punishes those who dishonor him. Just as those
people were destroyed, so would Antiochus and his people, who sacrificed a pig on the altar of God, be destroyed. When Cyrus the Persian
conquered Babylon and set the Jews free, he became their messiah as
Isaiah said, "Thus saith the LORD to his anointed, to Cyrus, whose right
hand have I holden" (Isaiah 45:1). *Messiah* means "the Anointed One"
and Isaiah hoped that Cyrus would convert to Judaism, but he didn't.

Even though there was no actual handwriting on the wall, it is such a good story that it has given rise to the modern expression, "I can see the handwriting on the wall." Because nothing was written on the wall there was no need of a supernatural hand.

The whole story was made up to encourage the Jews.

119　*Daniel in the Lion's Den*

◆　Daniel 6

> Then this Daniel was preferred above the presidents and princes, because an excellent spirit was in him; and the king thought to set him over the whole realm. . . . Then the presidents and princes assembled together to the king, and said thus unto him, "King Darius, live for ever. All the presidents of the kingdom, the governors, and the princes, the councellors, and the captains, have consulted together to establish a royal statute, and to make a firm decree, that whosoever shall ask a petition of any God or man for thirty days, save of thee, O king, he shall be cast into a den of lions." . . . Now when Daniel knew that the writing was signed, he went into his house; and his windows being open in his chamber toward Jerusalem, he kneeled upon his knees three times a day, and prayed, and gave thanks before his God, as he did aforetime. Then these men assembled, and found Daniel praying and making supplication before his God. . . . Then the king commanded, and they brought Daniel, and cast him into the den of lions. Now the king spake and said unto Daniel, "Thy God whom thou serveth continually, he will deliver thee."

Daniel was delivered from the lion's den and Darius proclaimed Daniel's God as the living God. "So this Daniel prospered in the reign of Darius, and in the reign of Cyrus the Persian." King Darius liked Daniel but was tricked into having Daniel thrown into the den of lions. When the lions didn't harm him, Daniel came out a greater hero and those who sought his death were put to death by the same lions. God won again, and more heathens believed in the God of the Jews.

This is the parallel story to the one in which the three Jews were saved from the fiery furnace. That was why Daniel was not in the furnace: he had his own story. The stories are similar in many ways. The three were loyal to God and disobeyed Nebuchadnezzar; Daniel was loyal to God and disobeyed Darius. The enemies of the three had them condemned; the enemies of Daniel condemned him. With the three it was the court sages; with Daniel it was the court officials. There was an angel in the fiery furnace; there was an angel who shut the mouth's of the lions. Those who put the three into the furnace were killed by the fire; those who caused Daniel to be in the lion's den died in the lion's den. The lesson of the story was loyalty to God's laws and obedience to his commands.

Because of the fictional nature of the story, no supernatural power was present, only the power of the pen to inspire courage.

120 *Appearances and Visions.*

The book of Daniel is full of dreams, visions, appearances of angels, beasts, men, watchers and celestial beings. In ancient days, those who experienced such visions and dreams were considered holy people of God. The fact that these were symptoms of hysteria was unknown to them. They needed all the help they could get so they counted visions as divine revelations. Hallucinations are experienced in all five senses, so a person can see, hear, feel, taste and smell things that are not reality. Conditions that initiated hysteria were very common in those days, and one of the symptom of hysteria is hallucinations. People who had visions and dreams were called prophets or seers. Visions were common in both Old Testament and New Testament stories. Even today people claim to see angels, Jesus, the Virgin Mary, or their own dead relatives. Because people are the same today as they were thousands of years ago, some will continue to have similar experiences.

The human mind is a wondrous thing we still scarcely understand. It was at the end of the 19th century that Freud began to understand hysteria. He tried to help us learn how and why people have these strange experiences. Only when we understand that appearances and visions are natural and not supernatural, can we begin to help one another.

In Daniel we have the first mention of angel's names, Gabriel and Michael. Scholars tell us that the idea of angels as intermediaries between God and man was not earlier than the Babylonian Exile. It was from the Babylonians and Persians that the Jews learned about angels. Any stories of angels we find in the Old Testament are added retrospectively after the Exile. Stories of angels appearing to Abraham and Jacob were added to existing stories. This was done to add power to the Jewish idea of their God.

These are lite*rary* visions rather than lite*ral* visions. The bulk of the visions in Daniel deal with the "last days" and the "time of the end." This meant the end of the present age, for soon God was to establish his kingdom, and his servants must prepare the way. In the time of Jesus, people were still expecting the end time. Jesus was made to say, "Verily I say unto you, that there be some of them that stand here, which shall not taste of death, till they have seen the kingdom of God come with power" (Mark 9:1).

Because the stories are the product of the human mind, there are no supernatural elements involved, just natural, man-made concoctions.

121   Daniel Writes of the Resurrection

◆ Daniel 12:1-3

> And at that time shall Michael stand up, the great prince which standeth
> for the children of thy people: and there shall be a time of trouble, such
> as never was since there was a nation even to that same time: and at
> that time thy people shall be delivered, every one that shall be found
> written in the book. And many of them that sleep in the dust of the
> earth shall awake, some to everlasting life, and some to shame and
> everlasting contempt. And they that be wise shall shine as the bright-
> ness of the firmament; and they that turn many to righteousness as the
> stars for ever and ever.

This is understood by some to pertain to physical resurrection, but it
must be remembered that Jews didn't then, and most still don't, believe
in physical resurrection. This story refers to "the time of the end" in
Daniel 11:40, and deals with the Syrian rule over the Jews. For Jews, the
main reason to have children was for the perpetuation of their heritage;
and this they considered "everlasting life." For those who died fighting
for Israel against the Syrians would be remembered and thus live on.
Those who refused to fight, or even worse, supported the Syrians, would
be remembered and live on in "shame and everlasting contempt."

The Jews have no heaven or hell in their Bible so they didn't believe
in them. Even the Sadducees in Jesus' time didn't believe in heaven,
hell, angels or other spirits. There was no doctrine of resurrection here
as taught in the New Testament. The Jewish idea of remembrance was
that "No one truly dies as long as someone is left who remembers." There
is an Egyptian proverb that says "To speak of the dead is to make them
live gain." This was the idea Jews had of resurrection.

There is no supernatural power involved in the natural process of
speaking of the dead.

122   Jonah and the Storm

◆ Jonah 1:1-16

> Now the word of the LORD came unto Jonah the son of Amittai,
> saying, "Arise, go to Nineveh, that great city, and cry against it; for
> their wickedness is come up before me." But Jonah rose up to flee unto
> Tarshish from the presence of the LORD, and went down to Joppa; and
> he found a ship going to Tarshish: so he paid the fare thereof, and went
> down into it, to go with them unto Tarshish from the presence of the
> LORD. But the LORD sent out a great wind into the sea, and there was
> a mighty tempest in the sea, so that the ship was like to be broken. . .
> And they said every one to his fellow, "Come, and let us cast lots, that
> we know for whose cause this evil is upon us." So they cast lots, and

the lot fell upon Jonah. . . . Then said they unto him, "What shall we do unto thee, that the sea may be calm unto us?" for the sea wrought, and was tempestuous. . . . So they took up Jonah, and cast him forth into the sea: and the sea ceased from her raging.

This story of Jonah trying to run away from God is very interesting. The only witness was Jonah—he wrote the book. No time element is given so we don't know when the story was supposed to have occurred. All we know is that for some reason God wanted to save Nineveh, the capital of Assyria, from itself and its wickedness. How Jonah was to do this was unknown because he probably didn't speak their language. It is difficult to imagine why a large city like Nineveh would listen to a foreigner tell them that his God was about to destroy their city. The story about their fasting, praying and turning away from evil is almost unbelievable. Even the animals wore sackcloth and fasted (Jonah 3:7-8).

As for the storm, that is hardly a problem. Storms are everyday occurrences. Why was a simple storm on the Mediterranean Sea called a miracle? There were dozens of storms each year and to pick out one and call it a miracle is arrant nonsense. It doesn't take supernatural influence for wind to blow and waves to come up at sea.

The book of Jonah was written as a parable. In this parable we see a nation, portrayed by Jonah, that has no concern for other lands. After the Exile, Israel was bitter toward other nations. As Jonah rebelled against going to help Nineveh, so did Israel against doing anything for other people. When we see Jonah offering his life for the safety of the others in the boat, we see the writer trying to change the attitude of Israel. As Jonah was unwilling that God should save Nineveh, Israel was to see itself turning against God and his great kindness. When Jonah showed compassion for a gourd and hatred for people, the message should be clear. Israel was to have seen itself as fighting against God who wanted all people to join Israel in worshiping him. The book was written between 400 and 200 B.C. when Israel had a vengeful attitude toward others. This writer took it upon himself to try to turn Israel from exclusiveness and selfishness to compassion. No longer were they to think only of themselves. It was time to share God's love with everyone.

In the Bible, the sea symbolized mankind and the turmoil of the sea was calmed by Jonah's sacrifice. If Israel also could show mercy toward other nations, their conflicts could also be resolved.

Even though Jonah is among the twelve minor prophets, it is evident that he differs vastly from them. The book of Jonah is more concerned with the man Jonah than with a prophetic message. The other eleven minor prophets have only brief stories of the prophets themselves, and the messages are longer.

123   *Jonah and the Great Fish*

◆ Jonah 1:17; 2; Matthew 12:38-41

> Now the LORD had prepared a great fish to swallow up Jonah. And Jonah was in the belly of the fish three days and three nights. . . . Then Jonah prayed unto the LORD his God out of the fish's belly. . . . And the LORD spake unto the fish, and it vomited out Jonah upon dry land.

Now that is some fish story! Jonah said it was a great fish, but Jesus said it was a whale; and a whale is not a fish. How could a man live inside a fish for three days? He couldn't, and he didn't. The story symbolizes Israel's Exile into Babylon. Jonah was the nation of Israel; the fish was the nation of Babylon. As Jonah was vomited out of the fish, so Israel was delivered out of its captivity.

Because the story of the fish is fiction, no supernatural power is needed to create the fish. The creative power of man's mind is all that is needed in this story.

124   *Jonah and the Gourd*

◆ Jonah 3; 4:1-6

> So Jonah arose, and went unto Nineveh, according to the word of the LORD. . . and he cried, and said, "Yet forty days, and Nineveh shall be overthrown." So the people of Nineveh believed God, and proclaimed a fast, and put on sackcloth, from the greatest of them even to the least of them . . . and God repented of the evil, that he had said that he would do unto them; and he did it not.

In Jonah's message there is no allowance made for repentance. Why would a heathen city decide to repent when it was clear they were going to be overthrown? The writer really turned the tables here, and when Nineveh repented, God also repented. Now Israel was on the spot. If they were not willing to accept those whom their God had pardoned, they themselves stood in danger of judgment.

Jonah was upset to the extent that he wanted to die. "So Jonah went out of the city, and sat on the east side of the city, and there made him a booth, and sat under it in the shadow, till he might see what would become of the city." Jonah decided to wait and see what would happen in the next forty days. Of course forty days was only an indefinite time—the Septuagint said three days, which makes more sense. "And the LORD God prepared a gourd, and made it to come up over Jonah, that it might be a shadow over his head, to deliver him from his grief. So Jonah was exceeding glad of the gourd." The story says the gourd grew suddenly but don't be confused. The booth was the rebuilt Temple, and Jonah was Israel sitting and waiting for the world to be destroyed.

The protection of the gourd was the freedom of Israel from 536 B.C. to 332 B.C. when Alexander the Great conquered Israel.

We need not look for a miracle—we are only looking at a fabrication.

125 The Worm Kills the Gourd

◆ Jonah 4:7

> But God prepared a worm when the morning rose the next day, and it smote the gourd that it withered.

In this parable, the worm is Alexander the Great, and when he came in 332 B.C. he conquered the nation of Israel. Israel had been a free country for 200 years, but because they didn't make friends and share their blessings, they lost their freedom.

The worm isn't a product of a miracle, it is only part of the story.

126 Jonah and the East Wind

◆ Jonah 4:8-10

> And it came to pass, when the sun did arise, that God prepared a vehement east wind; and the sun beat down upon the head of Jonah, that he fainted, and wished in himself to die, and said, "It is better for me to die than to live."

The scorching sirocco made it very uncomfortable with the intense heat and dust. Jonah wanted to die again as he did before the gourd. The metaphor continues as Israel, now under the rule of Alexander's Greece, wanted to give up and die.

As the heathens rejoiced in their salvation, Jonah was crushed by his God. This was how Israel felt after their freedom was lost. Jonah had compassion for the gourd for which he had not labored but he had no compassion for Nineveh. Israel had 200 years of peace for which it did not labor, but it was still without compassion for other nations. Now that freedom was gone, all Israel could do was "cry the blues."

The message of the story is now revealed. An Israel without compassion would be hard to imagine, but Israel could not accept God showing compassion to the heathen. "We live in a world, where, if we would save ourselves, we also must save others, and if we will not save others, ourselves we cannot save" (*The Interpreters Bible*). The story is a parable, and like all good parables it contains a powerful truth for us today and the nation of Israel: don't wait for God to do something. If something needs to be done, do it yourself.

If nothing supernatural happened before don't expect miracles today.

STORIES FROM THE

NEW TESTATMENT

Chapter 8

Gospel Stories

127 The Virgin Birth

◆ Matthew. 1:18-24; Luke 1, 2

> And in the sixth month the angel Gabriel was sent from God unto a
> city of Galilee, named Nazareth, to a virgin espoused to a man whose
> name was Joseph, of the house of David; and the virgin's name was
> Mary. . . . And when she saw him, she was troubled at his saying, and
> cast in her mind what manner of salutation this should be. And the
> angel said unto her, "Fear not, Mary: for thou hast found favor with
> God. And, behold, thou shalt conceive in thy womb, and bring forth a
> son, and shalt call his name JESUS."

This is Luke's story of an angel coming to Mary and telling of her
pregnancy. In Luke only Mary saw and talked to an angel. In
Matthew's story, Mary had nothing to do with an angel and only
Joseph saw an angel in his dream. The angel told Joseph that Mary was
pregnant by the Holy Ghost and that she would bear a son whom they
were to name Jesus. Here are two entirely different announcements of
why Mary was pregnant. Matthew and Luke used different sources for
their stories. The silence of Mark, John and Paul suggests that they never
heard any stories about the birth of Jesus.

Angelic announcements and virgin birth stories were common in the
Mediterranean world at that time. Most heroes, kings and rulers were
alleged to have been born of virgins. The mother of Hercules was a
virgin, the mother of Sosiosh the Persian was a virgin, and Nana was the
virgin mother of Attis. Rhea Silvia was the virgin mother of Romulus

and Remus by means of the god Mars. Bacchus, Aesculapius, Zarathustra and many others were born of virgins, so Jesus could have no less a supernatural origin.

Mark is the earliest gospel, and apparently he never heard the story because it hadn't been made up yet. John has Jesus pre-existent, so he wouldn't write about a virgin birth even if he had heard of it. John never even mentions that the mother of Jesus was named Mary. Matthew writes, "Behold, a virgin shall be with child, and shall bring forth a son." This was supposed to be quoted from Isaiah, but there is a problem in the translation. The Hebrew word translated virgin means "young woman," whether virgin or not. When it was translated into Greek for the Septuagint, it came out virgin. Because Matthew and Luke didn't read Hebrew, they used the Septuagint and so they were confused right from the start.

When we look at the genealogies of Jesus listed in Matthew and Luke, we see that they are entirely different from David on down to Joseph. They are from two separate sources. While Matthew has twenty-seven names from David to Jesus, Luke has forty-two. The genealogy would be of consequence only if Joseph were the father of Jesus anyway.

There are other interesting differences between the stories in Matthew and Luke that must be mentioned. Matthew has Jesus born in a house and visited by the Magi or wise men. Luke has Jesus born in a stable and visited by shepherds. Matthew says Jesus was a carpenter's son. Mark says Jesus himself was a carpenter. Matthew wrote of a royal Jesus. Luke wrote of Jesus as a common man. In Matthew, Joseph and Mary lived in Bethlehem when Jesus was born, went to Egypt for a year or two until Herod died and then went to live in Nazareth. In Luke, Joseph and Mary lived in Nazareth, and went to Bethlehem when Jesus was born, and returned to Nazareth shortly after that.

Those who use the quotation from Isaiah 7:14 about the Virgin Birth fail to read the rest of the verse that says, ". . . and shall call his name Immanuel." Nowhere in the New Testament is Jesus called Immanuel, so is it any wonder the Jews didn't respond to someone named Jesus and not Immanuel? Isaiah was writing to people in his own time and not to people 700 years in the future.

When people refer to Jesus today they often call him Jesus Christ as if that were his full name. Jesus is a name, and Christ is a title. *Christ* is the English word for the Hebrew term *Messiah*. Both *Messiah* and *Christ* mean "the anointed one" or simply "king." Properly used, it would be Christ Jesus or Jesus the Christ. It is not as if Mr. and Mrs. Christ announced the birth of their son, Jesus.

The two stories in Matthew and Luke are fabrications using bits and pieces from many sources. The angelic announcement, the Virgin Birth, the location of the birth, the visit of Magi or shepherds, the trip to Egypt, the genealogies—all were borrowed. They were taken from Old Testament stories. Babylonian, Persian, Greek, Roman and Oriental stories, and myths and legends were also blended in. The composite was then tailored to fit the pattern of both old and current ideas of divinity. It took over 300 years to put all of the stories together and still we have divergent accounts.

My view is that Mary was Jesus' mother and Joseph was his father. The rest was added to conform to 4th century ecclesiastic dogma.

There is nothing supernatural in the birth of Jesus. It was much later that the Virgin Birth story was added, and the only miracle is that people still believe it.

128   *The Baptism of Jesus*

◆   Matthew 3; Mark 1:1-11; Luke 3:1-23; John 1

> In those days came John the Baptist, preaching in the wilderness of Judea, and saying, "Repent ye: for the kingdom of heaven is at hand. I indeed baptize you with water unto repentance." . . . Then cometh Jesus from Galilee to Jordan unto John, to be baptized of him. But John forbad him, saying, "I have need to be baptized of thee, and comest thou to me?" . . . And Jesus, when he was baptized, went up straightway out of the water: and, lo, the heavens were opened unto him, and he saw the Spirit of God descending like a dove, and lighting upon him: And lo a voice from heaven, saying, "This is my beloved Son, in whom I am well pleased."

This was Matthew's story of the baptism of Jesus. All four gospels tell the story, but there are some important differences.

Mark says John didn't recognize Jesus and neither did John preach against the Pharisees and the Sadducees. Luke says John didn't recognize Jesus and he has John speak harshly against Herod, for which he was thrown into prison. John had John the Baptist firmly deny he was the Messiah, Elijah or even a prophet. There were rumors in John's day that John the Baptist was the Messiah. In John, John the Baptist recognizes Jesus, but later says he didn't recognize him until the Spirit descended on him. John does not tell of a voice from heaven when the Spirit descended on Jesus.

Here are four stories and they are all different in important details. It has been said that there is only one thing worse than having a witness to an act and that is to have several witnesses. In this case we are not dealing with witnesses but with story tellers. Matthew, Mark and Luke said the heavens opened and a voice was heard. Who heard the voice and who saw the dove? John reports a dove flying around but records no voice. I think the reason for this is clear. The dove was merely flying by and may have flown close to Jesus. Jesus alone heard the voice.

Until this time Jesus had been living in Nazareth of Galilee and had heard many stories of the Roman rulers of Israel. He heard of Judas of Galilee who attempted to free the country from bondage as the Hasmoneans had done 200 years earlier. Jesus was a student of the Hasmoneans and likely was a Hasmonean himself. He became so involved that he decided to do something to free his people. His emotionalism, repression, tension and need to do all he could led to his baptism. It was here that all these emotions may have caused him to experience a hysteric hallucination. Jesus saw the dove as the symbol of the Holy Ghost. He even heard a voice saying what he wanted to hear, "Thou art my beloved Son, in whom I am well pleased." Jesus was now ready to begin his ministry to free Israel from Rome.

There is no miracle or supernatural event here, only a natural occurrence produced by a traumatic experience of "opening night jitters" and a bit of stage fright. Jesus was about to become the main character in the struggle to free Israel from Roman rule.

129   *Temptation in the Wilderness*

◆ Matthew 4:1-11; Mark 1:12-15; Luke 4:1-13

> And immediately the Spirit driveth him into the wilderness. And he was there in the wilderness forty days, tempted of Satan; and was with the wild beasts; and the angels ministered unto him.

This report is from Mark. Matthew and Luke found another source, probably *Q*, a source book no longer extant, that told of three specific temptations. John, who was supposed to have been with Jesus at his baptism, doesn't even mention forty days in the wilderness. John has Jesus at the wedding in Cana three days after the baptism.

In Matthew and Luke, Jesus had been without food for forty days and the Devil said

> "If thou be the Son of God, command that these stones be made bread." Jesus said, "Man shall not live by bread alone, but by every word that proceedeth out of the mouth of God." Then the devil taketh him up into the holy city, and setteth him on a pinnacle of the temple. And saith unto him, "If thou be the Son of God, cast thyself down: for it is written, He shall give his angels charge concerning thee: and in their hands they shall bear thee up, lest at any time thou dash thy foot against a stone." Jesus said, "Thou shalt not tempt the Lord thy God." Again, the devil taketh him into an exceeding high mountain, and sheweth

him all the kingdoms of the world, and the glory of them; And saith unto him, "All these things will I give thee, if thou wilt fall down and worship me." Jesus said, "Thou shalt worship the Lord thy God, and him only shalt thou serve."

The story of the temptations is common to Buddha and Zarathrusta as they began their ministries. The reason it is in our Bible is because the writers wanted to show Jesus as a world-class religious hero.

If the three temptations in Matthew and Luke were known to Mark, he most assuredly would have included them, but they evidently had not been written in Mark's time. Mark does have forty days of tempting by Satan, but no details are given. For John to ignore such a good story is puzzling. John doesn't have the same idea of a devil as does Matthew, Mark and Luke.

John makes much of John the Baptist's denial of being Elijah, one of the prophets, or the Messiah. John the Baptist was a cousin of Jesus and six months older than Jesus. The last king of Israel was of the Hasmonean line, and some scholars think John the Baptist and Jesus were from this family. If so, they were in line for the throne of Israel. The Hasmoneans ruled Israel from 165 B.C. to 37 B.C.

When the wise men came to see Jesus they asked, "Where is he that is born King of the Jews?" It may have been asked of John the Baptist, because he was first in line, but the story was told of Jesus. Jesus said he was born to be a king. He lived with the hope of having a throne and even promised thrones to each of the twelve apostles (Matthew 19:28). Jesus was crucified because he aspired to be king of the Jews. Jesus did not deny John the Baptist's claim to the throne. "Now after that John was put in prison, Jesus came into Galilee, preaching the gospel of the kingdom of God." Jesus was the Messiah or king, but he never got to sit on the throne of Israel.

The reason Jesus went into the wilderness immediately after his baptism was probably because before that time he didn't know that John was still alive. After he was born, Elizabeth and Zechariah gave John to the Essenes at Qumran and the family lost track of him. Perhaps Jesus and his family got word of John baptizing in Judea and went to make sure it was really John. When Jesus was certain, he knew he could not put in his claim for the throne as long as John lived. When John was put in prison, Jesus, being next in line, began his challenge for the throne.

The temptation was only in the mind of Jesus; it was likely the result of a hysteric hallucination. Jesus was still excited from the hallucination at his baptism. Now with the news of John the Baptist being the pretender to the throne, he again became so anxious that the emotional conflict caused another hysteric hallucination. This time his hallucination produced a vision of the devil. As they talked, he was in such anguish that he imagined the devil offered him all the kingdoms of the world. Even in his hysteric condition, Jesus could still refuse to worship the devil. As he satisfied himself about his determination to follow God, he saw himself being ministered to by angels.

This whole episode of the temptation is the product of a natural hysteric hallucination. No miracle was involved.

130   The First Draught of Fishes

♦   Matthew 4:18-22; Mark 1:16-20; Luke 5:1-11; John 1:29, 35-43

> And it came to pass, that, as the people pressed upon him to hear the word of God, he stood by the lake of Gennesaret, and saw two ships standing by the lake: but the fishermen were gone out of them, and were washing their nets. And he entered into one of the ships, which was Simon's, and prayed him that he would thrust out a little from the land. And he sat down, and taught the people out of the ship. Now when he had left speaking, he said unto Simon, "Launch out into the deep, and let down your nets for a draught." And Simon answering said unto him, "Master, we have toiled all night, and have taken nothing: nevertheless at thy word I will let down the net." And when they had this done, they inclosed a great multitude of fishes: and their net brake. . . . And Jesus said unto Simon, "Fear not; from henceforth thou shalt catch men."

This story of the net full of fish was only put in to set the scene for the real drama. The story of the net being so full it broke is an exaggeration, but it is an illustration of something greater. The real story is the one where Peter, Andrew, James and John were caught and were changed from fishermen to "fishers of men." Here again the means are justified by the end, and the end of the story was the reason the rest of the story was made up. We are led to believe this was the first time Jesus ever saw these four fishermen and they immediately left all and followed him. Acts 1:21 tells us these men began to follow Jesus when he was baptized. One needs to be careful when reading these stories or one also will be caught in the writer's net.

There is nothing supernatural in this story. It is only made up, and fabrication is hardly supernatural.

131   Jesus Cures a Leper

♦   Matthew 8:1-4; Mark 1:40-45; Luke 5:12-15

> And, behold, there came a leper and worshipped him, saying, "Lord, if thou wilt, thou canst make me clean." And Jesus put forth his hand,

and touched him, saying, "I will; be thou clean." And immediately his leprosy was cleansed. And Jesus saith unto him, "See thou tell no man; but go thy way, shew thyself to the priest, and offer the gift that Moses commanded, for a testimony unto them."

In this story a leper came to Jesus and undoubtedly knew what Jesus had been doing. Hearing that Jesus had cured others, he believed Jesus could heal him, too. The story doesn't have any conversation, but I am sure they must have talked for a while and Jesus assured the man that he could be cured. The man had faith to believe in his cure, and when Jesus suggested he be clean, "immediately his leprosy was cleansed." In this story, Jesus touched the man and that point of contact was important, for it established a specific time when the man's faith could claim the cure.

Recall what leprosy meant in Bible times. For a leper to be cured, was as it were, going from death to life, so we can see how much it meant to the man to be cured. Jesus specifically told the man not to tell anyone about the cure, but I am sure the man couldn't keep such an obvious thing hidden. Mark said he "began to publish it much, and to blaze abroad the matter." Word of a healer spread fast and it was urgent to make known the fact that Jesus and the Kingdom of God were at hand. Did the man sin by telling others about his cure? That is a hard question. Perhaps Jesus was only protecting himself in case the man again became hysteric and the skin disorder returned.

Elisha cured a man named Naaman by sending him to wash in the Jordan River. Some think this is but a copycat story to make Jesus at least equal with Elisha. I think if Elisha did cure Naaman, Jesus also cured this leper of his problem. There is nothing supernatural in this story, because natural means handled the situation nicely.

132   *Jesus and the Centurion's Servant*

◆   Matthew 8:5-13; Luke 7:1-10

And when Jesus was entered into Capernaum, there came unto him a centurion, beseeching him, And saying, "Lord, my servant lieth at home sick of the palsy, grievously tormented." And Jesus saith unto him, "I will come and heal him." The centurion answered and said, "Lord, I am not worthy that thou shouldst come under my roof: but speak the word only, and my servant shall be healed. For I am a man under authority, having soldiers under me: and I say to this man, 'Go, and he goeth; and to another, Come, and he cometh; and to my servant, Do this, and he doeth it.'" When Jesus heard it, he marvelled, and said to them that followed, "Verily I say unto you, I have not found so great faith, no, not in Israel." And Jesus said unto the centurion, "Go thy way; and as thou hast believed, so be it done unto thee." And his servant was healed in the selfsame hour.

Luke tells the same story but with some major differences. Matthew says the centurion came to Jesus; Luke says the centurion sent "the elders of the Jews." Matthew says the servant was "sick of the palsy, grievously tormented" Luke says he was "sick and ready to die." Matthew has the centurion say Jesus could heal with his word and need not come to his home. Luke says the centurion sent friends to meet Jesus and says Jesus only needed to say the word and the servant would be healed. Both stories have Jesus praise the faith of the centurion, and because he was a Gentile, the Jews were chastised as unbelievers in the power of Jesus.

As long as the servant knew of Jesus and believed he was able to help, he was assured in his mind that he would be cured. There was probably a certain time arranged when the centurion or his friends were to talk to Jesus. When the time came and the servant was satisfied the meeting took place, his ailment was cured.

This story is more about the Roman centurion and his having built a synagogue for the Jews than about the healing. The fact that a Roman believed in the Jewish God and could have such faith in Jesus was a way to shame the Jews for rejecting Jesus. Matthew doesn't seem to be aware of the synagogue but Luke mentions it. Luke was a Gentile and wanted to portray Gentiles in the best light. By the time Luke was written, Paul had established his Gentile Christian churches and Luke himself had been with Paul. Matthew wrote mainly to Jews and he wasn't as interested in Gentiles; he did take a jab at the Jews for not having as much faith as the Roman Centurion. Matthew has Jesus threaten the Jews and says "the children of the kingdom shall be cast into outer darkness: there shall be weeping and gnashing of teeth." Whether the servant was healed or not, Matthew is more concerned with the message to the Jews: "Shape up or ship out."

If a healing of the servant's paralysis occurred, it is much like the last story and the same natural elements were used to cure hysteric paralysis.

No miracle is in evidence in the story.

133   *Peter's Mother-in-law Cured of a Fever*

◆   Matthew 8:14-15; Mark 1:29-31; Luke 4:38-39

> And when Jesus was come into Peter's house, he saw his wife's mother laid, and sick of a fever. And he touched her hand, and the fever left her: and she arose, and ministered unto them.

This short story deals with Jesus curing Peter's mother-in-law. She had a great fever and Jesus merely touched her hand and the fever was gone. Luke says Jesus, "rebuked the fever; and it left her." In any case, the result was instant relief from fever.

We are dealing with yet another classic case of hysteria. This was probably brought on by the fact that Jesus was coming to her home. Anxiety, fear of not pleasing him, stress in the preparations—any number of things could have caused her to experience hysteria with fever as its symptom. Try to imagine how you might feel if you believed that the Messiah would soon be a visitor in your home. Jesus spent a few moments calming her and assuring here everything was fine in the house and when he suggested that she was cured, "the fever left her." She would have had no problem believing he could help her and her faith in him had a palliative effect.

Mark was the first to write his gospel and Matthew and Luke copied liberally from it so all three of these stories are from one source: Mark. You may be interested to know that Mark's gospel contains 661 verses, and 606 of them have found their way into Matthew. Luke took 380 of Mark's verses and put them into his gospel. The idea of inspiration really didn't enter the picture in those days. Plagiarism was not a crime; it was very common to copy another person's work. Paul wrote "All scripture is given by inspiration of God" (2 Timothy 3:16). When Paul wrote that, he wasn't writing about the gospels being inspired because they hadn't been written yet. Only the Law and the Prophets in the Old Testament were scripture at that time. Preachers today use this verse to justify anything they want to tell you, and you will do well to remember this and catch them at their own game. Never let them get away with intellectual dishonesty.

The story of Peter's mother-in-law was natural in cause and cure and no miracle was performed.

134   *Many Healed by Jesus*

◆   Matthew 8:16-17; Mark 1:32-34; Luke 4:40-41

> And at even, when the sun did set, they brought unto him all that were diseased, and them that were possessed with devils. And all the city was gathered together at the door. And he healed many that were sick of divers diseases, and cast out many devils; and suffered not the devils to speak, because they knew him (Mark 1:32-34). When the even was come, they brought unto him many that were possessed with devils: and he cast out the spirits with his word, and healed all that were sick (Matthew 8:16). Now when the sun was setting, all they that had any sick with divers diseases brought them unto him; and he laid his hands on every one of them, and healed them (Luke 4:40).

This event took place on the same day as two other stories; the synagogue demoniac and Peter's mother-in-law. Faith was obviously at a high point all over town, and in this story we have three stages of development. Mark said they brought all the sick and he healed many of them. Matthew said they brought many of the sick and he healed them all. Luke said they brought all that were sick and he healed them all. Did you see the progression from all . . . many, to many . . . all, to all . . . all? In this process of mythical accretion, a story began and was embellished and grew as it was rewritten. Mark wrote first and Matthew and Luke copied and added what they felt would make a better story.

Here they were dealing with people afflicted with a variety of symptoms. By evening, news had rapidly spread and people were well aware of those already cured. As Jesus counseled and laid hands on them, their faith was adequate for them to accept a cure for themselves. I am of the opinion that Mark was probably closest to the truth when even though all were brought to him, not all were cured. Jesus was only able to help "many that were sick of divers diseases." Not everyone who was sick was suffering from hysteria. Some were probably victims of real leprosy, blindness, deafness or paralysis. Some may have had broken bones or open sores. Remember, Jesus didn't bring John the Baptist back to life when he was beheaded. Only hysteric symptoms can be cured by counseling, calming, and suggestion. Real physical problems were never cured and that was why only "many" were healed when "all were brought."

This is one of the two times that not everyone who was brought to Jesus was cured. Mark tells of Jesus going into his own country, "And he could there do no mighty work, save that he laid his hands upon a few sick folk, and healed them. And he marvelled because of their unbelief" (Mark 6:5). The reason for this was poor screening. When the confederates reported properly, only those with hysteric symptoms were dealt with, and they were cured. When all the sick were brought, only the hysteric were healed and the rest were condemned for their unbelief.

This story concerns only natural cures and no miracles were present here or all would have been healed on every occasion.

135 *Jesus Calms a Storm*

◆ Matthew 8:23-27; Mark 4:35-41; Luke 8:22-25

> And when he was entered into the ship, his disciples followed him. And, behold, there arose a great tempest in the sea, insomuch that the ship was covered with the waves: but he was asleep. And his disciples came to him, and awoke him, saying, "Lord, save us: we perish." And he saith unto them, "Why are ye fearful, O ye of little faith?" Then he arose, and rebuked the winds and the sea; and there was a great calm. But the men marvelled, saying, "What manner of man is this, that even the winds and the sea obey him!"

Jesus and his disciples got into a ship to cross the lake as they had frequently done. Jesus laid down on a pillow and fell asleep. A sudden gust of wind blew across the lake and caused a wave to sweep over the ship filling it with water. Quickly they woke Jesus and told him they were about to die. Jesus wasn't too concerned and he said something they took to be a rebuke of the wind. Peter, Andrew, James and John were aware of such squalls and they should have told the rest in the ship that this was common and would soon pass. Storms came up and calmed down quickly and it is strange that this story is even in the Bible.

I think the reason for the story has to do with a comparison of Jesus to Jonah. Jonah was asleep aboard ship when a storm arose. Jesus, too, slept as the storm arose. Jonah had to be thrown overboard to calm the storm, but Jesus simply rebuked the storm and it ceased.

The winds coming over the hills west of the Sea of Galilee sometimes swept down onto the surface stirring up sudden storms. The Valley of Doves acts like a funnel for the violent westerly winds and causes them to swirl over the surface of the shallow water. This happens in summer or winter, and lasts only a short time. Jesus knew what to expect and watched the calm part of the sea. When the calm approached the ship, Jesus said something about it being peaceful and still. After it was told and retold, Jesus was made to say, "Peace, be still."

Perfectly natural actions were misunderstood and turned into supernatural events. No miracle took place in the story.

136   *The Gadarene Demoniac*

◆   Matthew 8:28-34; Mark 5:1-20; Luke 8:25-40

> And they came over unto the other side of the sea, into the country of the Gadarenes. And when he was come out of the ship, immediately there met him out of the tombs a man with an unclean spirit, who had his dwelling among the tombs; and no man could bind him, no, not with chains. . . . But when he saw Jesus afar off, he ran and worshipped him, And cried with a loud voice, and said, "What have I to do with thee, Jesus, thou Son of the most high God? I adjure thee by God, that thou torment me not." For he said unto him, "Come out of the man, thou unclean spirit." And he asked him, "What is thy name?" And he answered, saying, "My name is Legion: for we are many." . . . And all the devils besought him, saying, "Send us into the swine, that we may enter into them." And forthwith Jesus gave them leave. And the unclean spirits went out, and entered into the swine: and the herd ran violently down a steep place into the sea, (they were about two thousand;) and were choked in the sea. . . . And they come to Jesus, and see him that was possessed with the devil, and had the legion, sitting, and clothed, and in his right mind: and they were afraid.

Mark and Luke set the scene in the country of the Gadarenes and have one man come out of the tombs. Matthew sets the scene in the country of the Gergesenes and has two men come out of the tombs. Here again, Matthew isn't satisfied with Mark's story so he felt free to edit liberally. The man was hysteric and showed several symptoms. He was crying, cutting himself with stones, violent, naked, and suffered from multiple personality disorder. The man was in very poor mental health. When they put chains on him, he broke them as he had great strength. Jesus was able to talk with the man, calm him down, understand his problem, and by suggesting that the man be normal again, he was cured. The hysteria was removed and the symptoms went with it.

About the same time, some swine herds came and brought some people from the city with them. They were very upset because the man in his frenzy, running around yelling and raising such a commotion, had stampeded a herd of about 2,000 pigs. As a result, "the whole herd of swine ran violently down a steep place into the sea, and perished in the waters." Somehow as the story was told and retold, it soon took on the idea that Jesus had sent the unclean spirits into the swine and that caused them to run into the sea. In this story we have a very strange concept: demons recognize Jesus and are permitted to enter the swine. If Jesus were more powerful than the demons why didn't he simply destroy them instead of the unfortunate pigs? Swine were unclean for Jews, and some think the story was to show displeasure toward Jews who raised them. A modern story might tell of a Christian's crop of opium poppies destroyed by flood.

This story as I have explained it in its natural setting is not difficult to understand, but I also find political overtones therein. There is a possibility that the story is a parable. The demon-possessed man would represent the nation of Israel in Roman bondage. The Legion would refer to the Roman Tenth Legion occupying Israel at that time: they were "possessing" Israel. The emblem on the banner of the famous Tenth Legion was a large boar. The image of the swine running into the sea could be a metaphor for the Romans leaving the country by ship. Israel was now free, calm, clothed with crops and in its right frame of worship.

When Jesus got back into the ship, the man wanted to go with him, but Jesus wouldn't let him. Instead he was told to go home and tell his friends what Jesus had done for him. Two things are different here as Jesus was usually looking for followers and he often told those cured not to tell anyone. What he was saying was that Israel was to tell other nations what God had done for them and convince them to follow Israel's God. I think that is a very good parable and it makes a lot of sense.

No miracle was performed here, but still it was a good story.

137 Jesus and the Paralytic

◆ Matthew 9:1-8; Mark 2:1-12; Luke 5:17-26

> And he entered into a ship, and passed over, and came into his own city. And, behold, they brought to him a man sick of the palsy, lying on a bed: and Jesus seeing their faith said unto the sick of the palsy; "Son, be of good cheer; thy sins be forgiven thee." And, behold, certain of the scribes said within themselves, "This man blasphemeth." And Jesus knowing their thoughts said, "Wherefore think ye evil in your hearts? For whether is easier, to say, 'Thy sins be forgiven thee;' or to say, 'Arise, and walk?' But that ye may know that the Son of man hath power on earth to forgive sins," (then saith he to the sick of the palsy,) "Arise, take up thy bed, and go unto thine house." And he arose, and departed to his house.

Four men carried a paralyzed man lying on a rug to the house where Jesus was. Again the story is brief, and says Jesus forgave the man's sins and then healed him. In Mark and Luke, the four men had to make a hole in the roof and lower the man to get him near Jesus; Matthew omits this. Jesus must have had a conversation with the man and when he understood the situation, he said something strange, "thy sins be forgiven thee." The man must have had guilt feelings and they may have been the cause of the hysteria that brought on the symptom of paralysis. We notice that when the man's sin was forgiven he was still paralyzed. There is no indication that any healing had taken place, even to the man himself. When Jesus suggested the man was able to take up his bed and walk home, the man was satisfied, got up and left.

Hysteria brought on by the guilt of sin rendered this man helpless, so it took a double dose to cure him. First the guilt had to be removed so the hysteria could be relieved, then the physical paralysis could be dealt with. This is the only instance where mental guilt and physical disability are considered together. No one had come to Jesus to asked forgiveness of sins up to that time. Many desired physical relief, but spiritual help was not a concern to them.

This story is about natural assurance and relief, and no miracle is involved in any way.

138 Jairus's Daughter Raised

◆ Matthew 9:18-26; Mark 5:22-43; Luke 8:41-56

> While he spake these things unto them, behold, there came a certain ruler, and worshipped him, saying, "My daughter is even now dead: but come and lay thy hand upon her, and she shall live." And Jesus arose, and followed him, and so did his disciples. . . . And when Jesus came into the ruler's house, and saw the minstrels and the people

making a noise, He said unto them, "Give place: for the maid is not dead, but sleepeth." And they laughed him to scorn. But when the people were put forth, he went in, and took her by the hand, and the maid arose. And the fame hereof went abroad into all that land.

This story is about Jairus and his twelve-year-old daughter. The girl died and her father asked Jesus to bring her back to life. Jesus went to the man's home, and after making everyone else leave, he took her by the hand, told her to get up, and she did. The girl was the victim of hysteric coma and was considered to be dead. There were no signs of life so the people had no way of knowing she was still alive. Jesus made it quite clear when he told the people she was "not dead, but sleepeth." It didn't do any good to tell the people the truth because they didn't believe him anyway. When he was alone with the girl, he talked to her and assured her he was able to help her. When he suggested she arise, she simply got up and all was back to normal.

Luke said, "her spirit came again" and that simply meant she took a deep breath. Remember, spirit means "air" or "breath," and when she took a deep breath, she revived.

This is a classic case of hysteric coma and the cure was purely natural.

This story is thought by some to be a copy of Elisha and the Shunammite's son. Here the father was a ruler of the synagogue and the Shunammite was called "a great woman." Both children were presumed dead when Elisha and Jesus arrived, they were alone with the child, or nearly so, and they suggested the children awake. Both children awoke and all was well. As in many stories, Jesus is made to do what the Old Testament prophets did so he could not only match but outdo all who came before him.

This story has only natural problems and natural solutions. No miracle took place in the story.

139 *The Woman With An Issue of Blood*

◆ Matthew 9:20-22; Mark 5:25-34; Luke 8:43-48

And, behold, a woman, which was diseased with an issue of blood twelve years, came behind him, and touched the hem of his garment: For she said within herself, "If I may but touch his garment, I shall be whole." But Jesus turned him about, and when he saw her, he said, "Daughter, be of good comfort; thy faith hath made thee whole." And the woman was made whole from that hour.

This episode happened while Jesus was on his way to the home of Jarius. A woman afflicted with a chronic hemorrhage or a continuous uterine discharge which she had had for twelve years, came up behind Jesus and touched his garment. She knew of his power and believed if she could just get close enough to touch his clothing she would be cured. She had spent all her money on doctors, but none had helped her. She had already conditioned herself to receive her healing and Jesus confirmed this as he said, "thy faith hath made thee whole." In this case, Jesus had nothing to do but to be there. He didn't have to talk with her and explain her hysteric condition or tell her about her symptom of hemorrhage. He was merely a point of contact and she served as her own psychotherapist.

This story is probably the basis for two other miracle stories in the Book of Acts. Luke has Peter's shadow heal people in Acts 5:11-16 and "handkerchiefs or aprons" from Paul healed diseases in Acts 19:11-12. As long as people believe strongly and the conditions of hysteria are right, a cure can take place. I can't emphasize enough that faith is the curative vehicle. Many times Jesus said "According to your faith be it unto you," or "thy faith hath saved thee." Jesus knew, if only unconsciously, what cured hysteric symptoms and his hope was to stimulate the faith and assurance the people lacked.

Another story in Matthew 14:35-36 tells of many diseased who "besought him that they might only touch the hem of his garment: and as many as touched were made perfectly whole." Healing by touch was common in those and Old Testament times. The Roman Emperor Hadrian is credited with a cure of a fever and blindness when an old blind man touched him. In all stories of relieving hysteric symptoms, the faith of the one suffering is the controlling factor in the relief of the symptoms. The woman in this story brought about her own healing and Jesus commended her for it.

This story has no supernatural element in it because all the results arise from natural physical and mental means.

140 Jesus and the Two Blind Men

◆ Matthew 9:27-31

> And when Jesus departed thence, two blind men followed him, crying, and saying, "Thou son of David, have mercy on us." And when he was come into the house, the blind men came to him: and Jesus saith unto them, "Believe ye that I am able to do this?" They said unto him, "Yea, Lord." Then touched he their eyes, saying, "According to your faith be it unto you." And their eyes were opened; and Jesus straitly charged them, saying, "See that no man know it." But they, when they were departed, spread abroad his fame in all that country.

These two blind men followed Jesus from the house of Jairus after he raised the young girl from the dead. The two men called Jesus the "son of David" and asked for mercy. When they got to the house they probably had a little talk about their blindness. When Jesus was sure he could help them he asked, "Believe ye that I am able to do this?" When he was satisfied they were assured he could help them, he suggested they could see "according to your faith" and they had their cure. These two men were told not to say anything, but of course they couldn't keep quiet and they too spread the word.

This blindness was obviously hysteric blindness so there was no physical damage to their eyes. With an attitude of faith and assurance, they could be helped. Jesus merely suggested that they be cured and the job was done. The system worked for Elijah, Elisha, Jesus, Peter, Paul and it works for psychotherapists today. The same circumstances that caused hysteric symptoms thousands of years ago still cause them today. The cure was the same then as it is today.

Whether there was one or two blind men in the source material is uncertain as Matthew again has a knack for doubling-up in his stories. In another story, we will find Mark telling about Bartimaeus, Luke telling about a certain blind man and Matthew had two blind men. It is hard to say why Matthew added to the stories he copied from Mark, but it seems to be just one of his quirks.

The story of these blind men dealt only with natural cures and no supernatural element entered the picture.

141 Jesus and the Dumb Demoniac

♦ Matthew 9:32-34; 12:22-37; Luke 11:14-26

> As they went out, behold, they brought to him a dumb man possessed with a devil. And when the devil was cast out, the dumb spake: and the multitudes marvelled, saying, "It was never so seen in Israel."

Here is another brief story of a dumb man possessed with a devil. It simply says that the devil was cast out and the man could speak. I imagine there was a little visit and chat before anything happened. When Jesus was aware of the man's problem, he was able to reassure the man and as he suggested a cure, the man was able to speak again.

This story is identical with the one in Matthew 12:22-37 except for the addition of blindness. "Then was brought unto him one possessed with a devil, blind, and dumb: and he healed him, insomuch that the blind and dumb both spake and saw." The stories are one, and Matthew simply added blindness and told it again. The cure for hysteric blindness is the same as the cure for hysteric dumbness so it was also an immediate cure. These two stories end with the same negative attitude, "But the Pharisees said, 'He casteth out devils through the prince of the devils. This fellow doth not cast out devils, but by Beelzebub the prince of the devils.'" That was some charge to make against a man who had just cured a blind and dumb man.

It would not seem to matter to some people how a person was cured, but the Pharisees were concerned. Jesus made a very important observation and threw it right back at them. "And if I by Beelzebub cast out devils, by whom do your children cast them out? therefore they shall be your judges. But if I cast our devils by the Spirit of God, then the kingdom of God is come unto you." This was all good reasoning, but it is based on a false premise. If there were devils, it would make sense to reason, "If Satan cast out Satan, he is divided against himself; how shall then his kingdom stand?" We are well aware that there are no devils, so we wonder why the omniscient Jesus was unaware of that fact. The answer is easy. Jesus knew no more than did the ones who wrote of him.

If devils caused blindness, deafness and dumbness then, what causes these things now? Eyeglasses, hearing aids and artificial larynxes cure the problems today for many people but if the problems are hysteric symptoms, psychotherapy is in order. When the church blames diseases and infirmities on the devil they claim they alone can cure such problems. It is simply a means of enhancing their power and prestige. In medieval times the church struck against medical advances because it proved that the real devils of diseases were invading pathogens. At the last half of the 19th Century Freud found hysteria to be the cause of many health problems; when he devised a cure, multitudes were benefited.

One of the main reasons for this book is to make people aware of how many ailments are symptoms of hysteria. It is my hope that many people find answers and help in this information and will seek the help of qualified professionals. Remember that the natural means of healing are adequate for natural hysteric problems, so don't sit around waiting for a miracle that will never happen.

142 Jesus Heals a Withered Hand

◆ Matthew 12:9-14; Mark 3:1-6; Luke 6:6-11

> And he entered again into the synagogue; and there was a man there which had a withered hand. And they watched him, whether he would heal him on the sabbath day; that they might accuse him. And he saith unto the man which had the withered hand, "Stand forth." And he saith unto them, "Is it lawful to do good on the sabbath days, or to do evil? to save life, or to kill?" But they held their peace. And when he had looked round about on them with anger, being grieved for the hardness of their hearts, he saith unto the man, "Stretch forth thine hand." And he stretched it out: and his hand was restored whole as the other.

Jesus went into the synagogue on the sabbath and saw a man whose hand was withered or paralyzed. This may have been the only man in the house who had a condition worthy of healing. Perhaps the scribes and Pharisees made sure the man was in the crowd. In either case, the man didn't ask for healing. Maybe Jesus preached that day and his sermon concerned healing. If he did preach about healing, perhaps the man with the withered hand was inspired by the message and came to realize that Jesus could help him. One thing led to another and finally Jesus asked the man to "Stand forth" and he came forward. By now the man's faith must have been at fever pitch. When Jesus said "Stretch forth thine hand," the man accepted the suggestion and reached out his hand.

This paralysis was hysteric in nature and all the conditions were met for a cure. Faith and assurance that Jesus was able to help, and the suggestion that the job was done enabled the man to accept the help he needed. Only the man's hand was affected but we shall see other cases in which legs and feet were paralyzed causing immobility.

What an exciting thing it must have been to watch someone you personally knew released from a condition that had caused suffering for years. No wonder when people saw this happen, they marveled at the man who made it happen and even worshiped him. Here though, "the Pharisees went forth, and straightway took counsel with the Herodians against him, how they might destroy him." Because Jesus didn't explain to the people just what he was doing, some misunderstood. He didn't even get his methods across to all the apostles and sometimes even they were unable to heal the sick.

If people understood how Jesus healed, they would never have called him the Son of God. I think that when Jesus told people not to tell about their healing he meant not to tell how they were healed. If word got out of how he used only natural means to heal he would have had no claim to fame. It is evident that Jesus was best known for the good works that he performed. If too many others learned how to heal the sick, Jesus would have lost much of his appeal and maybe some of his followers.

Back in the Old Testament we had a case of a withered hand. King Jeroboam wanted to offer incense but the priests wouldn't allow it and his hand withered. The man of God prayed for the king and his hand was restored (1 Kings 13:1-6). Some think this New Testament story is a copy of the Jeroboam story to make Jesus superior to the Old Testament. I think that hysteria was common in both time periods and I can accept both stories.

Again only natural methods were used and no supernatural means were necessary.

143   The Feeding of 5,000

◆ Matthew 14:13-21; Mark 6:31-44; Luke 9:10-17;
John 6:1-14

> And he said unto them, "Come ye yourselves apart into a desert place, and rest a while": for there were many coming and going, and they had no leisure so much as to eat. And they departed into a desert place by ship privately. And the people saw them departing, and many knew him, and ran afoot thither out of all cities, and outwent them, and came together unto him. And Jesus, when he came out, saw much people, and was moved with compassion toward them, because they were as sheep not having a shepherd: And he began to teach them many things. And when the day was now far spent, his disciples came unto him, and said, "This is a desert place, and now the time is far passed: Send them away, that they may go into the country round about, and into the villages, and buy themselves bread: for they have nothing to eat." He answered and said unto them, "Give ye them to eat." And they say unto him, "Shall we go and buy two hundred pennyworth of bread, and give them to eat?" He saith unto them, "How many loaves have ye? go and see." And when they knew, they say, "Five, and two fishes." And he commanded them to make all sit down by companies upon the green grass. And they sat down in ranks by hundreds, and by fifties. And when he had taken the five loaves and the two fishes, he looked up to heaven, and blessed, and brake the loaves, and gave them to his disciples to set before them; and the two fishes divided he among them all. And they did all eat, and were filled. And they took up twelve baskets full of the fragments, and of the fishes. And they that did eat of the loaves were about five thousand men.

Of all the miracle stories, this is the only one mentioned in all four gospels. Sounds great, but we must remember that Matthew and Luke copied from Mark, and John's gospel was written about thirty years after Mark wrote his account.

What we have here is a picture of the compassion Jesus had for people. He was genuinely concerned for their welfare, and knowing that some of them brought more food than others, some might still be hungry after eating what they brought. Jesus asked everyone to sit down in an orderly fashion, and when they were all comfortable on the green grass they had a big picnic, pot-luck style. By first sharing what the disciples had, everyone else shared too, and they had a great time and a good meal together. When everyone was satisfied, the leftovers were gathered and twelve baskets were filled.

Have you ever wondered why there were twelve empty baskets with them? A basket was a lunch basket large enough for one person for one day. People just didn't bring empty baskets to a get-together—they filled them with food. It was this food that was shared so all could be fed.

As to the number of 5,000 men plus women and children, we are definitely looking at inflation. Exaggeration is common in the Bible, but we may rest assured there was a good-sized crowd.

Looking closely at the story we notice that the disciples had just come from the burial of John the Baptist, and Jesus took them to this desert place. It was they who were hungry for "they had no leisure so much as to eat." It wasn't the crowd that was so hungry, for they had just come from their homes the same day. The situation was not as bad as some would have us believe and no one was in danger of starvation. When the people came out of the nearby cities, they brought their picnic baskets; they were more intelligent than most modern preachers give them credit.

It should be noted that no one seemed the least bit excited that so many had eaten when so little food was available. The absence of emotion is characteristic of almost all the miracle stories, and it leads one to the conclusion that they simply were not miracles. Even in the story of the manna, no one seemed to be amazed when they found it lying on the ground all around the camp.

While the explanation of a picnic may sound simple, consider a few verses in John's version. Some of the people had followed Jesus across the Sea of Galilee, and as they were talking with Jesus, they asked him to show them a sign or miracle. "They said therefore unto him, 'What sign shewest thou then, that we may see, and believe thee? what dost thou work? Our fathers did eat manna in the desert; as it is written, He gave them bread from heaven to eat.'" If Jesus had performed a miracle and had given them bread, they would not have asked for a miracle or Jesus would have related the one that just happened. Because there was no miracle to tell, no one mentioned the picnic. This was just the day after the picnic so it still would have been fresh in their minds.

After the picnic, the disciples were in a ship and were caught in a wind storm. Jesus got into the ship and calmed them down. At the same time, the wind calmed down and they were "sore amazed." "For they considered not the miracle of the loaves: for their heart was hardened" (Mark 6:52). In this verse, the word *miracle* is in italics because it was not in the original. We see very clearly they didn't take it as a miracle, so why should we.

The story is based on the Old Testament stories of Moses and the manna, and of Elisha when he fed 100 men with twenty loaves of bread and some ears of corn. No manna was left over, and Elisha did have a little bread left over, but after Jesus fed 5,000 men, there were twelve baskets full left over. In the contest between the Old and New Testaments, Jesus wins again.

There is no miracle here as it was only a natural sharing of food.

144 Jesus Walks on Water

◆ Matthew 14:22-36; Mark 6:45-52; John 6:15-21

> And when even was now come, his disciples went down unto the sea,
> And entered into a ship, and went over the sea toward Capernaum. And
> it was now dark, and Jesus was not come to them. And the sea arose
> by reason of a great wind that blew. So when they had rowed about
> five and twenty or thirty furlongs, they see Jesus walking on the sea,
> and drawing nigh unto the ship: and they were afraid. But he saith unto
> them, "It is I; be not afraid." Then they willingly received him into the
> ship: And immediately the ship was at the land whither they went.

This took place right after the feeding of the 5,000 and while Jesus
sent the people away, the disciples were in a ship crossing the sea of
Galilee. It was between three and four a.m., and in the blackness of night
they saw Jesus walking along by the sea. In the Bible we read "on the
sea" but it also could be translated "by the sea." Because of the great
wind blowing, the ship had been blown around so much that the disciples
had no idea where they were. As Jesus was "by the sea"—on the
shore—they took him "into the ship" and immediately the ship was at
the "land whither they went." It took them so long to row against the
wind that Jesus walked faster than they rowed.

Matthew tells us that Peter even stepped out of the ship and walked
with Jesus until he slipped off a rock and fell into the water. When they
had Jesus in the ship, it was only a short way to the dock and their journey
was over. The trip the ship took "on the sea" was not very far and neither
was the walk Jesus took "by the sea."

Try to picture Jesus walking on water during a time of big waves and
strong winds and you will have a problem. Do you see him on the crest
of the waves or in the trough between them? Because waves roll so
rapidly he would have bobbed up and down and it is hard to visualize
how the disciples could have seen him. It is better to reason things out
to try to determine what really happened. The translation of a single word
turns this from the Bible story of chaos to a prosaic story with a
semblance of order.

The reason this story was pushed into the miracle realm was simply
to match up to or outdo the Old Testament water feats: Moses and the
Red sea, Joshua crossing the Jordan and the little stories of Elijah and
Elisha walking across Jordon on the stepping stones left by Joshua. Jesus
is made to walk on the water instead of parting it and so he was superior
to the others.

The story is only of natural events—no miracle was performed.

145   *A Woman's Daughter Cured*

◆ Matthew 15:21-28; Mark 7:24-30

> Then Jesus went thence, and departed into the coasts of Tyre and Sidon. And, behold, a woman of Caanan came out of the same coasts, and cried unto him, saying, "Have mercy on me, O Lord, thou son of David; my daughter is grievously vexed with a devil." But he answered her not a word. And his disciples came and besought him, saying, "Send her away; for she crieth after us." But he answered and said, "I am not sent but unto the lost sheep of the house of Israel." Then came she and worshipped him, saying, "Lord, help me." But he answered and said, "It is not meet to take the children's bread, and cast it to dogs." And she said, "Truth, Lord: yet the dogs eat of the crumbs which fall from their masters' table." Then Jesus answered and said unto her, "O woman, great is thy faith: be it unto thee even as thou wilt." And her daughter was made whole from that very hour.

This story is most unusual in that it takes place outside of the nation of Israel. Tyre and Sidon were in Gentile territory and the woman was a Syro-Phoenician or Greek-speaking woman. All we know of the daughter was that she was "vexed with a devil." It seems like Jesus and his disciples tried to get the woman to leave them alone, but she kept after them. All she wanted was for Jesus to free her daughter from the devil. Jesus told her he was only sent to the Jews but still she persisted. Jesus said it was "not meet to take the children's bread, and cast it to the dogs." Some Jews called Gentiles "dogs" so the writer has Jesus say the same thing. The woman was clever and reminded Jesus that the "dogs eat of the crumbs which fall from their masters' table." Such good reasoning could not go unrewarded, so Jesus said, "O woman, great is thy faith: be it unto thee even as thou wilt."

The signal phrase is the demon possession—a sure sign of hysteria. This victim of hysteria was cured because the woman was able to understand the situation after Jesus explained it to her. Once she knew how to suggest the cure to her daughter we read "her daughter was made whole." By using the mother as an intermediary, Jesus didn't even have to meet with the daughter. This is another story where natural means were used to solve a problem and no miracle is needed.

146   *The Feeding of 4,000*

◆ Matthew 15:30-39; Mark 8:1-9

> In those days the multitude being very great, and having nothing to eat, Jesus called his disciples unto him, and said unto them, "I have compassion on the multitude, because they have now been with me three days, and have nothing to eat: And if I send them away fasting

to their own homes, they will faint by the way: for divers of them came
from far." . . . And he asked them, "How many loaves have ye?" And
they said, "Seven." . . . And they had a few small fishes: and he blessed,
and commanded to set them also before them. So they did eat, and
were filled: and they took up of the broken meat that was left seven
baskets. And they that had eaten were about four thousand: and he sent
them away.

Most scholars agree that this story is a doublet, or a retelling, of the
story of feeding the 5,000 told in Mark 6. When the gospel of Mark was
written, about 40 years after the crucifixion, the writer gathered material
from many sources. In this case two similar stories came to him, and
because the numbers are different he used both of them. The same story
was told and retold and somewhere along the way the facts changed. The
4,000 became 5,000 and the area changed from Bethsaida to Decapolis.
One heard five loaves and two fishes, another heard seven loaves and a
few small fishes. It all worked out the same: the people shared what they
had and the surplus was taken up to be used again.

Luke and John have the story of the 5,000 but did not include the story
of the 4,000. Perhaps they did not hear it or they considered the two
stories the same and simply picked the one over the other. When
Matthew took this story from Mark, he copied it almost word for word.
Remember that of the 661 verses of Mark, Matthew copied 606 of them.
Matthew uses over 90% of Mark's gospel. When you hear the stories of
how the Bible was inspired, consider how inspired Matthew was as he
took so much directly from Mark's gospel. This is not a criticism of
Matthew. It is a criticism of the preachers who want us to believe the
words men wrote down were told to them directly by God. With the Old
Testament sources of *J, E, D, P* and *R,* and the way Matthew and Luke
took the material Mark wrote, as well as the *Q* source, divine inspiration
is nowhere to be found. Natural manipulation of stories and not supernatural inspiration brought about the Bible we have today.

147   *The Transfiguration*

◆   Matthew 17:1-13; Mark 9:1-13; Luke 9:28-36

And after six days, Jesus taketh with him Peter, and James, and John,
and leadeth them up into a high mountain apart by themselves: and he
was transfigured before them. And his raiment became shining, exceeding white as snow; so as no fuller on earth can white them. And
there appeared unto them Elias with Moses: and they were talking with
Jesus. . . . And there was a cloud that overshadowed them: and a voice
came out of the cloud, saying, "This is my beloved Son: hear him."
And suddenly, when they had looked round about, they saw no man
any more, save Jesus only with themselves.

Jesus took his three favorite apostles and went up into a mountain. As he prayed, "his raiment became shining, exceeding white as snow." Matthew even said "his face did shine as the sun." Next thing we read there were two more men on the mountain and we are told that they were Elijah and Moses. I have no idea how they recognized Elijah and Moses because the Jews never made pictures of anyone because it was against their law. I have a notion that Jesus planned this rendezvous with a couple of his Essene friends, and he may have mentioned Elijah and Moses, and Peter, James and John misunderstood. We are not told what they discussed, though it would be of great interest to us. They had a short chat with Jesus and left. A voice was heard to say "This is my beloved son: hear him." It may well have been one of the visitors introducing his son to Jesus.

When they came down the mountain Matthew had Jesus say, "Tell the vision to no man." How about that! What we were told earlier was an appearance is now only a vision. There is a great difference between an appearance in which someone is actually there and a vision that takes place only in the mind.

There are several reasons I can think of why a story like this found its way into the Scriptures. One is to demonstrate Jesus' superiority over Moses who represented the Law and Elijah who represented the Prophets. In the Old Testament story of Moses' face shining as he was on Mt. Sinai, Jesus had his face and his raiment shine in Matthew's account. Elijah wasn't transfigured, but he did encounter the horses and chariot of fire. As King Saul had been able to get the witch of Endor to call Samuel from the dead, Jesus is said to have called back Elijah and Moses. All of this is interesting, but if Jesus, Peter, James and John saw anything, I believe it was a vision as Jesus said.

What could have happened was a mass hallucination. Because Peter, James and John were so excited about what Jesus had told them just before climbing the mountain, they were in a state of hysteria. When Jesus suggested the presence of Elijah and Moses, the three had a hysteric hallucination in which they saw and heard strange things. In hysteric hallucinations, visions and voices can be suggested and experienced by any number of people. Luke said the three were "heavy with sleep: and when they were awake, they saw his glory, and the two men that stood with him." This is a picture of a suggestive hysteric occurrence. Even as people can receive suggestions to remove hysteric symptoms, they also can take on symptoms by suggestion. We will see other cases of mass hysteria as we continue our study so be on the lookout for them.

The explanations I have given are logical, reasonable and natural. Because this story can be explained in the natural realm, there is no reason to look for anything supernatural.

148   A Demonic Boy Cured

◆ Matthew 17:14-21; Mark 9:14-29; Luke 9:37-43

> And when they were come to the multitude, there came to him a certain man, kneeling down to him, and saying, "Lord, have mercy on my son: for he is lunatick, and sore vexed: for ofttimes he falleth into the fire, and oft into the water. And I brought him to thy disciples, and they could not cure him." Then Jesus answered and said, "O faithless and perverse generation, how long shall I be with you? how long shall I suffer you? bring him hither to me." And Jesus rebuked the devil; and he departed out of him: and the child was cured from that very hour.

The boy in this story is really a sad case. The father had brought his son to the disciples but they could not help him. Peter is the only apostle who is recorded to have done specific miracles of healing and the others are characterized here as unable to cure the boy. A large crowd gathered and as Jesus and the three arrived, the disciples were perplexed. It appears that none of the nine understood how Jesus healed the sick.

In this story we see what probably took place in the other stories that were so briefly written. Mark has Jesus ask, "How long is it ago since this came unto him? And he said, Of a child." Jesus asked such questions of all he cured, but they are not always recorded. What a list of problems the boy had! Foaming at the mouth, trying to bite people, lunatic, falling into the fire, falling into the water, a dumb spirit, gnashing his teeth, convulsions and even malnutrition. When Jesus was familiar with the problem and gained the confidence of the father and the son, he calmed the boy's hysteria. "Jesus took him by the hand, and lifted him up; and he arose," cured of his symptoms. All that was needed was a calm reassurance and understanding the disciples were unable to match. All the problems listed are symptoms of hysteria, and as a result of the gentle suggestion by Jesus, they simply vanished. The boy was calmly, quickly restored to a condition of health.

It is interesting to notice how the three gospels differ about why the disciples were unable to cure the boy. Matthew says it was because of their unbelief. With "faith as a grain of mustard seed" they could have done it. But "this kind goeth not out but by prayer and fasting." Mark doesn't say anything about faith, "he said unto them, 'This kind can come forth by nothing, but by prayer and fasting.'" Luke only refers to "a faithless and perverse generation."

I think the main fault was in the inability to take control of the situation. That one quality so commonly mentioned concerning Jesus was that he spoke with authority. He took command, he was in control, he had the situation in hand at all times. This caused people to have confidence and gave them the assurance so they could accept the cure.

One final observation on this case is the fact that this boy was the only child of his father. We find that to be a characteristic in many healing stories. Whether this was the actual situation or only put in as a ploy for sympathy is hard to tell, but it does have an effect on the readers. In this story all the evidence shows a natural cure was effected and no supernatural means were used.

149   *The Fish and the Coin*

◆   Matthew 17:24-27

> And when they were come to Capernaum, they that received tribute money came to Peter, and said, "Doth not your master pay tribute?" He saith, "Yes." And when he was come into the house, Jesus prevented him, saying, "What thinkest thou, Simon? of whom do the kings of the earth take custom or tribute? of their own children, or of strangers?" Peter saith unto him, "Of strangers." Jesus saith unto him, "Then are the children free. Notwithstanding, lest we should offend them, go thou to the sea, and cast an hook, and take up the fish that first cometh up; and when thou hast opened his mouth, thou shalt find a piece of money: that take, and give unto them for me and thee."

This story is related only by Matthew, himself a tax collector. This is a strange story, both in its intent and in the fact that the action never happened. We are not told that Peter caught a fish with a coin in its mouth although, as a fisherman by trade, he may have. Perhaps all that was meant was to catch as many fish as necessary, sell them, and use the money to pay the tax. That would make good sense since Peter had been in the fish business for many years.

It would not be supernatural for a fish to have a coin in its mouth because it is perfectly natural for fish to strike at bright objects. This is why bright, shiny lures are on the market today. The story is probably based upon an actual event when someone, perhaps even Peter, caught a fish and found a coin in its mouth. To transfer the story to Peter in the discussion of taxes would be a very natural thing to do if one wanted to suggest some supernatural event.

As the event is not said to have really happened, there need be no miracle involved.

150 Blind Bartimaeus Healed

◆ Matthew 20:29-34; Mark 10:46-52; Luke 18:35-43

> And they came to Jericho: and as he went out of Jericho with his disciples, and a great number of people, blind Bartimaeus, the son of Timaeus, sat by the highway begging. And when he heard that it was Jesus of Nazareth, he began to cry out, and say, "Jesus, thou son of David, have mercy on me." . . . And Jesus stood still, and commanded him to be called. And they call the blind man, saying unto him, "Be of good comfort, rise: he calleth thee." And he, casting away his garment, rose, and came to Jesus. And Jesus answered and said unto him, "What will thou that I should do unto thee?" The blind man said unto him, "Lord, that I might receive my sight." And Jesus said unto him, "Go thy way; thy faith hath made thee whole." And immediately he received his sight, and followed Jesus in the way.

When Matthew copied this story in Mark, the same thing happened when Matthew copied the one about the Gadarene demonic. Matthew doubled up and has two men in each story. Mark even names the blind man Bartimaeus, but that really wasn't his name, for the name simply means "son of Timaeus." Matthew and Mark say Jesus was leaving Jericho when the story took place, and Luke says it was when Jesus was about to enter Jericho.

The basic story tells about the blind man crying out, and Jesus asks him what he wanted. The man asks for his sight and Jesus simply says "thy faith hath made thee whole," and the man received his sight immediately. Another classic case of hysteric blindness cured by a mutual understanding and the suggestion of a cure. Once the man with the problem and the man with the solution to that problem came to terms, the problem was solved immediately. Matthew says Jesus touched the eyes while Mark and Luke say Jesus only spoke the words. In either case, no miracle was used, only natural means cured the blind man.

151 The Withered Fig Tree

◆ Matthew 21:17-22; Mark 11:12-14, 20-24

> And on the morrow, when they were come from Bethany, he was hungry: And seeing a fig tree afar off having leaves, he came, if haply he might find any thing thereon: and when he came to it, he found nothing but leaves; for the time of figs was not yet. And Jesus answered and said unto it, "No man eat fruit of thee hereafter for ever." And his disciples heard it. . . . And in the morning, as they passed by, they saw the fig tree dried up from the roots. And Peter calling to remembrance saith unto him, "Master, behold, the fig tree which thou cursedst is withered away." And Jesus answering saith unto them, "Have faith in God."

This little story of the fig tree is puzzling to many people. If it was not the season for figs, why would Jesus hope to find figs on the tree? If it was not the time for figs, why curse the poor tree? The fact that the tree dried up by the next day certainly does not suggest a miracle. If Jesus had caused ripe figs to appear on the tree that would have been a miracle, for they would have been out of season. When he cursed the tree, "And his disciples heard it," they decided to help him out. That night they could have gone out and dug around the tree and cut the roots to kill the tree. Next day when they were passing by, Jesus had forgotten all about the tree but Peter pointed out that the tree was "withered away."

The story is either a parable in which Israel is the unfruitful tree and therefore condemned by Jesus, or the disciples took Jesus' curse and made it happen.

There is no miracle—natural means were adequate to kill the tree, assuming it was not intended as a parable.

152   *Malchus's Ear Cut Off*

♦   Matthew 26:51-56; Mark 14:47; Luke 22:50-51; John 18:10-11

> And one of them that stood by drew a sword, and smote a servant of the high priest, and cut off his ear.

When Mark wrote his story that was all that was known of the incident of the servant's ear. For Mark it was only a bystander that drew a sword and a servant of the high priest who lost an ear. Luke embellished and it became the servant's right ear. The physician Luke, has Jesus restore the slave's ear. When John wrote his account, the story had grown and it was now Peter who cut off the right ear of the servant, Malchus. As time passes, traditions grow.

It would seem that most information would have been available to the earliest account, Mark. When Luke wrote 15–20 years later, he had more information. By the time John wrote, about 30–40 years after Mark, he even had the names of the swordsman and the victim. This needn't be a problem when we realize that the writers felt free to add anything they believed would make the story more spiritual and supernatural. John clearly states, "these are written, that ye might believe that Jesus is the Christ." Anything was fair so long as it increased people's faith in Jesus.

There is no miracle in this story as written by Mark; miracles were added as exaggeration gave license to almost any literary whim. Only Luke heard of and included it in his story, and if it had actually happened the others would have eagerly written about it.

Only natural means of exaggeration and embellishment are necessary to explain this story and its growth.

153   *The Story of Calvary*

◆   Matthew 27 & 28; Mark 14 & 15; Luke 23 & 24; John 18-20

The story of the trial, sentencing and crucifixion involve only a short period of time but a lot of confusion. The only thing worse than having a witness to these events is to have two witnesses. We have it twice as bad because we have *four* witnesses, or at least they wrote as if they were eyewitnesses. To begin with, all four have Jesus dressed in royal apparel and mocked. The reason he was tried, convicted and crucified was because he was a king. Specifically, he was the King of the Jews.

Now sentenced to crucifixion and starting toward Golgotha, a strange thing happened. "And as they came out, they found a man of Cyrene, Simon by name: him they compelled to bear his cross." This is what Matthew, Mark and Luke say, but look at what John says. "And they took Jesus, and led him away. And he bearing his cross went forth into a place called the place of a skull, which is called in the Hebrew Golgotha: Where they crucified him." John says specifically "And he that saw it bare record, and his record is true: and he knoweth that he saith true, that ye might believe." Gnostics had a story in which not only did Simon carry the cross, but he was also the one who was crucified on it. John did not want to deal with this argument so he simply eliminated any mention of Simon.

Once Jesus was crucified, they gambled for his garments, and a title was nailed to the cross over Jesus. All four agree on that but all four have a different wording of what it said. Mark writes "THE KING OF THE JEWS." Luke has it "THIS IS THE KING OF THE JEWS." Matthew's version is "THIS IS JESUS THE KING OF THE JEWS." John reports "JESUS OF NAZARETH THE KING OF THE JEWS." Why would Matthew and Luke change the wording that Mark wrote? Weren't they satisfied or did they really know more than Mark did? The evidence shows that none of them knew what it really said so they made up their own wording.

All four gospels have thieves crucified on either side of Jesus, but here too we have crucial differences. Matthew and Mark have both men railing on Jesus while Luke has one railing and the other accepting Jesus. Luke took this opportunity to preach a sermon and had the repentant thief say, "'Jesus, Lord, remember me when thou comest into thy kingdom.' And Jesus said unto him, 'Verily I say unto thee, To day shalt thou be with me in paradise.'" John saw the two thieves but didn't hear them say anything.

At this point, Matthew, Mark and Luke have a story of great interest. "Now from the sixth hour there was darkness over all the land unto the ninth hour." Luke goes as far as to say the darkness was "over all the earth." Strange to say but, John, whose "record is true," didn't notice three hours of darkness. In his book, Josephus made an interesting comment in a footnote. "This clause plainly alludes to that well-known but unusual and very long darkness of the sun which happened upon the murder of Julius Caesar by Brutus and Cassius, which is greatly taken notice of by Virgil, Pliny, and other Roman authors" (*Antiquities of the Jews,* Book XIV, Chapter XII). To my way of thinking, this story of darkness on the day Jesus died was made up by Mark and copied by Matthew and Luke. The gospel of Mark was written in Rome and the story was added to make Jesus match up to or surpass Julius Caesar in power.

As far as the veil of the temple being torn in two, Mark wrote it, Matthew and Luke copied it and John never heard of it. The episode of the earthquake was coupled with the veil story in Matthew. "And, behold, the veil of the temple was rent in twain from the top to the bottom; and the earth did quake, and the rocks rent; and the graves were opened; and many bodies of the saints which slept arose, and came out of the graves after his resurrection, and went into the Holy City, and appeared unto many." All this happened when Jesus died and evidently only Matthew knew about it.

Here a stupendous event with an earthquake and many dead people raised to life and walking around town and Mark, Luke, and John miss the whole thing. If the story was written, or at least told, by an eyewitness, he probably had a hysteric hallucination and saw graves open and bodies come out and walk around. This was a very emotional time and it would not be out of the question for many to have had hysteric experiences.

In John's gospel, the story is told of a soldier piercing Jesus' side with a spear and blood and water came out. Could it be that what John saw was what Mark recorded? "And one ran and filled a sponge full of vinegar, and put it on a reed, and gave him to drink." John may have seen the man reach up with the reed. There being too much vinegar in the sponge, it ran down Jesus' side and appeared to be blood and water. Red vinegar would look like blood and water from a distance, and the reed would look like a spear.

Where were the women when Jesus was on the cross? Matthew, Mark and Luke say they were "beholding afar off"; John says they "stood by the cross." How could they be at odds on such a thing? They are not even in accord about where the crucifixion took place. Matthew, Mark and Luke say it was on a barren hill shaped like a skull, while John says it was in a garden. The garden must have belonged to Joseph of Arimathea because his tomb was there.

All four writers mention Joseph, but only John knew that Nicodemus came to help Joseph of Arimathea bury Jesus. It was John who told us that Nicodemus "came to Jesus by night," and because he was a Pharisee he could not be seen openly as a disciple of Jesus. Nicodemus brought "a mixture of myrrh and aloes, about a hundred pound weight." They took the body, "wound it in linen clothes with the spices, as the manner of the Jews is to bury. Now in the place where he was crucified there was a garden; and in the garden a new sepulchre, wherein was never man yet lain. There laid they Jesus." Since the spices were already wrapped up with Jesus, why would the women come to do the same thing later? Maybe only John knew these things and he didn't tell anyone else. More likely these were later traditions and they hadn't been made up when the other three gospels were written.

One other story known only to Matthew was the sealing of the tomb.

> Now the next day, that followed the day of the preparation, the chief priests and Pharisees came together unto Pilate, Saying, "Sir, we remember that that deceiver said, while he was yet alive, 'After three days I will rise again.' Command therefore that the sepulchre be made sure until the third day, lest his disciples come by night, and steal him away, and say unto the people, 'He is risen from the dead': so the last error shall be worse than the first."

A watch was set and the tomb sealed, but they were too late. The body was probably removed from the tomb a few hours after it was put into the tomb. When the tomb was sealed, it was empty. It was no problem to take the body the same night he was crucified, because no one was guarding the tomb until the next day. I think Joseph of Arimathea and Nicodemus were the ones who took the body, but they may have had help from some Essenes. I do not think the Apostles had any knowledge of what went on at the tomb because they were still scattered and hiding.

Why was Jesus crucified and the Apostles allowed to remain free? If the Jews were so upset with Jesus that they turned him over to the Romans, it seems strange that they would have allowed the Apostles to worship in the Temple for forty years after the crucifixion. Even though The Twelve taught what Jesus taught, they were not in any danger from the Jews or from Rome. Remember, Jesus was crucified because he was "The King of the Jews."

Matthew tells of wisemen coming to see Jesus at his birth and they ask "Where is he that is born King of the Jews." They didn't see his star. They heard from the Hasmoneans of his birth. When Jesus was baptized, John has Nathanael say "thou art the King of Israel." Many knew Jesus was the legitimate King of Israel, but when it came time to take the country by storm, not enough turned out and Jesus was crucified.

The church teaches the necessity of Jesus' death for the forgiveness of sins but way back in Ezekiel we read (Ezekiel 18:20-22)

> The soul that sinneth, it shall die. The son shall not bear the iniquity of the father, neither shall the father bear the iniquity of the son: the righteousness of the righteous shall be upon him, and the wickedness of the wicked shall be upon him. But if the wicked will turn from all his sins that he hath committed, and keep all my statutes, and do that which is lawful and right, he shall surely live, he shall not die. All his transgressions that he hath committed, they shall not be mentioned unto him: in his righteousness that he hath done he shall live.

Sins were forgiven in the Old Testament. In 2 Chronicles 7:14 God told Solomon that if the people would humbly pray and turn from wickedness he would forgive their sins. When John the Baptist came, he preached "the baptism of repentance for the remission of sins." In John's time people were baptized and their sins were forgiven. Jesus preached repentance and forgave people their sins while he was alive. If people could have sins forgiven before Jesus died, why did he have to die?

Some see in the crucifixion fulfillment of Old Testament prophesies. The stories in the New Testament were made up with the Old Testament prophesies as their patterns. The idea of Jesus being crucified with thieves, no bones broken and the Romans gambling for his clothes were written just so they would match the corresponding Old Testament prophesies. After believing the stories in the Old testament and seeing himself as the Messiah, Jesus went through all the steps he felt necessary to free his people. He had only one problem: a shortage of soldiers to press his claim for the throne. As a result of the failure, he was crucified. On the cross he "cried with a loud voice," the most heart-rending question a man could ever ask: "My God, my God, why hast thou forsaken me?" With that his spirit was broken and he "yielded up the ghost."

I think he died a sad, disillusioned, defeated man. One of the finest, noblest and most altruistic men who ever lived became the victim of his nation's myths. He read the stories, heard the cry of his people and decided to do all he could to help, but it just wasn't enough. Today we see people who would rather worship Jesus than to do as Jesus did in helping those in need. People are willing to die for him, but not ready to do as he asked them to do in service to others. What a sad commentary on Christianity as it takes his name but rejects his message.

It wasn't a miracle that happened on Calvary, it was a shame, and one of earth's finest men died.

154 The Resurrection Story

◆ Matthew 28:1-10; Mark 16:1-11; Luke 24:1-12; John 20:1-8

> And when the Sabbath was passed, Mary Magdalene, and Mary the mother of James, and Salome, had bought sweet spices, that they might come and anoint him. And very early in the morning the first day of the week, they came unto the sepulchre at the rising of the sun. And they said among themselves, "Who shall roll us away the stone from the door of the sepulchre?" And when they looked, they saw that the stone was rolled away: for it was very great. And entering into the sepulchre, they saw a young man sitting on the right side, clothed in a long white garment; and they were affrighted. And he said unto them, "Be not affrighted: Ye seek Jesus of Nazareth, which was crucified: he is risen; he is not here: behold the place where they laid him. But go your way, tell his disciples and Peter that he goeth before you into Galilee: there shall ye see him, as he said unto you." And they went out quickly, and fled from the sepulchre; for they trembled and were amazed: neither said they any thing to any man; for they were afraid.

This story from Mark is the earliest and most simple of the gospels. We will compare this to the others. Again we have four separate stories so we will find some interesting variances. What time of day did the story begin? Matthew says "as it began to dawn." Mark claims "at the rising of the sun." Luke says "very early in the morning." John reports "when it was yet dark." These are all close enough. Who came to the tomb? Matthew says "Mary Magdalene, and the other Mary." Mark says "Mary Magdalene, and Mary the mother of James, and Salome." Luke relates "Mary Magdalene, and Joanna, and Mary the mother of James, and other women that were with them." John tells us "Mary Magdalene." Quite a difference here.

Why did they come to the tomb? Matthew says "to see the sepulchre." Mark says they "brought sweet spices, that they might come and anoint him." Luke claims they came "bringing the spices which they had prepared." John says nothing at all about why they came. Very interesting variances. Where was the stone when they arrived? Matthew says it was still in place. Mark says "they saw the stone was rolled away." Luke recounts "And they found the stone rolled away." John says "And seeth the stone taken away from the sepulchre." Only Matthew has the door closed.

All four agreed that the body of Jesus was gone, but there is no agreement on what happened next. Matthew says "And, behold, there was a great earthquake: for the angel of the Lord descended from heaven, and came and rolled back the stone from the door, and sat upon it. His countenance was like lightning, and his raiment white as snow." Mark says "they saw a young man sitting on the right side, clothed in a long white garment." Luke differs "behold, two men stood by them in shining garments." John says Mary Magdalene saw the empty tomb, ran and told Peter and the disciple Jesus loved. They came, saw the empty tomb and left. Then Mary Magdalene "as she wept, she stooped down, and looked into the sepulchre, And seeth two angels in white sitting, the one at the head, and the other at the feet, where the body of Jesus had lain." How interesting! One angel, one young man, two men and two angels: take your pick. Whenever you read in the Bible about a man dressed in white, it is more than likely an Essene. Their public dress outfits were long white garments such as described here. They were certainly not angels.

What message was given to the women and how did they respond? Matthew says the angel said not to fear, Jesus was risen, and go tell the disciples to go to Galilee. "And they departed quickly from the sepulchre with fear and great joy; and did run to bring his disciples word." Mark says the young man said not to be afraid, Jesus was risen, go tell his disciples to go to Galilee. "And they went out quickly, and fled from the sepulchre; for they trembled and were amazed: neither said they any thing to any man; for they were afraid." Luke says the two men said Jesus was risen, and reminded them that Jesus had told them these things would happen. "And they returned from the sepulchre and told all these things unto the eleven. . . . And their words seemed to them as idle tales, and they believed them not." Peter went and saw the empty tomb. John says the two angels asked Mary Magdalene why she cried. She answered them, "Because they have taken away my Lord." There are some irreconcilable differences here.

As for the burial clothes only Luke and John mention them. John says the napkin that had been around his head was not with the linen clothes, "but wrapped together in a place by itself." No mention is made of the hundred pounds of spices.

When all four stories are considered, there is no substantive evidence of a resurrection at all. Because the tomb was not sealed or guarded until some time the next day, the body could easily have been removed during the first night. No one was expecting Jesus to rise—even John wrote, "For as yet they knew not the scripture, that he must rise again from the dead." The only indication of any consequence was when Jesus said the only sign would be concerning Jonah. "For as Jonah was three days and three nights in the whale's belly; so shall the Son of man be three days and three nights in the heart of the earth" (Matthew 12:40). If the crucifixion and burial were on Good Friday at sunset, as we are taught to believe, three days and three nights would mean the resurrection took place 72 hours later. That would mean the resurrection could only have taken place at sunset on Monday, but the tomb was already empty on Sunday morning. If the only sign was the 72 hours in the tomb, and Jesus staked his reputation on that one sign, there is only one inescapable conclusion: Jesus was mistaken.

We must remember that Jesus never planned on a resurrection because he never planned to die. His plan was to take his rightful place on the Hasmonean throne and rule over Israel as its King, just as Mattathias had done in 167 B.C. The problem was that Jesus did die and with his death the idea of the resurrection of the nation of Israel was put on the back burner. There was no resurrection, and as we read in Mark, the women didn't say anything to anyone. It was many years before the story of a resurrection was fabricated, and Paul was the one who did it. The trial, crucifixion and death of Jesus were all natural events and the story ended there for many years.

When we look at the story of the post-crucifixion appearances of Jesus a little later, we will have more to say on the subject.

155   *The Synagogue Demoniac*

◆   Mark 1:21-28; Luke 4:33-36

> And there was in their synagogue a man with an unclean spirit; and he cried out, Saying, "Let us alone; what have we to do with thee, thou Jesus of Nazareth? art thou come to destroy us? I know thee who thou art, the Holy One of God." And Jesus rebuked him, saying, "Hold thy peace, and come out of him." And when the unclean spirit had torn him, and cried with a loud voice, he came out of him. And they were all amazed, insomuch that they questioned among themselves, saying, "What thing is this? What new doctrine is this? for with authority commandeth he even the unclean spirits, and they do obey him."

Here was "a man with an unclean spirit" in the synagogue and Jesus saw him. The man said, "Let us alone," but Jesus didn't pay any attention to him and cast out the spirit and the man was cured. This was a case of hysteria with symptoms of multiple personality and falling down without getting hurt. This man spoke in the plural because he took on other personalities in his hysteric state. Perhaps you have heard people say, "He's beside himself with anger," this can be hysteria brought on by anger manifesting in multiple personality.

In the *San Francisco Chronicle*, March 6, 1990, there is a story of two exorcisms performed in the past several months to cure "demonic possessions." Cardinal John O'Connor in his sermon March 5, 1990 at St. Patrick's Cathedral blamed heavy metal rock music for the problems. He may be right because some people get so emotionally involved in this type of music that they go into hysterics. If their symptoms include multiple personalities, it gives the impression of "demonic possession."

More than likely, Jesus calmed the man down and reasoned with him about his problem. With gentle suggestions, which the man accepted, he was able to remove the hysteria and the man returned to normal. I find it of interest that Matthew, Mark and Luke tell stories of demonic possession, but not John. Nowhere in John is there any mention of evil spirits, unclean spirits or any demonic possession of people or animals.

This story is only natural in cause and cure and no supernatural events took place.

156   *The Deaf and Dumb Man at Decapolis*

◆   Mark 7:31-37

> And they bring unto him one that was deaf, and had an impediment in his speech; and they beseech him to put his hand upon him. And he took him aside from the multitude, and put his fingers into his ears, and he spit, and touched his tongue; And looking up to heaven, he sighed, and saith unto him, "Ephphatha," that is, "Be opened." And straightway his ears were opened, and the string of his tongue was loosed, and he spake plain. And he charged them that they should tell no man: but the more he charged them, so much the more a great deal they published it.

The man in this story has two problems; he was deaf and had a speech impediment. He lost his hearing and his speech was hard to understand because only through hearing do we learn to speak properly. The reason for his deafness was probably hysteric in nature. So many people of that time were subject to a number of circumstances that brought on hysteria. Deafness was a common symptom that manifested itself during such a condition. Because the speech problem was part of the hearing problem, they were cured simultaneously.

Jesus took the man aside and was able to show him the concern he had for his needs. The man was able to relax and when Jesus went through a couple of gestures of touching the ears and tongue of the man, the cure was effected. The point of contact was adequate for the man to believe and receive his healing. Immediately his hearing was restored and his speech was cleared up at the same time. Again he gave the strict order to keep the healing quiet, but again the order was disregarded and the word spread like wildfire. This story is one of a natural technique of soothing guidance by one who really understood the psychology of hysteric symptoms.

No miracle is needed when natural means were used in such a fine manner.

157 The Blind Man at Bethsaida

◆ Mark 8:22-26

> And he cometh to Bethsaida; and they bring a blind man unto him, and besought him to touch him. And he took the blind man by the hand, and led him out of the town; and when he had spit on his eyes, and put his hands upon him, he asked him if he saw ought. And he looked up, and said, "I see men as trees, walking." After that he put his hands again upon his eyes, and made him look up: and he was restored, and saw every man clearly.

The people were so well acquainted with the way Jesus healed, they even told Jesus what to do and who to heal. Here they brought a blind man and "besought him to touch him." Jesus knew that touching the man at that time would do no good, so "he took the blind man by the hand, and led him out of the town." Jesus had to get the man away from all the noise and excitement of the multitudes. When they were alone, Jesus talked with the man to understand his problem. When the man was calm and assured Jesus could help him, Jesus suggested the man might be able to see. The first glance the man took was blurred. I think the verse itself tells us why. When Jesus "spit on his eyes," everything was blurred because of the spit. "After that he put his hands again upon his eyes," and wiped away the spit, "he was restored, and saw every man clearly."

This is a classic case of hysteric blindness easily cured by gentle treatment and calm suggestion. Soon the man was willing to accept the cure that was suggested, his sight was restored and all was well. In hysteric blindness there is no physical damage to the eyes. Mental conditions brought on by hysteria often manifested as blindness, deafness, paralysis, fever, and coma. Because no deterioration of body organs takes place in hysteric symptoms, the sight, hearing, movements, etc., can be restored the instant the person accepts the suggestion of a cure.

This healing is completely natural—no supernatural event took place.

158 The Omniscience of Jesus

◆ Mark 11:1-11; Luke 19:1-10; John 1:45-51; 4; 5:1-9

> Then cometh he to a city of Samaria. . . . There cometh a woman of Samaria to draw water: Jesus saith unto her, "Give me to drink." . . . Jesus saith unto her "Go call thy husband, and come hither." The woman answered and said, "I have no husband." Jesus said unto her, "Thou hast well said, 'I have no husband': For thou hast had five husbands; and he whom thou now hast is not thy husband: in that saidst thou truly." . . . The woman then left her waterpot, and went her way into the city, and saith to the men, "Come, see a man, which told me all things that ever I did: is not this the Christ?"

In Matthew 10:5, Jesus told the Apostles not to go into Samaria. In this story, Jesus was at Jacob's well, in the city of Sychar, right in the middle of Samaria. Jesus met with a Samaritan woman and sent her to get her husband. When she admitted she had no husband at the time, Jesus told her about her five husbands. She went to the men of the city and told them she met a man who knew about her past. Because Jesus knew about her five previous husbands, she figured he must be the Christ.

How did Jesus know so much about this Samaritan woman? How did Jesus know it was Zacchaeus up in the tree? How did Jesus know about the donkey at Bethphage? Some said Jesus was omniscient, that he knew all things. There is a very simple verse that I will quote a little later that will explain all these stories. First let's look at some reasons people thought Jesus was omniscient.

The day after Jesus was baptized, Nathanael came toward Jesus and Jesus said

> Behold an Israelite indeed, in whom is no guile. Nathanael saith unto him, "Whence knowest thou me?" Jesus answered and said unto him, "Before that Philip called thee, when thou wast under the fig tree, I saw thee." Nathanael answered and saith unto him, "Rabbi, thou art the Son of God; thou art the King of Israel."

This little story shows that Nathanael was surprised that Jesus knew about him so he said, "Thou art the King of Israel." Nathanael was from Cana, about three miles from Nazareth. Jesus was told about Nathanael by Philip, a mutual friend.

When Jesus went to Jericho there was a short man named Zacchaeus who climbed a tree so he could see Jesus. "And when Jesus came to the place, he looked up, and saw him, and said unto him, 'Zacchaeus, make haste, and come down; for to day I must abide at thy house.'" Zacchaeus was surprised when Jesus called him by name, but Jesus knew all about him.

"And a certain man was there, which had an infirmity thirty and eight years. When Jesus saw him lie, and knew that he had been now a long time in that case, he saith unto him, 'Wilt thou be made whole.'" Jesus seemed to know all about this lame man even though he had never seen him before. Jesus knew about the man with the water pitcher who had an upper room in Jerusalem where they had the Last Supper.

All these and more seem to tell us Jesus knew everything all by himself, but let me quote one verse of scripture that answers all these questions: "After these things the Lord appointed other seventy also, and sent them two and two before his face into every city and place, whither he himself would come" (Luke 10:1). Earlier he had sent out the Twelve, now he sent out seventy more. What we learn from this is that all these men were his agents. They were to gather all the information they could and bring it back to him. When Jesus went to the places later, they told him all he needed to know.

"That man in the tree is Zaccheus. He is rich and you need to meet him." "That is the man who has been lame for 38 years, stop and talk to him." "There is a donkey in Bethphage, send your disciples and they can have it." "At noon today a Samaritan woman will come to this well, this is her story." All the information Jesus needed would have been at his beck. There is no need of magic or miracles, just good intelligence. Moses and Joshua sent spies into Canaan. Elijah and Elisha sent spies to keep themselves informed. There is little reason to believe Jesus did any differently to keep himself posted on what was going on in every city he was to enter.

There is no problem here; no deceit or trickery, just good business. Jesus was a very intelligent man and since he had been trained to be the King of Israel, he had a good education and following. Many people knew who he was: he was often called "Messiah," "Christ," and "King of Israel."

James and John knew him personally because they were his first cousins. Their mother, Salome, was Mary's sister and Salome was the wife of Zebedee. To find this relationship compare Matthew 4:21, Matthew 27:56; Mark 15:40; and John 19:25. Another apostle named James, his brothers Judas (not Iscariot), and Levi (or Matthew) were also cousins of Jesus. Their mother Mary was married to Alphaeus (or Cleophas, which is the Greek form of Alphaeus.) Alphaeus was a brother of Joseph, Jesus' father. For this relationship compare Matthew 10:3; Matthew 27:56; Mark 15:40; John 19:25; and Acts 1:13. Peter and Andrew were partners with James and John in their fish business. Philip was from Bethsaida, the town of Peter and Andrew. Bartholomew is another name for Nathanael of Cana. Simon the Zealot was from Cana about three miles from Nazareth. Judas Iscariot was the son of Simon who may have been the Simon of Bethany and friend of Mary, Martha and Lazarus. The Twelve were family or very close friends of Jesus, probably even from childhood.

There is evidence of at least fourteen who were with Jesus from the time he was baptized until he died. After Judas Iscariot committed suicide, the apostles decided to replace him. Two men were candidates: "Wherefore of these men which have companied with us all the time that the Lord Jesus went in and out among us, Beginning from the baptism of John, unto that same day that he was taken up from us, must one be ordained to be a witness with us of his resurrection. And they appointed two, Joseph called Barsabas, who was surnamed Justus, and Matthias" (Acts 1:21-22). This clearly shows that at least these fourteen were with Jesus from beginning to end.

Jesus knew what was going on, not because of a supernatural omniscience, but by a natural intelligence network.

159 *Mary Magdalene*

♦ Mark 16:9; Luke 8:1-3

> And it came to pass afterward, that he went throughout every city and village, preaching and shewing the glad tidings of the kingdom of God: and the twelve were with him. And certain women, which had been healed of evil spirits and infirmities, Mary called Magdalene, out of whom went seven devils, and Joanna the wife of Chuza Herod's steward, and Susanna, and many others, which ministered unto him of their substance.

Mary Magdalene is one of the most important women in the New Testament. She supported Jesus during his ministry, was present when Jesus was crucified, and was the first person to see Jesus after his resurrection. That is about all we were told about Mary except the short statement, "out of whom went seven devils." Mark also referred to "Mary Magdalene, out of whom he [Jesus] had cast seven devils." What did these verses mean to people of that day? What do they mean to us now?

Several New Testament stories refer to people possessed with devils or vexed with unclean spirits. It must be pointed out that Matthew, Mark, and Luke write about devils and spirits but John does not mention them. There were no devils or spirits mentioned in the Old Testament because the Jews didn't believe in such things. This idea of spirits came to the Jews during the Exile and was not accepted by all the Jews. The Pharisees believed in spirits but as Acts 23:8 shows, the Sadducees did not believe in them.

In any event we know there are no devils or spirits that cause disease, so how can we understand these stories? One story tells about a man who regained the power of speech when a spirit was cast out (Matthew 9:33). Another man regained both sight and speech when a devil was cast out (Matthew 12:22). Mary Magdalene was possessed by seven devils. One man lived in the tombs and was possessed by so many devils he called them Legion. When all the devils were cast out of him, they entered 2,000 swine (Mark 5:1-20). We may tend to think of such stories as products of the time two millennia ago. Do such stories have any meaning to us today?

Let's look at what we have learned and see if we can now understand what these stories mean.

In recent years we read accounts of people with various numbers of distinct personalities. These personalities cause the individual to dress, act, and speak in as many ways as there are personalities. In *The Three Faces of Eve* there were three personalities. In *Sybil,* there were sixteen. An article in *Woman's Day* magazine, August 8, 1990, told about a woman with twenty-three personalities. Some people have even more. The term used to describe these psychoses is Multiple Personality Disorder (MPD). The New Testament writers did not have our medical knowledge, so they called such disorders devils or spirits.

Behind almost all MPD is a background of abuse: physical, mental, or sexual. MPD is a mechanism to dissociate the person from the abuse. The abused person splits off the feelings and forms another personality to absorb the pain of the attack. When a stressful circumstance arises, the personalities switch places and one of the others takes control of the body. Each personality is well defined and consistent in character. Some are infantile, some adolescent, some mature. Some are friendly, some are hostile. Some are withdrawn, some outgoing. Because there is no communication between personalities, the person lacks memory of actions carried out by the alternate characters.

Of over 20,000 people afflicted with MPD in the United States, about 90% are women. The problem with MPD is that it goes unrecognized in many instances. When a person does get treatment, about 75% can be cured. The stories we read in the Bible were stories of cures. Jesus recognized the problem and could explain it to the person and suggest a cure. Psychotherapists can help people today in the same way.

Mary Magdalene was probably abused as a child, became hysterical, and the symptom she demonstrated was MPD. When she met Jesus, he understood her problem, and through his assurance of protection, she experienced kind and gentle care. When she calmed down, her hysteria went away. With the suggestion of mental health, the devils vanished and she was cured. This was perhaps one of the earliest recorded cases of a cure for MPD.

I believe such stories hold the key to help us unlock past mysteries of human behavior so we can better understand ourselves today. If one has symptoms of MPD and one wants to be cured, one mustn't just sit and wait for a miracle. One must see a psychotherapist.

There were no devils in the time of Jesus, and there aren't any today. This story of Mary Magdalene was about a natural cure and no supernatural element was involved.

160   The Ascension Story

◆   Mark 16:19; Luke 24:50-52; Acts 1:4-23

> So then after the Lord had spoken unto them, he was received up into heaven, and sat on the right hand of God.

This verse in Mark is brief and to the point, but almost all scholars agree it was an appendix added many years after the book was written in 70. No importance can be put on this verse. "And it came to pass, while he blessed them, he was parted from them, and carried up into heaven." This verse from Luke is also suspect because the words "and carried up into heaven," are missing in the oldest text of *Codex Sinaiticus* and also from *Codex Bezae*. These are the earliest texts we have of the New Testament and they date from the 4th and 5th centuries. Over 300 years after the crucifixion the story was only then finding its way into some copies of the books. The only other story we have was recorded by Luke in Acts. Paul never knew any ascension stories. Paul wrote up until about 65, and no indication of an ascension appears in any of his letters. The gospels were written between 70 to 110 and the references to an ascension were added later.

> When they therefore were come together, they asked of him, saying, "Lord, wilt thou at this time restore again the kingdom to Israel?" And he said unto them, "It is not for you to know the times or the seasons, which the Father hath put in his own power. But ye shall receive power, after that the Holy Ghost is come upon you: and ye shall be witnesses unto me both in Jerusalem, and in all Judea, and in Samaria, and unto the uttermost part of the earth." And when he had spoken these things, while they beheld, he was taken up; and a cloud received him out of their sight.

This record in Acts was written about 100 and it is strange that no one else said anything about an ascension.

Acts is very specific about the fact that at least thirteen men were present to witness the event. "Wherefore of these men which have companied with us all the time that the Lord Jesus went in and out among us, Beginning from the baptism of John, unto the same day that he was taken up from us, must one be ordained to be a witness with us of his resurrection. And they appointed two." This suggests that all the Apostles remaining plus these two were at the ascension, yet not one made use of this information. Matthew and John were certainly there, but no mention of it is in their gospels.

If you choose to accept the account in Luke's gospel, the ascension took place the same day as the resurrection: Easter Sunday. The action of the whole chapter of Luke 24 is without a break in time and so you must believe the ascension was not forty days after the resurrection. This is certainly inadequate coverage for an event that is the most important part of the Christian faith. The Virgin Birth, the Resurrection, and the Ascension, are the keystones of the faith and it is strange that all three are surrounded by such a cloud of contradiction and suspicion.

The real story here is that this small group of people had only about three days to come to terms with the fact that Jesus was dead. Because this was almost more than they could handle, they acted as if he were still with them. As they went to Bethany that Sunday afternoon, they saw someone they thought was Jesus exchange a blessing with them and walk away. As the man walked up the road, over a hill and into a low cloud bank, they thought, in their own confused minds, he had gone up "into heaven." When they told and retold the story, it came to be believed and eventually included in the Bible as we now have it. The reason Matthew, Mark, John, and Paul never knew firsthand or wrote about the ascension is simply because the story had not been made up when they wrote.

One other explanation is that the group there on the Mount of Olives was so upset, confused and anxious over the death of Jesus that they were in a state of hysteria. When someone said he saw Jesus, the group was subject to a mass hallucination and they all saw him. Someone suggested he arose in a cloud and the others accepted the suggestion. The story spread until it finally became accepted many years later and became part of the recorded history. The story of the forty days of appearances is not to be understood literally. Forty days means only an indefinite number.

The whole story is the result of natural causes leading to hysteric reactions and nothing supernatural played any part in the drama.

161 *Zacharias and the Angel*

◆ Luke 1

> There was in the days of Herod, the king of Judea, a certain priest named Zacharias, of the course of Abia: and his wife was of the daughters of Aaron, and her name was Elisabeth. . . . And they had no child, because that Elisabeth was barren, and they both were now well stricken in years. . . . And there appeared unto him an angel of the LORD standing on the right side of the altar of incense. . . . But the angel said unto him, "Fear not, Zacharias: for thy prayer is heard; and thy wife Elisabeth shall bear thee a son, and thou shalt call his name John. And, behold, thou shalt be dumb, and not able to speak, until the day that these things shall be performed, because thou believest not my words, which shall be fulfilled in their season."

This story is known to only Luke. No other mention of the family of John the Baptist is found in any other literature. Luke gathered information from many sources and compiled his gospel. Luke even says, "It seemed good to me also, having had perfect understanding of all things from the very first, to write unto thee in order, most excellent Theophilus." Luke asserts that he knows everything in proper chronological order.

Zechariah and Elizabeth "were both righteous before God." As Zechariah burned incense, he saw an angel who told him Elizabeth was to have a son and that they should name him John. Zechariah was also told he would be unable to speak until after the child was born. What we have here is a strange story of an angel, a barren old woman bearing a son, and a man stricken with temporary dumbness. How could such things be? The answer is somewhat complicated, but I believe we can understand it if we take each piece in order.

When Zechariah went into the Temple to burn incense, he was also praying that Elizabeth would have a child. His anxiety and need, coupled with the smell of the incense, could have put him into a state of hysteria and he had a hallucination. Hallucinations can occur in any of the senses, and in this case sight and hearing were affected. Zechariah saw an angel and heard the angel speak. The birth of a child was very important to Zechariah. He heard the angel say, "Fear not Zacharias: for thy prayer is heard; and thy wife Elisabeth shall bear thee a son." Because he questioned the angel, he had a guilty conscience and this guilt manifested itself in hysteric aphonia. Zechariah was unable to speak for about nine months. Built into his hysteric hallucination was the suggestion that after the child was born, he would be able to speak again. When John was born, Zechariah was ready "And his mouth was opened immediately, and his tongue loosed, and he spake, and praised God."

As for Elizabeth, her need to have a child was so great it overwhelmed her. The greatest fear of a Jewish woman in those days was her inability to bear children for her husband. Because of her anxiety, fear, need and guilt for not having a child, she suffered hysteric barrenness. There was nothing physically wrong with her reproductive system, but her hysteria prevented her from conceiving. We read of several women in the Old Testament who had the same problem. Sarah, Rebecca, Hannah and the wife of Manoah are some of the more important ones. When Zechariah finished his job at the Temple and went home, he wrote notes to Elizabeth telling her she was to have a child. The calming effect of such reassurance relieved her anxiety. The suggestion that she would bear a son removed the hysteria and she conceived and bore John. It is necessary to realize that to a Jewish couple, the birth of children was extremely important and most considered barrenness a curse from God. No wonder the women were hysterical. Only as the fear was removed and the suggestion given by a husband, priest or angel in a vision, was the woman able to conceive.

There is little doubt that Luke compiled this story of the birth of John the Baptist from many sources. These sources from the Old Testament were used to suit Luke's purposes, and as in the other instances, the child was destined for greatness.

This story is based on natural events. There is nothing supernatural in it and no miracle happened.

162   *The Widow of Nain's Son Raised*

◆ Luke 7:11-17

> And it came to pass the day after, that he went into a city called Nain; and many of his disciples went with him, and much people. Now when he came nigh to the gate of the city, behold, there was a dead man carried out, the only son of his mother, and she was a widow: and much people of the city was with her. And when the Lord saw her, he had compassion on her, and said unto her, "Weep not." And he came and touched the bier: and they that bare him stood still. And he said, "Young man, I say unto thee, Arise." And he that was dead sat up, and began to speak. And he delivered him to his mother. And there came a great fear on all.

Jesus and his disciples went to Nain and met the funeral procession of a man who was the only son of a widow. Jesus told the woman "Weep not," but that must have sounded callous to her since her son just died. I imagine they had a brief conversation and when Jesus understood the circumstances of the man's death, he knew what he was going to do. When Jesus "touched the bier," it is possible that he didn't just gently touch it, but knocked loudly on the side of the casket. When he said, "Young man, I say unto thee, Arise," he didn't speak quietly, but shouted to get the man's attention. When the young man was startled out of his coma, he "sat up, and began to speak." I imagine he said, "What am I doing here? I just laid down to take a nap and I wake up in a coffin. What's going on here?"

What we have here is a classic case of hysteric coma. In this symptom the victim imitates all the appearances of death itself. Extremely shallow breathing, very faint heartbeat, and the skin takes on the waxy pallor of a corpse. If the man were buried in such a condition he would die of starvation or suffocation. There have been many cases of people coming out of hysteric comas during their funerals and of some awaking in their graves. Scratches inside caskets dug up long after burial suggest the people tried to get out. The call to awaken the man and the suggestion to arise were adequate to bring him to consciousness and save his life.

It seems inexplicable that only Luke knew about this story because it was the first restoration to life performed by Jesus. Why Matthew, Mark and John never heard of it is unbelievable if it really happened. Stranger yet are the amazing similarities with the story of Elijah and the son of the widow of Zarephath. Both stories begin, "and it came to pass: when he came to the gate of the city, behold, the widow woman was there." Elijah's story is longer, but they come to the same climax where both the sons were dead. Elijah and Jesus both raised the sons and delivered them to their mothers. If we don't see this as a copy of Elijah's story we make a mistake. There were no limits to which some of the Bible writers would not go for a good story. Luke simply borrowed Elijah's story, set it in Nain, and made Jesus the hero.

No miracle took place because no action took place—only the stroke of the copy-cat's pen.

163 *The Infirm Woman Cured*

◆ Luke 13:10-17

> And he was teaching in one of the synagogues on the sabbath. And, behold, there was a woman which had a spirit of infirmity eighteen years, and was bowed together, and could in no wise lift up herself. And when Jesus saw her, he called her to him, and said unto her, "Woman, thou art loosed from thine infirmity." And he laid his hands on her: and immediately she was made straight, and glorified God.

This woman had been stooped over and couldn't straighten up for eighteen years. Jesus was teaching in the synagogue and he happened to see her in the crowd. He called her over and they talked for a while so they could understand the situation. When Jesus was satisfied that the woman had confidence and could be helped he "laid his hands on her." At the gentle suggestion that she was now able to straighten up "immediately she was made straight." The eighteen years of suffering were over "immediately."

Luke was a physician, and his diagnosis was that she "had a spirit of infirmity." What she really had was hysteric paralysis of the back and needed only to be relaxed and given the suggestion of healing. The marvelous thing about hysteric paralysis is that even after eighteen years, there was no muscular atrophy, and when cured she could straighten up immediately. Don't misunderstand if I speak of Luke unflatteringly. He was a product of his time and very few people knew any better. It wasn't until the last half of the 19th century that Freud was able to understand the problems.

In the time of Jesus, it was believed that nearly all illnesses were caused by spirits, demons, or devils. That was why the Bible is written in those terms. Today we know better, and it is my hope this book will serve as a means of helping people know more about hysteria and getting help if they need it. So many people with hysteric symptoms are not helped medically and as a result say "It's God's will that I be sick." Others who are prayed for and not healed are told they don't have enough faith. Some churches say the day of miracles has passed.

These are all cop-outs, and we need to let people know that if their problem is hysteric, there are people who can help them. Psychotherapists are able to understand and give the proper suggestions to help those in need. If you suffer with a problem similar to one of those in the Bible, make an appointment today and get on the road back to health.

This cure was natural and your cure also may be the result of natural means. Don't wait for a miracle for they never happen.

164 The Man With Dropsy Cured

◆ Luke 14:1-6

> And it came to pass, as he went into the house of one of the chief Pharisees to eat bread on the sabbath day, that they watched him. And, behold, there was a certain man before him which had the dropsy. And Jesus answering spake unto the lawyers and Pharisees, saying, "Is it lawful to heal on the sabbath day?" And they held their peace. And he took him, and healed him, and let him go; And answered them, saying, "Which of you shall have an ass or an ox fallen into a pit, and will not straightway pull him out on the sabbath day?" And they could not answer him again to these things.

Here is another case of Jesus healing on the Sabbath day. Seven healings are recorded on the Sabbath and in all cases the Pharisees were upset—except in this one. In this story, Jesus was in the house of one of the chief Pharisees for lunch, and there was a man sick of the dropsy. They invited this man just to see what Jesus would do. Jesus was aware of their scheme, so he took the offensive and asked if it was lawful to heal on the Sabbath day. When they didn't answer his question, he made his move and healed the man. (Contrary to common belief, the Jews had no proscription against medical attention on the Sabbath. If the condition was an emergency the law not only allowed, but *required*, treatment. The Pharisees had every right to question Jesus, an acknowledged rabbi, on the law about these healings.)

Again we have only an abbreviated story, and we must understand that Jesus spoke with the man until they understood each other. Dropsy is a condition that causes fluid retention in the body. Often it is urine that is not processed by the kidneys and is retained causing the body to swell. No indication is given of how long the man had been afflicted, but when he was cured he left, undoubtedly to relieve himself of the fluids. The case is one of hysteria and the symptom was dropsy.

The cure was the natural suggestion of healing and the result was immediate. It is a natural cure and no supernatural involvement was necessary.

165   *Jesus and the Ten Lepers*

♦ Luke 17:11-19

> And as he entered into a certain village, there met him ten men that were lepers, which stood afar off: And they lifted up their voices, and said, "Jesus, Master, have mercy on us." And when he saw them, he said unto them, "Go shew yourselves unto the priests." And it came to pass, that, as they went, they were cleansed. And one of them, when he saw that he was healed, turned back, and with a loud voice, glorified God, and fell down on his face at his feet, giving him thanks: and he was a Samaritan. And Jesus answering said, "Were there not ten cleansed? but where are the nine? There are not found that returned to give glory to God, save this stranger." And he said unto him, "Arise, go thy way: thy faith hath made thee whole."

What a great story! Ten men healed simultaneously. These ten lepers asked Jesus for mercy and all he did was to send them to see the priest. One was a Samaritan and he couldn't go see the priest because he was not welcome in the Temple. He alone came back to thank Jesus "when he saw that he was healed." Mark has one account of a leper being cleansed and Luke copied that one in Luke 5:12-15. This seems to be a retelling with a variation in which there are now ten lepers.

This story is not so much about healing, but about gratitude. Luke, a Gentile, showed only one of the ten giving thanks to Jesus: the Samaritan. I think the reason the nine Jews didn't return and thank Jesus might be because they weren't healed. Without proper counseling, hysteric symptoms might not be cured. It is possible the other nine just went along for the ride and didn't understand or believe Jesus could help. Another, perhaps better explanation is that they may have had real leprosy, Hansen's disease.

The cured Samaritan had only a skin disorder resembling leprosy and his real problem was hysteria. When one is afflicted with hysteric skin disorder, the symptom could appear very much like leprosy. But there would not be the microorganism that produced the lesions in the skin, the mucous membranes and the nervous system. All that appeared was a scaly, scabby and rough appearance to the skin. Such conditions were sufficient to cause separation and require them to cry "unclean, unclean."

If the Samaritan was healed, it was because he understood and accepted his cure, for as Jesus said, "thy faith hath made thee whole."

This cure was by natural means and no miracle is in evidence here.

166 The Logos or the Word of God

◆ John 1:1-18

> In the beginning was the Word, and the Word was with God, and the Word was God. The same was in the beginning with God. All things were made by him; and without him was not any thing made that was made. In him was life; and the life was the light of men.

John wrote his book to show the preexistence of Jesus. John's idea of Logos was the same as the idea of Wisdom was to the writers of Genesis and Proverbs. To the earlier writers, Wisdom was preexistent. Wisdom and Logos were, "In the beginning," the creative force behind everything that was created. Much of Proverbs deals with Wisdom and her (Wisdom is personified and feminine) attributes, and John claims all of these attributes for his Logos. Take a few moments right now and read Proverbs 7, 8, and 9. See how John copied the ideas in his prologue. John is more eloquent and his phrasing is excellent, but it is only a reworking of older ideas. Logos is substituted for Wisdom and applied to Jesus, who was then called the Christ.

John perceived that his task was to show that Jesus was not only Christ, but also eternal, and coexistent with God from the beginning. If one believes God always was, even before there was light, you must wonder why God spent eons alone and in total darkness. Before the cosmos was created there was only a void. It was in this state of nothingness that God spent countless eternities alone. If Jesus was the preexistent Word and the Son of God, there obviously was a time when he was not. A father and his son cannot both coexist from the beginning. Jesus therefore had to have been created and was of a different substance than the Father. The whole intent of John's gospel is summed up in one verse. "But these are written, that ye might believe that Jesus is the Christ, the Son of God; and that believing ye might have life through his name" (John 20:31). Understanding this, we now know John wrote anything he thought would make people believe in Jesus as the Son of God.

To understand these stories we must understand their source. The nation of Israel began with Moses during the Exodus. Israel had no history before that time. During the Exile (586-536 B.C.), the Jews learned about history from the Babylonians, and decided they should have a history of their own. They borrowed names of some of the Babylonian heroes and tribal leaders. Other names from the Canaanites, other times and other places were fair game. They put them together and claimed to be descendants of all these great people.

To add effect, Jewish historians assigned each name a life of hundreds of years. Adam is alleged to have lived 930 years, Seth, 912; Enos, 905; Jared, 962; Methuselah, 969; Noah, 950; etc. People did not live longer in those days—it is only a ploy to extend their history. When we look at the genealogies of Jesus as recorded in Matthew and Luke we find not only different names, but a different number of generations. Matthew has 61 generations and Luke has 76, from Adam to Jesus. Taking an average of 66 generations and allowing 30 years for each generation, we cover about 2,000 years. By extending the life of each of their early heroes, the number reached 4,000 years. Archbishop Usher figured the date of Adam's creation as 4004 B.C. The Jews pushed their history all the way back to the creation. The Christians accepted that and looked forward to eternal life in heaven, "henceforth and even forevermore."

The history of God's people was now completed as Jesus was "in the beginning" and shall be "alive for evermore" (Revelations 1:18). So they have it covered from eternity to eternity, and you just can't get a more comprehensive history than that. Recognizing the source of these stories and the intent of the writer, we realize there is only one conclusion we can reach. There is no supernatural, preexistent, Logos or Son of God in reality, but only in concept. John borrows from the ancient stories and makes his gospel fit their mold. Whether it be called Wisdom or Logos, it is only a literary device to personify the indescribable.

No miracle is required to write a new story based on old ideas.

167 The Wedding at Cana

◆ John 2:1-12

> And the third day there was a marriage in Cana of Galilee; and the mother of Jesus was there: And both Jesus was called, and his disciples, to the marriage. And when they wanted wine, the mother of Jesus saith unto him, They have no wine. Jesus saith unto her, "Woman, what have I to do with thee? mine hour is not yet come." . . . Jesus saith unto them, "Fill the waterpots with water." And they filled them to the brim. And he saith unto them, "Draw out now, and bear unto the governor of the feast." And they bare it. When the ruler of the feast had tasted the water that was made wine, and knew not whence it was: (but the servants which drew the water knew;) the governor of the feast called the bridegroom, and saith unto him, "Every man at the beginning doth set forth good wine; And when men have well drunk, then that which is worse: but thou hast kept the good wine until now." This beginning of miracles did Jesus in Cana of Galilee, and manifested forth his glory; and his disciples believed on him.

John says this is the first miracle Jesus performed. It is puzzling that only John seems to know about this remarkable miracle, which makes one wonder if it was indeed a miracle. Cana was only about three miles from Nazareth and Jesus was very familiar with the city. In the story we learn that Jesus' mother was there, Jesus himself, at least fourteen disciples according to Acts 1:21, his brothers and many other guests. It is hard to tell for sure how many people were at the marriage, but we get some idea when we see how much wine Jesus produced. The six stone jars each held between twenty and thirty gallons, so there would have been about 150 gallons in all. As the wine provided by the host was already used up, and Jesus supplied 150 additional gallons, we can surmise that it must have been a very large wedding. Wedding feasts usually lasted seven days, and if this took place about the middle of the affair, there could have been about 150 gallons already consumed.

Because Mary, who is never mentioned by name in the entire gospel of John, was concerned with the wine, some suppose she was in charge of the affair. There is some conjecture that the wedding was Jesus' and Mary Magdalene's, which would account for Mary's concern over the shortage of wine. If Jesus had been responsible for the wine, he would simply have sent his servants to bring in more to satisfy the guests.

It is interesting that Jesus says, "Mine hour is not yet come." This is something like the wine commercial Orson Welles narrated a few years ago in which he said, "We will sell no wine before its time." Here Jesus said, "I will make no wine before its time," and all of a sudden, "It is time." I can see why Jesus would stage such an event because it was to be his first miracle and he wanted it to be spectacular.

One clue to the miraculous wine may be in the remark about its source. The ruler of the feast, "knew not whence it was: (but the servants who drew the water knew)." The servants probably knew because they went and got the extra wine. The wine in the pots may have been too strong, so when the water was added, it diluted it to the proper proportions and it tasted better than the strong wine. Some see the story as a fabrication to show Jesus superior to Moses who turned water to blood. Others see it as a story of outdoing Dionysus, the Greek god of wine, who was reputed to have turned water to wine.

Cana was the home base of the remaining Hasmoneans. Jesus was the next in line as pretender to the throne and this may have been his "coming-out party." The Zealots were the protectors of the Hasmonean line and one of the Apostles was Simon the Zealot. It was from this group of Zealots that a fresh supply of wine could easily have been obtained.

There are several ways this natural event of supplying more wine could have been accomplished. No supernatural method was needed. If it was a miracle, the other gospel writers would surely have made the most of it and reported it too.

168 *The New Birth*

♦ John 3:1-16

> Jesus answered and said unto him, "Verily, verily, I say unto thee, Except a man be born again, he cannot see the kingdom of God." Nicodemus saith unto him, "How can a man be born when he is old? can he enter the second time into his mother's womb, and be born?" Jesus answered, "Verily, verily, I say unto thee, Except a man be born of water and of the Spirit, he cannot enter into the kingdom of God. That which is born of the flesh is flesh; and that which is born of the Spirit is spirit. Marvel not that I said unto thee, Ye must be born again. The wind bloweth where it listeth, and thou hearest the sound thereof, but canst not tell whence it cometh, and whither it goeth: so is every one that is born of the Spirit."

This story is not about a miracle that happened; it is a story of a miracle Jesus would like to have seen happen. The phrase "Ye must be born again" was not only unintelligible to Nicodemus then, it is still unintelligible to us now. Nicodemus asked, "How can a man be born when he is old?" His question was never answered. Jesus merely told stories about the wind blowing, but nothing about a new birth. If this meant the spirit goes and does whatever it wants to, then we haven't any choice in the matter. There is hardly any reason to bother.

Jesus continues in his enigmatic treatise: "That which is born of the flesh is flesh; and that which is born of the Spirit is spirit." What a peculiar concept. If it means that flesh is human life and that spirit is life to come, then we can't be born of the spirit while in the flesh. If you are in doubt about whether you are flesh or spirit, let me suggest a simple test to make that determination. All you need is a large straight pin. Jab it into your finger, and if you feel pain and your finger bleeds, you are still in the flesh and haven't become spirit yet.

In Hebrew and Greek, "wind," "air," and "breath" are all the same as "spirit." The phrase "Spirit of God" is indistinguishable from "breath of God." "Your body is the temple of the Holy Ghost" or spirit (1 Corinthians 6:19), simply means that you inhale the spirit—air, breath, or wind which comes from God. Notice that *spirit* and *ghost* are interchangeable in the Bible. Inspire means to inhale spirit or air. "Give up the ghost" means to die because spirit, ghost, and breath, are all the same. This whole subject of spirit, holy or otherwise, is little more than a play on words.

In Genesis "the spirit of God moved upon the face of the deep" (Genesis 1:2), and God formed man from dust and "breathed into his nostrils the breath of life" (Genesis 2:7). The notion that air, wind, breath, spirit, ghost, or any other synonyms are of more consequence than simply the air we breathe is simply misguided. To inflate a common word by putting a capital letter up front is a ploy to make it into something it isn't.

For all practical purposes, the Holy Spirit is nothing more nor less than a big wind, the "rushing mighty wind" of Acts 2:1-4. Some people think the experience of the early church must be repeated even now. There is such a searching, such a confusion, such an emotional desire, such a need to recapture the past that it becomes overwhelming. The ones who "must be born again" will be, as they experience it in a hysteric condition. Hysteric glossolalia (speaking in tongues) is the experience many in Pentecostal churches seek, and when emotions rise to a fever pitch, they experience it.

There is nothing supernatural in the story because nothing really happened. Jesus was giving advice to Nicodemus to take a deep breath, catch his second wind, and become a better person.

169   The Nobleman's Son Cured

◆ John 4:46-54

> So Jesus came again into Cana of Galilee, where he made the water wine. And there was a certain nobleman, whose son was sick at Capernaum. When he heard that Jesus was come out of Judea into Galilee, he went unto him, and besought him that he would come down, and heal his son: for he was at the point of death. . . . Jesus saith unto him, "Go thy way; thy son liveth." . . . And as he was now going down, his servants met him, and told him, saying, "Thy son liveth."

Jesus returned to Cana and met a nobleman whose son was sick in Capernaum, about fifteen to twenty miles away. The nobleman wanted Jesus to travel the distance before his son died. The boy appeared to have had a fever, and rather than travel so far, Jesus simply said to him, "Go thy way; thy son liveth." When the father was on his way home he was met by servants that told him his son was alive and well. The fever had broken at about the same time the man had talked with Jesus.

This may have been a case of hysteria in which the symptom was manifested in a high fever. We cannot know what caused this attack of hysteria, but we know that fever is a common symptom. We remember the story of Peter's mother-in-law having had a fever cured by Jesus. Hysteria due to any number of psychological, as well as physical causes, can imitate all types of physical ailments, and fever is one of the more simple ones. When the nobleman came to Jesus for help, there must have been some reason to believe Jesus could do something about it. He said the boy was at the point of death and he was vitally concerned. If we can believe what John wrote, the only miracle Jesus had performed up to this time was turning water to wine. What made this man think Jesus could heal his son?

Only John seems to know this story about curing the fever, but a similar story appears in Matthew and Luke. That story deals with a centurion and his servant but the circumstances are similar. In the centurion's story, it is his paralyzed servant that needed help, and the spoken word was adequate to cure the servant. In cases of remote cures, the fact that the suffering person knew that someone had gone for help tended to calm the person. The suggestion that they would be cured caused them to be well. The treatment for hysteria is usually as simple as reassurance and suggestion of a cure. Many stories of miracles in the New Testament are duplicates. Only the bare bones of the story was in circulation, and each writer took it upon himself to flesh out his version. Because each setting and cast of characters were different, the stories appear to be distinct, but they are only reformulations of the same events.

In stories of healing hysteric conditions, only natural means are used and no supernatural events occurred.

170 *Jesus and the Man at Bethesda*

♦ John 5:1-9

> After this there was a feast of the Jews; and Jesus went up to Jerusalem. Now there is at Jerusalem by the sheep market a pool, which is called in the Hebrew tongue Bethesda, having five porches. In these lay a great multitude of impotent folk, of blind, halt, withered, waiting for the moving of the water. For an angel went down at a certain season into the pool, and troubled the water: whosoever then first after the troubling of the water stepped in was made whole of whatsoever disease he had. And a certain man was there, which had an infirmity thirty and eight years. . . . Jesus saith unto him, "Rise, take up thy bed, and walk." And immediately the man was made whole, and took up his bed, and walked: and on the same day was the sabbath.

This is one of the more pathetic stories in the entire Bible! "A great multitude of impotent folk" were waiting, and once a year "an angel" would "trouble the water" and the first one in would be cured. An almighty, loving, caring God who supposedly could heal any and all, allowed only one of a multitude to be healed. I can sense the frustration of the multitude, and yet they continued to believe in such a God.

The informants Jesus had sent out told him about the man who had been there for thirty-eight years waiting to be cured of his paralysis, but no one helped him. Jesus asked him if he wanted to be healed and this raised his hope and assurance that something was going to happen. When Jesus suggested to the man, "Rise, take up thy bed, and walk," this was all it took, and immediately he was cured and walked.

This man was the victim of hysteric paralysis, and the salient factor in this type of paralysis is that there is no muscular atrophy. The muscles do not waste away and become useless. When the hysteria was calmed, and the suggestion of healing was accepted, the man immediately stood and walked. It must be noted that only people suffering from hysteric paralysis can be cured in this manner. Because there is no physical damage, the body is able to function when the mental condition is addressed. A person with paralysis due to nerve damage cannot be helped by psychology alone.

In this story no supernatural means are necessary because the natural process was adequate to deal with the problem.

171 Jesus Cures a Blind Man

◆ John 9

> And as Jesus passed by, he saw a man which was blind from his birth. And his disciples asked him, saying, "Master, who did sin, this man, or his parents, that he was born blind?" Jesus answered, "Neither hath this man sinned, nor his parents: but that the works of God should be made manifest in him. I must work the works of him that sent me, while it is day: the night cometh, when no man can work. As long as I am in the world, I am the light of the world." When he had thus spoken, he spat on the ground, and made clay of the spittle, and he anointed the eyes of the blind man with the clay. And said unto him, "Go, wash in the pool of Siloam, (which is by interpretation, Sent)." He went his way therefore, and washed, and came seeing.

John alone records this healing of the man born blind. In none of John's stories is a disease attributed to demons, devils or evil or unclean spirits. John never implies that anyone was possessed of devils or tormented by evil spirits, or bothered in any way by spirit beings. Jesus is not asked to cure this blind man nor did he ask if the blind man wanted to be cured. Jesus simply made clay from dust and spit and put it on the man's eyes and sent him to wash the clay from his eyes.

Very strange that Jesus and the blind man spoke not a word between them until he was sent to wash. I find it difficult to believe such an instance actually occurred because Jesus didn't work that way. There was obviously a time of visiting, getting acquainted and exchanging information about the man's blindness and Jesus' abilities.

Even though the man claimed to have been born blind, there is evidence that part of the story was made up to elicit sympathy as he begged for money. Begging was a well-exercised profession in Bible times. When the parents were asked about their son, they merely acknowledged his story so they wouldn't "blow his cover." As long as the story worked for him, they would go along with it. As we look at the parent's response when they learned their son was no longer blind, we are astounded to find no emotion at all from them. There was no hint of happiness, surprise or any other response. They barely acknowledged he was their son and let him tell his story.

Once the situation was understood and Jesus had a chance to get acquainted with the blind man, the cure was almost routine. The anointing with clay and washing were similar to Elisha sending Naaman to wash in the Jordan. When people have to do something themselves it enhances their faith and establishes a point when the healing can take place. This was a classic case of hysteric blindness cured by the suggestion that when the clay was washed away, sight would be restored.

Nothing supernatural is required as natural means were sufficient to get the desired results.

172   *The Raising of Lazarus*

◆ John 11:1-46

> Now a certain man was sick, named Lazarus, of Bethany, the town of Mary and her sister Martha. (It was that Mary which anointed the Lord with ointment, and wiped his feet with her hair, whose brother Lazarus was sick.) Therefore his sisters sent unto him, saying, "Lord, behold, he whom thou lovest is sick." When Jesus heard that, he said, "This sickness is not unto death, but for the glory of God, that the Son of God might be glorified thereby." Now Jesus loved Martha, and her sister, and Lazarus. When he heard therefore that he was sick, he abode two days still in the same place where he was. Then after that saith he to his disciples, "Let us go into Judea again. . . . Our friend Lazarus sleepeth; but I go, that I may awake him out of sleep." Then said his disciples, "Lord, if he sleep, he shall do well." Howbeit Jesus spake of his death: but they thought that he had spoken of taking rest in sleep. Then said Jesus unto them plainly, "Lazarus is dead."

This story of Lazarus is probably one of the more familiar and least understood of the New Testament miracles. Only John seems to know the story of Lazarus. Jesus spent quite a bit of time in Bethany and stayed in the home of Mary, Martha and Lazarus. Outside of his disciples, these three were probably his best friends, so it is unthinkable that Luke would know nothing about Lazarus and that only Luke and John should know about Mary and Martha. When Jesus was told Lazarus was sick, he didn't seem concerned—only after two days did he leave to go to Bethany. Jesus told the disciples that Lazarus would be all right because he was only asleep. Later he said Lazarus was dead, but I believe Jesus was right the first time.

By the time Jesus arrived at Bethany, Mary and Martha were understandably upset with Jesus because by then Lazarus had been "dead" for four days. Jesus tried to assure them

> "Thy brother shall rise again;" but they didn't understand. Jesus asked "Where have ye laid him?" and they took him to the tomb. Jesus said, "Take ye away the stone." Martha, the sister of him that was dead, saith unto him "Lord, by this time he stinketh: for he hath been dead four days." And when he thus had spoken, he cried with a loud voice, "Lazarus, come forth." And he that was dead came forth, bound hand and foot with graveclothes: and his face was bound about with a napkin. Jesus saith unto them, "Loose him, and let him go."

How could a man be dead, in his tomb for four days, and then come out alive? Surely something miraculous happened *this* time. What is of real importance here is that Jesus told the disciples that Lazarus was asleep and they didn't believe him. In order to satisfy them, he changed the story and told them Lazarus was dead and that seemed to satisfy them. How often people choose to believe something other than the truth when it is told to them.

When Jesus was back in Bethany, he talked with Mary and Martha and they showed him the tomb; but they didn't expect anything to happen. The Jews believed that the spirit or breath of a person hovered over the body for three days after the person died, and then left. Lazarus had been dead for four days so they were sure it was too late for him. Jesus was aware of something that none of the rest knew about and so he made a move no one expected. When the stone was rolled away from the tomb, Jesus hollered out to Lazarus and told him to come out of the tomb, which he did.

Note carefully that Martha says, "Lord, by this time he stinketh." Martha assumes, with good reason, that after four days a corpse would be rank. Just as revealing is the fact that no one mentions any powerful stench that would have saturated Lazarus's funeral clothes had he been indeed dead. There was no stink as Martha expected, because Lazarus wasn't dead. He was merely the victim of a hysteric coma. The symptoms approximate death in that the breathing is very shallow and the heartbeat is all but gone. The reason Jesus had to yell was so he could get Lazarus' attention and wake him up. Hysteric coma is as easy to cure as any of the rest of the symptoms of hysteria, but it is much more dramatic to observers. Some preachers like to say that if Jesus only said "Come forth" all the dead would have risen, so Jesus had to say "Lazarus, come forth."

Jesus knew Lazarus well enough to know that he was a person who could become hysteric. That is probably why Jesus was not concerned when he heard that Lazarus was sick. While raising the dead was one of his best feats, Jesus was well aware that only in the case of hysteria was this possible. There was no attempt to bring John the Baptist back from death. When a man's head is cut off he is *dead.* No one who was physically killed has ever brought back to life; only hysteric coma allowed such a restoration. No one shot to death with an arrow, stabbed to death with spear or sword was brought back. Jesus relied on his agents to give him pertinent information about people and their conditions before he attempted any cure. Only on a couple of occasions were failures recorded, and a testimony that not even Jesus had perfect intelligence. Some slipped through the cracks. In raising Lazarus, no supernatural event was necessary—the natural method was adequate.

173   *The Second Draught of Fishes*

♦ John 21:1-13

> After these things Jesus shewed himself again to the disciples at the sea of Tiberias; and on this wise shewed he himself. There were together Simon Peter, and Thomas called Didymus, and Nathanael of Cana in Galilee, and the sons of Zebedee, and two other of his disciples. Simon Peter saith unto them, "I go a fishing." They say unto him, "We also go with thee." They went forth and entered into a ship immediately; and that night they caught nothing. But when the morning was now come, Jesus stood on the shore: but the disciples knew not that it was Jesus. Then Jesus saith unto them, "Children, have ye any meat?" They answered him, "No." And he said unto them, "Cast the net on the right side of the ship, and ye shall find." They cast therefore, and now they were not able to draw it for the multitude of fishes. Therefore that disciple whom Jesus loved saith unto Peter, "It is the Lord." Now when Simon Peter heard that it was the Lord, he girt his fisher's coat unto him, (for he was naked,) and did cast himself into the sea. And the other disciples came in a little ship; (for they were not far from land, but as it were two hundred cubits,) dragging the net with fishes. As soon as they were come to land, they saw a fire of coals there, and fish laid thereon, and bread. Jesus saith unto them, "Bring of the fish which ye have now caught." Simon Peter went up, and drew the net to land full of great fishes, an hundred and fifty and three: and for all there were so many, yet was not the net broken. Jesus saith unto them, "Come and dine." And none of the disciples durst ask him, "Who art thou?" knowing that it was the Lord.

Seven disciples were fishing in the Sea of Tiberias, or Galilee, and after fishing all night had no fish. They saw a man on the shore and he asked if they caught anything. When they said no, he told them to throw the net on the right side of the boat. They did so and caught 153 fish. Because of the catch of fish someone told Peter it was Jesus. No one knew it was Jesus up until then. Peter jumped into the water and made his way to shore and he also helped the others drag in the net of fish. Jesus invited them to eat and then a most bizarre statement is recorded: "And none of the disciples durst ask him, 'Who art thou?' knowing it was the Lord."

Catching fish was no big deal—most of these men were fishermen by trade. The count of 153 great fish is a good catch, but then again, when a school of fish swims into a net, it was easy to catch them. This was only a natural event because the fish were not created just before being caught.

What is hard to imagine is that no one recognized Jesus, which raises the possibility that the man was *not* Jesus. Only when one of them suggested that it was Jesus did they recognize him, or at least pretend to recognize him. Because no one dared to ask "Who art thou?" there is reason to believe they did not know him.

What we have in this story is a case of mass hysteria. After the stress of fishing all night, the anxiety and hunger may have built up into hysteria. When someone suggested the man on the shore was Jesus, the rest of them accepted the suggestion and believed they saw Jesus.

If the man on the shore wasn't Jesus, who could it have been? It was common in those days for fish merchants to greet fishermen on their return from a night of fishing in order to buy their catch. For the man to have a warm fire burning and a hot meal prepared was good business. To tell the men to cast their net on the right side of the boat, because he had seen some fish jump, was very helpful advice.

This story has a purely natural explanation and to call it a miracle is a bigger fish story than the one in the Bible.

174 Post-Resurrection Appearances

The subject of resurrection was central to the early church and remains so today, so the writers gathered evidence of it in any way they could. Luke says that Jesus visited the Apostles "To whom also he shewed himself alive after his passion by many infallible proofs, being seen of them forty days, and speaking of the things pertaining to the kingdom of God" (Acts 1:3). Appearances of Jesus are found in several places in the Gospels, Acts, and 1 Corinthians 15. When the tomb was found empty, no one considered that Jesus was alive, "For as yet they knew not the scripture that he must rise from the dead" (John 20:9). Jesus never taught them he was to rise from the dead because he didn't plan on dying.

Let's look at some of the stories and see if we can find any similarities. When Mary Magdalene went to the tomb and found it empty, she "saw Jesus standing, and knew not that it was Jesus. She, supposing him to be the gardener" (John 20:14-15); that supposition was probably correct. This was the first time Jesus is reported to have been seen after his burial. Later that day, two disciples were on their way to Emmaus, about seven miles from Jerusalem. One of them was Cleopas, the uncle of Jesus according to Hegessipus, a second century writer. As they walked and talked, "Jesus himself drew near, and went with them. But their eyes were holden that they should not know him," then "their eyes were opened, and they knew him; and he vanished out of their sight" (Luke 24:13-35). When these two "went and told it unto the residue; neither believed they them" (Mark 16:12-13). "And as they thus spake, Jesus himself stood in the midst of them, and saith unto them, 'Peace be unto you.' But they were terrified and affrighted, and supposed that they had seen a spirit. And while they yet believed not for joy, and wondered, he said unto them, 'Have ye here any meat?'" (Luke 24:36-41). "Then the eleven disciples went away into Galilee, into a mountain where Jesus had appointed them. And when they saw him, they worshipped him: but some doubted" (Matthew 28:16-20). "After these things Jesus showed himself again to the disciples at the sea of Tiberias. . . . When morning was now come, Jesus stood on the shore: but the disciples knew not that it was Jesus." . . . "And none of the disciples durst ask him, 'Who art thou?'" (John 21:1-14).

Notice that in all those passages the same theme runs through them: one of doubt and unbelief. Mary Magdalene, standing face to face with him, "knew not that it was Jesus." Cleopas, his uncle didn't recognize him. The disciples "supposed they had seen a spirit." The eleven saw him "but some doubted." By the sea, the seven "knew not that it was Jesus," and didn't dare ask "who art thou?" How can we invest credibility in these reports when those who knew Jesus for one to three years couldn't recognize him when face to face?

Look closely as we study some of the events in more detail to see what we can find. The women at the tomb were said to have "seen a vision of angels" (Luke 24:23). Jesus, Peter, James, and John were said to have seen Moses and Elijah, but we read, "Jesus charged them saying, 'Tell the vision to no man'" (Matthew 17:1-9). In these stories we see how visions can be seen and accepted by several people simultaneously. What we are reading about are cases of mass hysteria when people experienced the shock of Jesus' death. When someone suggested that Jesus was present he participated in the vision and thought he saw Jesus. Not all were taken in by the hysteria and hallucination, and that is why we read "but some doubted," some "supposed they had seen a spirit," and some "knew not that it was Jesus."

Visions were very common to people in Bible stories as you will find when you look up these passages: Zechariah in Luke 1:9-22. Paul in Acts 16:9; 18:9; 22:17-18; 26:12-21; II Cor 12:1-3; Gal 1:12. Peter in Acts 10:9-18. Cornelius in Acts 10:30-33.

In 1 Corinthians 15 we find a list of appearances that is substantially different from those in the Gospels. 1 Corinthians 15:5 says "he was seen of Cephas" (Peter), and that isn't in the Gospels; "then of the twelve," but Jesus never appeared to the Twelve, only to the ten or eleven. After that, he was seen by more than "five hundred brethren at once" (1 Corinthians 15:6), that never got into the gospels either. "After that, he was seen of James" (1 Corinthians 15:7), that is not in the gospels. Paul said "he was seen of me also" (1 Corinthians 15:8), and that obviously is not in the Gospels, but Paul tells us about it in his letters and Luke tells us in Acts. While some appearances were added, some were also omitted. Paul does not mention the appearances to Mary Magdalene and the other women. This is almost incomprehensible because the women were the first ones to have seen the risen Jesus, and Paul didn't even know about it.

Even today we have similar events reported in our newspapers and on our radios and TV screens. On August 16, 1977, Elvis Presley died and in the thirteen years since he has been reportedly seen by hundreds, if not thousands of people. These reports come from people who were so taken by Elvis that they cannot believe he could possibly be gone. When some of these people hear his music, see his picture, or even just think about him, they have hysteric hallucinations of him. They are firmly convinced that he is present with them—some even talk with him. This is exactly the same experience people had in Israel 2,000 years ago.

On Dec. 9, 1531, Juan Diego saw a vision of the Virgin of Guadalupe in Mexico. On February 11, 1858, Bernadette Soubirous saw a vision of the Virgin at Lourdes, France. In 1917, Lucia, Francisco and Jacinta saw a vision of the Virgin Mary at Fatima, Portugal. Oral Roberts said he saw a 900-foot-tall Jesus at exactly 7 p.m. on May 25, 1980 in Tulsa, Oklahoma. Not to be outdone by Cristendom, Saddam Hussein is reported to have said, "The prophet Mohammed visited me in my sleep all dressed in pure white" on October 21, 1990. All appearances can be attributed to hysteric hallucinations, mistaken identity, trickery or pure fabrication.

No supernatural appearances took place and only natural events are necessary for people to see anything they choose to see.

Chapter 9

Stories From Acts

175   The Day of Pentecost

◆ Acts 2

> And when the day of Pentecost was fully come, they were all with one
> accord in one place. And suddenly there came a sound from heaven as
> of a rushing mighty wind, and it filled all the house where they were
> sitting. And there appeared unto them cloven tongues like as of fire,
> and it sat upon each of them. And they were all filled with the Holy
> Ghost, and began to speak with other tongues, as the Spirit gave them
> utterance.

The three yearly feasts the Jews celebrated when all the men of
Israel went to Jerusalem were Passover, Pentecost, and the Feast
of Tabernacles. As with all the other feast days, Jerusalem was
filled with Jews from all over the Mediterranean area on this Pentecost.

About 120 people were together in an upper room of a house and were
praying about who should replace Judas as the 12th Apostle. The other
eleven were there with the women and Mary, the mother of Jesus, and
his brothers. I propose the following scenario as an explanation. All of
a sudden a gust of wind blew into the room and the noise startled them.
The hot dry wind blew through the house and caused a great deal of static
electricity. As people moved about and touched each other the sparks
and shocks of the static charges caused the people to become hysteric.
This hysteria brought on a strange symptom that is known as glossolalia,
or speaking in tongues. This glossolalia is a sort of gibberish. The sparks

of static electricity were called "tongues of fire" to match the phrase "speak with other tongues."

This case of mass hysteria was interpreted by some as a drunken brawl and some said "The men are full of new wine." By now the disciples were in the streets and a large crowd gathered to see what was going on. Luke adds a bit of propaganda and has Peter preach a sermon to the Jews and "they that gladly received his word were baptized: and the same day there were added unto them about three thousand souls." Quite a day for what came to be called "the birthday of the church."

Some people felt the speaking in tongues, or glossolalia, was a result of the apostles being "filled with the Holy Ghost." The Gospels tell of others who had been filled with the Holy Ghost and never spoke in tongues. Elizabeth, John the Baptist, Zacharias and Jesus were all "filled with the Holy Ghost." The disciples were together on Easter Sunday when Jesus came and filled them with the Holy Ghost. Here were at least sixteen people who were filled with the Holy Ghost and didn't speak in tongues.

When one understands the words *air, wind, breath, spirit* and *ghost* all mean the same thing, one can see how the writer put his story together. He simply put capital letters on "spirit" and "ghost" and made them holy. The "rushing mighty wind" became the "Holy Ghost" or "Holy Spirit." The actual meaning of *Holy Spirit* is only a "big wind." What could be more clear than John 20:22 when Jesus "breathed on them, and saith unto them, 'Receive ye the Holy Ghost.'" Jesus called his breath the Holy Ghost.

Nothing supernatural occurred on the day of Pentecost for it was only a product of natural hysteria and human nature.

176   *Peter and the Lame Man*

◆ Acts 3:1-26

> Now Peter and John went up together into the temple at the hour of prayer, being the ninth hour. And a certain man lame from his mother's womb was carried, whom they laid daily at the gate of the temple which is called Beautiful, to ask alms of them that entered into the temple; Who seeing Peter and John about to go into the temple asked an alms. And Peter, fastening his eyes upon him with John, said, "Look on us." And he gave heed unto them, expecting to receive something of them. Then Peter said, "Silver and gold have I none; but such as I have give I thee: In the Name of Jesus Christ of Nazareth rise up and walk." And he took him by the right hand, and lifted him up: and immediately his feet and ankle bones received strength. And he leaping up stood, and walked, and entered with them into the temple, walking, and leaping, and praising God.

Peter and John were on their way into the temple when they saw a lame man begging alms at the temple gate. They stopped and healed the man and he went into the temple with them. A short, quick story but we need to look at it a little closer to see just what took place. Peter and John had seen Jesus cure such ailments before, so they were trained to perform the same cures. The story says the man was lame from birth, but it was a common practice to embellish ailments to elicit more sympathy and therefore get more alms. The man was no doubt a hysteric paralytic, and as Peter recognized the condition he knew he could help the man. There was obviously a bit of conversation so Peter could explain how the man could be cured.

Peter cured the man "In the Name of Jesus Christ of Nazareth." This is interesting because using a name in religious formulas comes from a very old tradition. People believed that by using a person's name they also could claim the power and authority of that person. The baptism in the church is done in "The name of the Father, the Son and the Holy Spirit" to claim their power. Luke, as a physician, was careful to point out that "Peter took him by the right hand" and "his feet and ankle bones received strength." An immediate cure was possible because in hysteric paralysis there is no muscular atrophy and there was no delay in the healing.

The miracles Luke credits to Peter were duplicated by Paul, and as we continue you will see this several times. The reason for the double miracles was to equate Paul with Peter, giving him authority in the church. It was very peculiar that Luke recorded all of Paul's miracles in Acts, but Paul never claimed any miracles in his epistles. This case of a man born lame is identical with the lame man at Lystra, and we will see Paul heal him in Acts 14.

Nothing supernatural takes place in this story as it is the natural suggestion of healing that made the man whole.

177 *A Second Pentecost*

◆ Acts 2-5

> And when they had prayed, the place was shaken where they were assembled together; and they were all filled with the Holy Ghost, and they spake the word of God with boldness. And the multitude of them that believed were of one heart and of one soul: neither said any of them that ought of the things which he possessed was his own; but they had all things common.

Notice the similarity between this passage and Acts 2:1-4. Not only is this one event similar but the whole story is the same. Acts 2:1 through Acts 4:30 is almost the same as Acts 4:31 through Acts 5:42. Read and compare these two sets of verses and you will see they were duplicate stories. Both told of the outpouring of the Spirit, communal living, fear in the church, signs and wonders, healings, gathering in Solomon's Portico, arrest of the apostles, Peter's speech to his accusers, the council deliberating, the apostles warned and freed, the community rejoicing. How could Luke put both stories in and not realize they were the same?

Just as nothing supernatural happened in the first telling, nothing supernatural occurred in the retelling.

178   *Ananias and Sapphira*

◆ Acts 4:32-5:11

> But a certain man named Ananias, with Sapphira his wife, sold a possession, and kept back part of the price, his wife also being privy to it, and brought a certain part, and laid it at the apostles' feet. But Peter said, "Ananias, why hath Satan filled thine heart to lie to the Holy Ghost, and keep back part of the price of the land? While it remained, was it not thine own? and after it was sold, was it not in thine own power? Why hast thou conceived this thing in thine heart? thou hast not lied unto men, but unto God." And Ananias hearing these words fell down, and gave up the ghost: and great fear came on all them that heard these things. And the young men arose, wound him up, and carried him out, and buried him.

About three hours later Sapphira came in and Peter asked her the same questions and she too fell dead and was buried. "And great fear came upon all the church, and upon as many as heard these things." The mood of unity was so great in the group that "they had all things common." Some sold what they had and brought the money in and gave it to the group. Ananias and Sapphira sold some land and decided to keep some of the money, but pretended to give the whole amount. Peter knew they were lying because his spies had told him, and so he condemned them. Their fear and guilt was so great they both became hysterical and went into hysteric comas. Because they appeared to be dead, they were buried and that is the last we hear of them. Because both these people were only in hysteric comas, they were actually buried alive. Because they were "wound up" in the burial clothes, they either died of suffocation or of starvation several days later.

The real impact of the story lies in the conclusion of the telling. "And great fear came upon all the church, and upon as many as heard these things." How could anyone hear these stories and still decide to hold back anything? Whether this actually happened or not, the effect was the same. Just as in the Old Testament when the priests wanted to enhance their power and prestige, this New Testament story enhanced the power and prestige of the Apostles. This story was copied for Paul, but tamed down quite a bit, which we will discuss when we come to the story of Elymas in Acts 13:4-12.

In the story of Ananias and Sapphira, there was no supernatural activity. If they were buried it was because in the state of hysteric coma they appeared to be dead. If the story was made up, as I think it was, it too was natural. In either event, no miracle took place.

179 Peter's Shadow Heals the Sick

◆ Acts 5:12-16

> And by the hands of the apostles were many signs and wonders wrought among the people. . . . Insomuch that they brought forth the sick into the streets, and laid them on beds and couches, that at the least the shadow of Peter passing by might overshadow some of them.

This was a strange story because it doesn't say anyone was healed by having been in the shadow of Peter. The verse says "by the hands of the apostles were many signs and wonders wrought," but nothing is said of anyone being helped in any way by a shadow. The idea of someone being cured in this way is not out of reason, however. A person with hysteric symptoms could use the suggestion of a cure with the shadow being the method of contact. I am not denying that cures could be received, I am only showing that the Bible does not say any such cures actually took place.

No miracle appeared in this story. All the cures were natural by the hands of the apostles.

180 The Apostles Freed From Prison

◆ Acts 5:17-42

> Then the high priest rose up, and all they that were with him, (which is the sect of the Sadducees,) and were filled with indignation, And laid their hands on the apostles, and put them in the common prison. But the angel of the Lord by night opened the prison doors, and brought them forth, and said, "Go, stand and speak in the temple to the people all the words of this life."

The high priest and the Sadducees were the men who took care of the temple. The early Apostolic Christian church met in the temple from the time shortly after the Crucifixion until the temple was destroyed in 70. There is a small problem because the Apostles were teaching and healing in Jesus' name and the Sadducees had asked them not to. When the apostles continued to teach in Jesus' name, the Sadducees had them imprisoned.

That same night "the angel of the Lord by night opened the prison doors" and the apostles were set free and told to go back and speak in the temple. After they were confronted, beaten, and told not to speak in the name of Jesus, they still disobeyed. "And daily in the temple, and in every house, they ceased not to teach and preach Jesus Christ." Because the apostles were preaching about the resurrection of Jesus and casting out unclean spirits in his name, the Sadducees were "filled with indignation." The Sadducees didn't believe in a resurrection or unclean spirits. "For the Sadducees say that there is no resurrection, neither angel, nor spirit: but the Pharisees confess both" (Acts 23:8).

When the apostles were arrested they were put in the common prison of the Romans. The Jews never had jails or prisons because there were no crimes in their law that required them. If a Jew committed a capital crime he was stoned to death right away if found guilty. If the law called for repayment for theft or damage, the guilty party either paid or became a slave of the person to whom the payment was due. It was a much simpler system than we have today.

An angel set the Apostles free from prison. *Angel* simply means "messenger," so we need to look around to find who the messenger was. It could well have been someone from the church who got a guard drunk and took his keys. It could have been someone who bribed a guard to open the doors. It could even have been one of those in prison who simply picked the lock and opened the door. Because it all happened in the middle of the night any of several natural means could have been used. No supernatural event is necessary in this case. We will see a couple more prison escapes as an angel helps Peter in Acts 12, and an earthquake sets Paul free in Acts 16.

181   *The Death of Stephen*

◆ Acts 6-7

> And in those days, when the number of the disciples was multiplied, there arose a murmuring among the Grecians against the Hebrews, because their widows were neglected in the daily ministration. Then the twelve called the multitude of the disciples unto them, and said, "It is not reason that we should leave the word of God, and serve tables. ..." And they chose Stephen, a man full of faith and of the Holy Ghost.

Stephen was a Hellenist Jew who was appointed one of seven to care for the Grecian widows in the church. Stephen was a good man and "did great wonders and miracles among the people." What these wonders and miracles were, we are not told.

Some people in the synagogue accused Stephen of blasphemy,

And they stirred up the people, and the elders, and the scribes, and came upon him, and caught him, and brought him to the council, And set up false witnesses, which said, "This man ceaseth not to speak blasphemous words against this holy place, and the law: For we have heard him say, that this Jesus of Nazareth shall destroy this place, and shall change the customs which Moses delivered us."

Stephen then told the whole history of Israel from Abraham to Jesus. When Stephen said the Jews had killed Jesus and that he had been resurrected, they would hear no more. "Then they cried out with a loud voice, and stopped their ears, and ran upon him with one accord, And cast him out of the city, and stoned him." Stephen may not have been guilty of anything more than a lack of good sense, or they may have thought he blasphemed—a capital offense. In either case, condemnation of the Jews led to his own condemnation.

Some people have the notion that the Jews could not put people to death in those days and that was why they turned Jesus over to the Romans. This story makes it very clear that they could and did put Stephen to death. The crime of Jesus was against Rome because he claimed to be the King of Israel. The crime of Stephen was against Israel because he blasphemed. His acts of service to the church were commendable, but discretion is the better part of valor, and Stephen lacked discretion. While Stephen was being stoned, he claimed to see a vision of "the glory of God, and Jesus standing on the right hand of God." Under the stress of stoning and the fear of death, it is plausible that Stephen experienced a hysteric hallucination of Jesus.

While there may have been no supernatural occurrence in evidence, it was a sad end to an exemplary life. Notice that the apostles did not come to the aid of Stephen, nor did they even try to raise him from the dead.

182 *Philip and his Cures*

◆ Acts 8

And at that time there was a great persecution against the church which was at Jerusalem; and they were all scattered abroad throughout the regions of Judea and Samaria, except the apostles. . . . Then Philip went down to the city of Samaria, and preached Christ unto them. And the people with one accord gave heed unto those things which Philip spake, hearing and seeing the miracles which he did. For unclean spirits, crying with loud voice, came out of many that were possessed with them: and many taken with palsies, and that were lame, were healed. And there was great joy in that city.

Philip was one of the seven selected with Stephen to minister to the Grecians, but now Stephen was dead and the rest had to leave town.

Notice carefully that while the church at Jerusalem was persecuted and scattered, the Apostles were not bothered by the Jews. This was very important because the teaching of the Apostles was different from the teaching of the Greeks. While the Apostles taught that Jesus was the Messiah, the Grecians, and later Paul, taught that Jesus was the Son of God. The Jews would not have allowed the Apostles to teach in the temple if they taught that Jesus was the Son of God. Jews could not accept such an idea, but it was easy for Gentiles to accept, for it was common in their Greek myths.

When Philip went to Samaria, he worked miracles and cured those with "unclean spirits" and "many taken with palsies, and that were lame." Philip had been taught how to calm such people and to suggest that they accept a cure. The power of suggestion could set them free from their hysteric ailments. Symptoms such as multiple personalities and paralysis are common among hysterics, and Philip did his job well and cured many. Certainly there was "great joy in that city" when Philip set people free from their hysteria and other psychological problems. Even Simon the Sorcerer was impressed by Philip and his cures, and he wanted to learn this magic. What Philip did was neither magic nor miracle, but only natural means were used to accomplish his cures.

Let's look at Simon the Sorcerer now and see how Philip helped him.

183 Peter and Simon the Sorcerer

◆ Acts 8:9-24

> But there was a certain man, called Simon, which beforetime in the same city used sorcery, and bewitched the people of Samaria, giving out that himself was some great one: To whom they all gave heed, from the least to the greatest, saying, "This man is the great power of God." And to him they had regard, because that of long time he had bewitched them with sorceries. . . . Then laid they their hands on them, and they received the Holy Ghost. And when Simon saw that through laying on of the apostles' hands the Holy Ghost was given, he offered them money, Saying, "Give me also this power, that on whomsoever I lay hands, he may receive the Holy Ghost."

Simon Magus, as he was called by his contemporaries, was a man of great standing because of his magic. He had a large following and it is thought by many scholars, that he, like many others, saw himself as Messiah. He "bewitched the people of Samaria," and was able to do marvelous things so that many admired him. When Simon saw Philip heal people, he was impressed, believed the preaching of Philip, was baptized, and "continued with Philip." As Simon bewitched people, he probably caused much of the hysteria Philip cured. Simon may only have known how to cause the hysteria and was unable to cure it himself and that was why he followed Philip.

When Peter and John came to town and brought the Holy Ghost with them, it was more than Simon could match. He offered to buy the power so he also could bestow the Holy Ghost, but Peter cursed him. Simon wanted this power because even Philip didn't have the power to give the Holy Ghost. Simon had bought and sold magic tricks before; he saw this the same as any other trick. Simon believed and was baptized and tried to get Peter's and John's power so he would be better able to dazzle the crowds. At that time the whole Mediterranean world abounded with seers, astrologers, spiritualists, exorcists, magicians, and miracle workers. To get to the top—Simon was well on his way—one needed to have state-of-the-art gimmicks, and the "Holy Ghost" was among the best he had seen.

For all his greatness in Samaria, Simon was also honored when he went to Rome. There was a statue erected for him and inscribed "To Simon the Holy God." Pretty good for a country boy, but it seems that from then on his popularity faded and we don't know what became of him. There is one final item from Simon's story that has lasted even to the present. *Simony* is a derogatory word meaning "the use of money to attain spiritual ends."

Simon used only natural means to impress people, and there are no miracles in the story.

184   *The Conversion of Saul*

◆ Acts 9:1-31

> And Saul, yet breathing out threatenings and slaughter against the disciples of the Lord, went unto the high priest, And desired of him letters to Damascus to the synagogues, that if he found any of this way, whether they were men or women, he might bring them bound unto Jerusalem. And as he journeyed, he came near Damascus: and suddenly there shined round about him a light from heaven: And he fell to the earth, and heard a voice saying unto him, "Saul, Saul, why persecutest thou me?" And he said, "Who art thou, Lord?" And the Lord said, "I am Jesus whom thou persecutest." . . . And the men which journeyed with him stood speechless, hearing a voice, but seeing no man. And Saul arose from the earth; and when his eyes were opened, he saw no man: but they led him by the hand, and brought him into Damascus. And he was three days without sight, and neither did eat nor drink.

Saul is first mentioned as being present at the stoning of Stephen and "Saul was consenting to his death." Now we find Saul on his way to Damascus, with permission from the high priest, to kill disciples of the

Lord. Suddenly there was a great light and a voice from heaven, and that was enough to convert Saul. He was blinded for three days, and during those three days he didn't eat or drink anything. Ananias, a disciple of the Lord living in Damascus, went to Saul and restored his sight. Saul was baptized and filled with the Holy Ghost, "And straightway he preached Christ in the synagogue, that he is the Son of God." Not too much later, however, "the Jews took counsel to kill him."

Here we have the turning point in the life of the real founder of Christianity. Based on this one short episode in his life, the world has been affected—for better or for worse—by this man's ideas. What really happened that day to Saul, later to be called Paul, that so impressed him? Luke tells us "And the men which journeyed with him stood speechless, hearing a voice, but seeing no man." Luke later writes, "And they that were with me [Saul] saw indeed the light, and were afraid; but they heard not the voice of him that spake to me" (Acts 22:9). Again Luke wrote, "At midday, O king, I [Saul] saw in the way a light from heaven, above the brightness of the sun, shining round about me and them which journeyed with me. And when we were all fallen to the earth, I heard a voice speaking unto me, and saying in the Hebrew tongue, Saul, Saul, why persecutest thou me?" (Acts 26:13-14). The stories differ about who heard the voice. One account says all of them heard it, the other two accounts say only Saul heard it.

Even though there are discrepancies, the story is clear enough for us to make some sense of it. Saul experienced a definite psychological event on that road to Damascus. From later information found in Paul's epistles, we are made aware that Paul had several problems, both physical and mental. While they were not major problems, they may explain why he acted as he did. On the road to Damascus there apparently was a flash of lightning that everyone in the group saw. It startled them so much that they all fell to the ground. Paul alone was temporarily blinded: it may have been the lightning. It may have been such a terrifying event that, coupled with his emotional state, he suffered a hysteric attack. Symptoms of the attack could have resulted in a hallucination in which he saw and spoke to Jesus. Everyone in the group may have heard the sound of thunder, but only Saul heard it as a voice. Even the blindness may have resulted from the hysteria, and when Ananias suggested that it be cured, it immediately left him. If the blindness was from the lightning and was only temporary, three days would have been sufficient for his vision to return. Some scholars suggest Saul was a victim of epilepsy, and a flash of light may trigger seizures in epileptics. I am inclined to stick with the hysteria hypothesis. We will see Saul (or Paul) having more experiences later.

Whatever it was that caused Saul to change from one who championed the law to one who preached against it, it brought him many problems with the Jews. His conversion was quick, but complete—there was no thought of turning back. Once Saul was convinced that he was on the right track he never looked back. Saul is to be greatly admired for his perseverance if not his theology. No miracle need be involved in this story. Natural occurrences may have caused this man to become the founder of present-day Christianity.

185   *Peter Heals Aeneas*

◆ Acts 9:32-35

> And it came to pass, as Peter passed throughout all quarters, he came down also to the saints that dwelt at Lydda. And there he found a certain man named Aeneas, which had kept his bed eight years, and was sick of the palsy. And Peter said unto him, "Aeneas, Jesus Christ maketh thee whole: arise, and make thy bed." And he arose immediately.

Peter just happened upon a paralytic, and without asking or being asked, he healed him. This story is very similar to Jesus' healing of the paralytic in Luke 5:18-26. Both cures took place without asking or being asked, both principals were told to take up or make up their beds. This man had been paralyzed for eight years, but when Peter suggested he was whole, "he arose immediately." There was obviously a short conversation between Peter and Aeneas, and when they understood each other, the power of Peter's suggestion may have been all that was needed to effect the cure.

The manifestations of hysteric paralysis are indistinguishable from neural paralysis. The only difference is that hysteric paralysis is mental. In neural paralysis the muscles atrophy and waste away; in hysteric paralysis there is no atrophy. When the hysteric paralytic understood his condition and the cure was suggested and accepted, he could immediately stand and walk. Even though it can be easily described, I don't mean to leave the impression just anyone could have accomplished the cure. Even today not all psychotherapists can deal successfully with hysteric patients. The problem must be identified, understood, and explained to the patient in order for the cure to be accomplished. Not even all of Jesus' disciples could cure such cases because some didn't understand the fundamental nature of the problem.

This story is similar to one in which Jesus was involved in Luke 5:18-26, and we will also see another in which Paul was involved in Acts 28. Luke seems to take stories about Jesus and transfer them to Peter and Paul so we would see all of them as miracle workers. Such parallel accounts recall the miracles of Elijah and Elisha from the Old Testament. In some instances, one Old Testament miracle story could account for four or five miracle stories scattered throughout the New Testament. It is possible that the forty or fifty stories of healings in the Bible, stem from only five or six in the Old Testament. As the story was told and retold, the teller transformed the identity of the healer to a current hero. We have seen too many similarities to dismiss this idea of copycat miracles. Keep this in mind as we look at more healing stories.

The fact that this story dealt with natural means of healing makes it clear that no miracle is necessary.

186 *Peter Raises Dorcas*

◆ Acts 9:36-42

> Now there was at Joppa a certain disciple named Tabitha, which by interpretation is called Dorcas: this woman was full of good works and almsdeeds which she did. And it came to pass in those days, that she was sick and died: whom when they had washed, they laid her in an upper chamber. . . . But Peter put them all forth, and kneeled down, and prayed; and turning him to the body said, "Tabitha, arise." And she opened her eyes: and when she saw Peter, she sat up. And he gave her his hand, and lifted her up, and when he had called the saints and widows, presented her alive.

Joppa was about six miles from Lydda, and when those in Joppa heard about Peter's miracle they sent for him. Dorcas was already dead, but Peter came to her room, and after sending everyone out he talked to her, she opened her eyes and sat up. When Peter presented her alive, the saints and widows didn't even get excited. They were more excited when she was dead than when she was revived; at least they "stood by him weeping" when Peter arrived. Dorcas was probably a victim of hysteric coma, and while Peter talked to her and explained her condition, she listened and understood. When Peter suggested she was cured, she accepted the suggestion and arose.

The similarity between this story and the raising of Jairus's daughter in Mark 5 is doubly interesting. Not only is one raised from the dead, but there is a similar word used in both stories. In Mark 5:41 we read "And he took the damsel by the hand, and said unto her, '*Talitha cumi*'; which is, being interpreted, 'Damsel, I say unto thee, arise.'" Luke has the same story and the woman was called Tabitha, and Peter is made to say "Tabitha, arise." Could Luke have used the same story for Peter that Mark used for Jesus? That is certainly a possibility. The echoes of Elijah and the widow's son, and Elisha and the Shunammite's son are also in our consciousness as all these stories may stem from one source. In Acts

20, we shall see Paul raise Eutychus from the dead to match this story of Peter raising Dorcas.

Not only was the cure of hysteric coma natural, but also the copying of miracles from character to character was natural in those days.

It is likely that no supernatural event took place in any of these stories.

187 Peter's Trance and Vision

◆ Acts 10:1-48

> On the morrow, as they went on their journey, and drew nigh unto the city, Peter went up upon the housetop to pray about the sixth hour: And he became very hungry, and would have eaten: but while they made ready, he fell into a trance, And saw heaven opened, and a certain vessel descending unto him, as it had been a great sheet knit at the four corners, and let down to the earth: Wherein were all manner of fourfooted beasts of the earth, and wild beasts, and creeping things, and fowls of the air. And there came a voice to him, "Rise, Peter; kill and eat." But Peter said, "Not so, Lord; for I have never eaten any thing that is common or unclean." And the voice spake unto him again the second time, "What God hath cleansed, that call not thou common." This was done thrice: and the vessel was received up again into heaven.

Can you imagine anyone being on a rooftop at high noon in desert country? Peter was: and "he became very hungry, and would have eaten." Peter was so hungry "he fell into a trance." This was very serious for a man to be so hungry that he passed out and went into a trance on a rooftop in the heat of the day. In his trance, he saw all kinds of animals and was told to "kill and eat." It is not uncommon for a hungry man to dream about food. Because Peter was so conscious of his diet, as were all strict Jews, he would not break dietary laws even in a dream.

Peter was in a compromising position: he was staying in the house of "Simon a tanner." To touch the carcasses or hides of dead animals was enough to render one unclean. To stay in the house was enough for a guilty conscience, at least. So under such stress and "very hungry," Peter fell into a hysteric trance. Struggling with his conscience about dietary laws, being near unclean animal hides, and in extreme hunger caused Peter to see a vision and hear a voice. Luke, a Gentile himself, uses this vision to allow Peter to meet with and sanction Cornelius as a legitimate Gentile Christian. It is strange that Luke makes Peter the pioneer of Gentile missions, even though Paul claimed to be the original Apostle to the Gentiles. Some scholars believe Luke confused his sources or put his stories in the wrong sequence in Acts.

When Peter awoke, servants sent by Cornelius confronted him. He decided that visions of animals represented people, and that justified his acceptance of the Gentiles by saying God showed him Jews and Gentiles were equals. What a masterful case of rationalization Luke put on Peter, and what a change it made in the new Christian Church. Even though it was a natural hysteric trance and vision, it came to be called a supernatural event and changed the course of history. If this had been inspired by the God of the Old Testament, or even by Jesus in the New Testament, the Gentiles would have needed to convert to Judaism. Jesus was very specific as he told the Twelve to go only to the Jews. As it turned out, the Gentiles won by an error Peter made interpreting his dream. Today not only the Jewish people, but the whole world is plagued by Christianity.

188 *Peter's Deliverance From Prison*

◆ Acts 12:1-19

> Now about that time Herod the king stretched forth his hands to vex certain of the church. And he killed James the brother of John with the sword. And because he saw it pleased the Jews, he proceeded further to take Peter also. (Then were the days of unleavened bread.) And when he had apprehended him, he put him in prison. . . . And, behold, the angel of the Lord came upon him, and a light shined in the prison: and he smote Peter on the side, and raised him up, saying, "Arise up quickly." And his chains fell off from his hands. . . . When they were past the first and the second ward, they came unto the iron gate that leadeth unto the city; which opened to them of his own accord: and they went out, and passed on through one street; and forthwith the angel departed from him.

Here again Peter was put into prison and sixteen soldiers were stationed to guard him. He was chained with two chains and set between two guards, but just like in Acts 5 an angel appeared and set him free. We are asked to believe an angel unlocked the chains, opened the gates, walked through the prison, and didn't stir any of the guards. As a result of this prison break, all sixteen guards were put to death by Herod. Its fairly obvious that the guards were drunk, so they would be sound asleep when the disciples came to free Peter. Rather than admit drugging the guards, Luke uses an angel-of-the-Lord story so common in the Bible. He had to make up a story so far beyond reason that people would have to believe it.

If God was so concerned with having Peter freed from prison, why didn't he do something for James instead of allowing him to be killed by Herod? It hardly seems fair that God played favorites, allowing James to be killed and Peter to go free. The reason James died and Peter escaped from prison had nothing to do with God. Because James had been killed, the church was just making sure the same thing didn't happen to Peter. They knew what they had to do and they simply went ahead and did it. They were not concerned that sixteen guards would die, only that Peter would live. After all, the guards were just expendable Romans.

When we get to Acts 16, we will see yet another prison break when Paul was set free. There is nothing supernatural in this episode—prison breaks are rather mundane occurrences.

189 The Death of Herod

◆ Acts 12:20-25

> And upon a set day Herod, arrayed in royal apparel, sat upon his throne, and made an oration unto them. And the people gave a shout, saying, "It is the voice of a god, and not of a man." And immediately the angel of the Lord smote him, because he gave not God the glory: and he was eaten of worms, and gave up the ghost.

Herod gave a speech and the people, in common Oriental fashion, praised his speech as divine. This was the accepted conduct: Egyptians, Romans and others deified their rulers. If God killed every deified king or emperor there would have been very few rulers in ancient times. Divine rulership had a long history before Herod's death.

For a person to get sick and die was, is, and always will be a natural event. No miracle is required for a sick person to die. Sometimes people were sick for a long time before death came. To say "an angel of the Lord smote him" is a common Bible phrase, and angels are often the agents of divine retribution. Some terrible disease evidently afflicted Herod, and if the description was correct, "he was eaten of worms" and died a horrible death. To say God had to kill him by means of an angel, because there was no way to convert him, makes God less powerful.

The real miracle for such a story would be to allow Herod to become a Christian and proclaim the gospel of Christ. To teach that God will kill anyone who does not do just what God wants him to do is to control by fear.

We have in post-biblical times as many examples of fear used as a means to control the faithful as one has the patience to search. At one time the Roman Catholic Church threatened people with eternal punishment in hell for not believing arbitrary, man-made rules like not eating meat on Friday. If this is how God intended to keep people in line he can hardly be a God of love.

This is not a story of a supernatural death, but only nature taking its course.

190   *Paul and Elymas the Sorcerer*

◆ Acts 13:4-10

> And when they had gone through the isle of Paphos, they found a
> certain sorcerer, a false prophet, a Jew, whose name was Bar-Jesus:
> Which was with the deputy of the country, Sergius Paulus, a prudent
> man; who called for Barnabas and Saul, and desired to hear the word
> of God. But Elymas the sorcerer (for so is his name by interpretation)
> withstood them, seeking to turn away the deputy from the faith. Then
> Saul, (who also is called Paul,) filled with the Holy Ghost, set his eyes
> on him, And said, "O full of all subtility and all mischief, thou child
> of the devil, thou enemy of all righteousness, wilt thou not cease to
> pervert the right ways of the Lord? And now, behold, the hand of the
> Lord is upon thee, and thou shalt be blind, not seeing the sun for a
> season." And immediately there fell on him a mist and a darkness; and
> he went about seeking some to lead him by the hand. Then the deputy,
> when he saw what was done, believed, being astonished at the doctrine
> of the Lord.

The deputy of Paphos wanted to hear Paul preach but Bar-Jesus, or
Elymas, didn't want him to. This was a simple case of difference of
opinion. Paul was trying to convert Sergius Paulus and Elymas didn't
want this to happen. Paul couldn't preach until he got rid of this rival,
Elymas, so he tried to insult him. It is interesting that Paul calls him
"child of the devil" while his name was Bar-Jesus, or "son of salvation."
Not satisfied with just calling him names, Paul looks him straight in the
eye and tells him he would be blind for a while. Elymas was in such an
emotional state of rage, tension, and fear that he may have become
hysteric and accepted the suggestion of blindness and "immediately"
became hysterically blind.

Since Elymas was a sorcerer, he was acquainted with magic and
trickery, but Paul was ready with a little trick of his own. Once he got
Elymas into a state of hysteria, Paul only needed the power of suggestion
and the man was blinded. Because of this little trick, Sergius Paulus
"believed, being astonished at the doctrine of the Lord." This is the same
phrase used in Luke when Jesus taught in Capernaum: "And they were
astonished at his doctrine: for his word was with power" (Luke 4:32).
When Luke uses the same phrase, he sometimes uses the same story,
and this may have been one of those times. By having people marvel at
Paul's doctrine as well as Jesus' doctrine, Luke raised Paul to a similar
level as Jesus. Luke was very concerned to have all three, Jesus, Peter,
and Paul, equal in preaching, healing, and raising the dead.

No supernatural power is used in this story. The natural power of the
mind is adequate.

191   Paul Cures a Cripple at Lystra

◆ Acts 14:1-18

And there sat a certain man at Lystra, impotent in his feet, being a cripple from his mother's womb, who never had walked: The same heard Paul speak: who stedfastly beholding him, and perceiving that he had faith to be healed, Said with a loud voice, "Stand upright on thy feet." And he leaped and walked.

This man at Lystra had been lame from birth and Paul immediately made him whole. There had to have been a short talk so they could understand one another, and when Paul "perceiving that he had faith to be healed," suggested he "stand upright" he "leaped and walked." The same formula is used over and over because it worked. The man was in the same hysteric paralytic state as all the others we have seen, and he too could respond to the suggestion to be healed.

This case is almost identical to the story in which Peter cured a cripple at the Beautiful Gate in Acts 3. Both men were "cripple from his mother's womb," and "lame from his mother's womb." Paul was "stedfastly beholding him." And "Peter fastening his eyes on him." Paul said, "Stand upright on thy feet," and Peter said, "Rise up and walk." Paul's man "leaped and walked," Peter's man "leaping up stood and walked." In neither case did the men seek healing—they were both just sitting and begging. It is not a coincidence that the stories are similar: they are identical. Luke is again building Paul to be every bit as good as Peter, for Luke was a Gentile and Paul was about to become the Apostle to the Gentiles. Also, Luke went on Paul's missionary journeys and Luke wanted Paul to be perceived as superior to the other Apostles.

Nothing supernatural here, only the same, natural, copycat stories.

192   Paul's Recovery From Stoning

◆ Acts 14:8-20

And there came thither certain Jews from Antioch and Iconium, who persuaded the people, and, having stoned Paul, drew him out of the city, supposing he had been dead. Howbeit, as the disciples stood round about him, he rose up, and came into the city: and the next day he departed with Barnabas to Derbe.

This was a close call. The people who were about to worship and offer sacrifice to Paul and Barbabas as gods now stoned Paul in an attempt to kill him. Paul had rejected their calling him a god and they were so upset they turned on him. They stoned him and dragged him out of the city, leaving him for dead. Nobody attempted to restore him to life. They just "stood round about him." Paul was just unconscious, so when he awoke, he got up and was all right. This situation brought Paul as close as he had ever been to death.

There is no doubt that he was hit all over his body with stones, bloodied and unconscious. He would certainly have appeared to have been killed. Paul was fortunate the mobs were easily satisfied with their supposition that he was dead or the church would likely have come to an early end. As it happened, Paul was able to continue his ministry and live many more years.

There is no miracle here, only the good fortune of bad judgment on the part of the people about Paul's condition.

193   Paul's Vision at Troas

◆ Acts 16:6-15

> And they passing by Mysia came down to Troas. And a vision appeared to Paul in the night; there stood a man of Macedonia, and prayed him, saying, "Come over into Macedonia, and help us." And after he had seen the vision, immediately we endeavored to go into Macedonia, assuredly gathering that the Lord had called us for to preach the gospel unto them.

Paul had a vision one night in which a man from Macedonia asked him to come preach to his city. Who was the man Paul saw in his vision? It was probably Luke himself who persuaded Paul to go to Macedonia because Luke was from "Philippi, which is the chief city of that part of Macedonia." Paul saw a man of Macedonia, but when he got there, it was a "certain woman named Lydia, a seller of purple, of the city of Thyatira," who heard and accepted Paul's preaching.

What we have here is a perfect match for Peter's vision of the clean and unclean animals he interpreted to be Gentiles. Both Peter and Paul had visions sending them on missions to convert Gentiles. It was very important to Luke that Paul be every bit as Spirit-directed as Peter so the Jews would accept Paul's preaching to the Gentiles. When you understand that this was written after Jerusalem and the temple were destroyed in 70, you can appreciate why the Jews had to get along with the Gentiles. The Jews in their synagogues outside of Jerusalem were meeting more Gentiles. The Jewish Christians were in Gentile Christian churches established by Paul.

The reason we have a Christian church today is because Paul's churches survived the fall of Jerusalem. As a result, we no longer have *Apostolic* Christianity but rather *Pauline* Christianity. Paul was very proud that he did not learn about Jesus from the Apostles: "But I certify you, brethren, that the gospel which was preached of me is not after man. For I neither received it of man, neither was I taught it, but by the revelation of Jesus Christ" (Galations 1:11-12). Now we see why it was so important for Luke to write these stories. Paul needed validity, and it was up to Luke to give him the necessary credentials in the book of Acts.

If there was a dream or vision it was a product of Paul's hysteric hallucination. When a person as intense as Paul had a dream, either awake or asleep, it would be based upon what was current in his mind. Paul was a very dedicated man, and being subject to visions, we can see how he could see whatever he chose. When Martin Luther King Jr. said, "I have a dream," he wasn't speaking of a sleeping dream, but of a waking, conscious, sought-after dream. King directed all his life energy to attain his goals. Paul was the same sort of person. Paul's visions were the natural products of hysteric hallucinations, but he seemed to base them on his own desires and goals. No miracle entered the picture.

Only natural dreams shaped and directed Paul's life.

194 *Paul and the Female Soothsayer*

◆ Acts 16:16-24

> And it came to pass, as we went to prayer, a certain damsel possessed with a spirit of divination met us, which brought her masters much gain by soothsaying. The same followed Paul and us, and cried, saying, "These men are servants of the most high God, which shew unto us the way of salvation." And this did she many days. But Paul, being grieved, turned and said to the spirit, "I command thee in the name of Jesus Christ to come out of her." And he came out the same hour.

While in Philippi, Paul and his group, including Luke, stayed in the house of Lydia. The damsel seemed to follow Paul everywhere he went and even though she said Paul and his group were "the servants of the most high God," Paul had had enough of her. He exorcised the spirit and was immediately in trouble with her masters. They promptly had Paul and Silas thrown into prison. The girl was apparently a victim of multiple personality disorder and acted as an oracle in giving people guidance for the future. Today we would call her a fortune teller. She may have been a very young girl, and when she heard and understood Paul she may have been sincere in calling him a servant of God.

Why did Paul become so upset when she advertised for him? Paul may have reasoned, because she was a victim of hysteria, that her symptoms could be cured. She may have been too young to understand that even though she was trying to help, she was too noisy and disruptive to his preaching. In her hysteria, she was also emotionally excited, and excessively anxious which Paul saw as being negative toward his preaching. In any event, he decided to calm her down, and when she quieted down her hysteria dissipated and she was made well.

Even though it was normal for young children to be excitable and noisy, this girl was able to help her masters make a good living. When she could no longer be of use to her masters, they had Paul and Silas thrown into prison. The girl was a ventriloquist according to many scholars, but it is important to note that multiple personality is one of the symptoms of hysteria. This symptom is often the basis for "trance channelers" and mediums who speak in different voices and appear to manifest several types of character. This was a natural—though not too desirable characteristic—and Paul's cure for it was also strictly natural.

195 *Paul and Silas Freed from Prison*

◆ Acts 16:19-40

> And when her masters saw that the hope of their gains was gone, they caught Paul and Silas, and drew them into the marketplace unto the rulers, And brought them to the magistrates, saying, "These men, being Jews, do exceedingly trouble our city, and teach customs, which are not lawful for us to receive, neither to observe, being Romans." . . . And when they had laid many stripes upon them, they cast them into prison, charging the jailer to keep them safely: Who, having received such a charge, thrust them into the inner prison, and made their feet fast in stocks. And at midnight Paul and Silas prayed, and sang praises unto God: and the prisoners heard them. And suddenly there was a great earthquake, so that the foundations of the prison were shaken: and immediately all the doors were opened, and every one's bands were loosed.

Once again we find the disciples in prison and again they were freed in a marvelous way. This time Paul and Silas prayed and sang at midnight. A great earthquake caused the prison to shake, the doors to open, and the prisoners bands to be loosed. This sounds like a copy of Acts 12 where Peter was freed by an "angel of the Lord." There is one major difference between the two stories and I find that difference of great interest. When Peter was freed, he left the prison and sixteen Roman soldiers were killed for allowing his escape. When Paul was set free, he stayed, and, as a result, the keeper of the prison was converted and his household as well. There may have been an earthquake but if Paul and Silas were set free from their chains it was probably with the help of Lydia's friends. Luke wrote both stories, but he showed mercy to the Philippian jailer and his family because Luke himself was from Philippi. In the story of Peter, Luke allowed sixteen soldiers to die because they were Romans.

When it was daytime "the magistrates sent the serjeants, saying, 'Let those men go.'" At that time Paul told the magistrates he and Silas were

Romans and the magistrates apologized to them and asked them to leave the city. After they said goodbye to Lydia they left Philippi.

This copycat story was written to show that Paul, too, could be put into prison and God would set him free, just as he did Peter. Scholars regard all the escape stories with suspicion because of the similarity of circumstances. The Apostles were imprisoned not for breaking laws, but because of good deeds they had done. They never had to spend more than a few hours in prison. Their freedom came in unusual ways: Peter was twice freed by angels, and Paul by a midnight earthquake. If these stories are not fabrications, we can be certain there were disciples who drugged or bribed the guards to set the prisoners free.

Why look for supernatural means when natural methods are more than adequate to set the prisoners free?

196   *Paul's Vision of Encouragement*

◆ Acts 18:1-17

> Then spake the Lord to Paul in the night by a vision, "Be not afraid, but speak, and hold not thy peace: For I am with thee, and no men shall set on thee to hurt thee: for I have much people in this city."

Paul had another of his visions "in the night." In this vision he heard words of encouragement from Jesus. In the strength of this vision "he continued there a year and six months, teaching the word of God among them."

No miracle is needed for Paul to have had a vision. Paul was quite capable of dreaming up his own visions of the Lord. All he had to do was to go into a trance state and in his mind he would dream about the Lord. Paul was a driven man—there was nothing more important to him than spreading the word of God. In his zeal he was without equal. He didn't let anything stand in his way even if it meant hardship or physical pain.

In this episode, Paul had just been thrown out of the synagogue and said, "From henceforth I will go unto the Gentiles." Paul was brought before Gallio, the deputy of Achaia, and the Jews brought charges against him, "Saying, 'This fellow persuadeth men to worship God contrary to the law.'" Paul taught against the "law" a great deal and was proud of himself for it. In his Epistles he wrote, "But if ye be led of the Spirit, ye are not under the law" (Galations 5:18). Probably one of his strongest teachings against the law was this one: "Stand fast therefore in the liberty wherewith Christ hath made us free, and be not entangled again with the yoke of bondage" (Galations 5:1).

Paul *did* preach against the Jewish law, and as a result, the Jews threw him out. It was for this reason he decided to turn to the Gentiles. Paul knew that to reach the Gentiles he could not expect them to become Jews and keep all the laws of the Old Testament. Paul therefore opened the way for them to become Christians without having to keep the Jewish law. This of course angered the Jews. The Apostles in the Jerusalem Church kept the laws, worshiped in the temple, and were in good standing with the Jews. The Sadducees who ran the temple caused trouble once in a while, but for the most part the Apostles were not in any danger from the Jews. We read earlier that Saul persecuted the church in Jerusalem, "and they were all scattered abroad throughout the regions of Judea and Samaria, except the apostles" (Acts 8:1). Remember, we do not have Apostolic Christianity today, but Pauline Christianity. Some of what Paul taught was contrary to the teaching of Jesus and the Apostles, but Paul's teachings outlasted Jerusalem.

As far as Paul's vision of encouragement, I think it was the result of hysteria. Because of all his stress, anxiety, fear, persecution, and emotionalism, Paul experienced a hysteric hallucination, saw and heard Jesus say just what he wanted and needed to hear. Nothing supernatural occurred here; only the natural working of Paul's mind.

197 *Paul and the Disciples At Ephesus*

◆ Acts 19:1-20

> And it came to pass, that, while Apollos was at Corinth, Paul having passed through the upper coasts came to Ephesus: and finding certain disciples, He said unto them, "Have ye received the Holy Ghost since ye believed?" And they said unto him, "We have not as much as heard whether there be any Holy Ghost." And he said unto them, "Unto what then were ye baptized?" And they said, "Unto John's baptism." Then said Paul, "John verily baptized with the baptism of repentance, saying unto the people, that they should believe on him which should come after him, that is, on Christ Jesus." When they heard this, they were baptized in the name of the Lord Jesus. And when Paul had laid his hands upon them, the Holy Ghost came on them; and they spake with tongues, and prophesied. And all the men were about twelve.

When Paul got to Ephesus he found "certain disciples" who had been baptized "unto John's baptism," but had never even heard of the Holy Ghost. Paul taught them about Jesus, of whom they had not heard, and they were baptized again; this time "in the name of the Lord Jesus." Paul then "laid his hands upon them" and they received the Holy Ghost as the disciples did at Pentecost. This group "spake with tongues and prophesied," because that was what Paul taught them. There were only twelve men in this group, but it was a good start for the church at Ephesus.

From whom did these twelve learn of John's baptism? It could be that they were in Judea twenty-five years earlier when John the Baptist was preaching and baptizing. That would really be outstanding, but they may have learned it only a short time before from Apollos who had just been there. As is obvious in the story, these twelve had not heard of Jesus so they were not Christians. Once Paul told them about Jesus, they believed and were baptized, and when Paul laid hands on them they received the Holy Ghost. That is speedy action. Once again Luke wanted Paul to be on a par with Peter, so he has Paul bring the Holy Ghost to disciples outside of Judea. Peter had twice bestowed the Holy Ghost in Acts 2 and Acts 4, but those two times were in Jerusalem.

Paul also was able to work some miracles in Ephesus, "So that from his body were brought unto the sick handkerchiefs or aprons, and the diseases departed from them, and the evil spirits went out of them." We aren't told why the sick weren't brought to Paul or why Paul didn't go to the sick, but at least they got the job done. This sounds like sympathetic magic: handkerchiefs cure people. Whether this actually happened or if it was just fabricated by Luke to match the healing power of Peter's shadow we don't know. Both stories have the flavor of the day when things closely associated with great people became powerful and communicated the power of the person. Jesus is in a similar story of a woman with an issue of blood who was healed when she touched the hem of his garment in Luke 8. Such was the magical belief of ancient people, and maybe Luke was just "carried away" and attributed such powers to Peter and Paul.

There is also the possibility that the people cured were all afflicted with hysteric symptoms which could be alleviated by the suggestion that handkerchiefs were their point of contact. Many diseases are hysteric in nature, and "evil spirits" were almost always the result of hysteric symptoms. Because the people did not understand mental illness, they often referred to those suffering in terms of spirits, demons and devils. I am inclined to believe that the faith of the hysteric person, properly conditioned, could account for such cures. As long as the person suggesting the cure properly prepares the patient, there would be no problem receiving it. Psychotherapists are able to help people suffering from hysteric disorders today. Once the therapist understands the problems and has the confidence of the patients, about 80% are cured of their disorders.

In this story only natural means are used—the same means we use today to cure hysteric problems. No miracle actually took place.

198 *Seven False Exorcists*

◆ Acts 19:13-20

> Then certain of the vagabond Jews, exorcists, took upon them to call over them which had evil spirits the name of the Lord Jesus, saying, "We adjure you by Jesus whom Paul preacheth." And there were seven sons of one Sceva, a Jew, and chief of the priests, which did so. And the evil spirit answered and said, "Jesus I know, and Paul I know; but who are ye?" And the man in whom the evil spirit was leaped on them, and overcame them, and prevailed against them, so that they fled out of that house naked and wounded.

This story deals with seven Jewish brothers, the sons of a chief of the priests whose name was Sceva, and their attempt to exorcise an evil spirit. No doubt they had witnessed exorcisms and decided to try it themselves. They made one mistake in their presentation and used the name of "Jesus whom Paul preacheth." They used second-hand information. When the man heard them attempt to cure him in someone else's name, he turned on them and overcame them. He acknowledged Jesus and Paul, but recognized that these seven men had no authority. Sounds somewhat scary, doesn't it.

What happened here requires a little bit of explanation so we may see it clearly. The man was a victim of hysteria with the symptom of multiple personality disorder. Because his condition was not properly explained to him he could not be cured. He was not prepared to accept any suggestion of a cure because he didn't even know who these seven men were. You remember that in all cases we discussed, I made comments that Jesus, or whoever was doing the healing, had to talk with the person and come to an understanding. Unless both parties knew what the problem was and the afflicted one believed the healer could do the job, nothing would happen. Because the man with the "evil spirit" had no knowledge of, or confidence in these seven men, he turned on them. With the strength "of a man possessed," or under hysteric control, he beat up the seven men who were probably not as strong as the man anyway. These seven men believed that knowing the right spell or name would give them magic powers, and the name of "Jesus, whom Paul preacheth" seemed like a good name to use.

There is nothing supernatural in the story; only the first time we have seen a healing improperly executed. It is extremely important that in such cases today, only highly qualified psychotherapists be allowed to deal with hysteric symptoms. The deeper attitudes and motivations of the person must be understood to effect a real cure of hysteria.

199   *Paul Raises Eutychus*

◆   Acts 20:1-12

> And upon the first day of the week, when the disciples came together
> to break bread, Paul preached unto them, ready to depart on the
> morrow; and continued his speech until midnight. And there were
> many lights in the upper chamber, where they were gathered together.
> And there sat in a window a certain young man named Eutychus, being
> fallen into a deep sleep: and as Paul was long preaching, he sunk down
> with sleep, and fell down from the third loft, and was taken up dead.
> And Paul went down, and fell on him, and embracing him said,
> "Trouble not yourselves; for his life is in him." When he therefore was
> come up again, and had broken bread, and eaten, and talked a long
> while, even till break of day, so he departed. And they brought the
> young man alive, and were not a little comforted.

You may have thought your preacher kept you in church too long, but
consider Paul. He preached until midnight and may have gone on longer
if Eutychus hadn't fallen out of the window. This young man was
overcome by the fumes from the "many lights" (oil-burning lamps), or
just because it was midnight. In either case he fell "into a deep sleep"
and "fell down from the third loft." We are told he "was taken up dead,"
but Paul was careful to say "his life is in him." Paul "fell on him, and
embracing him," just like Elijah and Elisha had done in the books of
Kings. A happy ending came as "they brought the young man alive."

The story was not written to tell about a miracle because none
happened. The story was to show a little bit about life in the early
Christian Church. Because the sacrament of the Lord's Supper had not
yet been formalized, the *agape,* or love feast, was simply called "breaking bread." The service took place at night because the business of the
day had to be completed before the service could begin.

The story of Eutychus is incidental to the meeting. Because there were
so many oil lamps burning and giving off toxic fumes and depleting the
oxygen, Eutychus fell asleep. He was sitting in a window high up on the
wall, and as fumes affected him he fell out the window. When Paul
reached him, the others thought he was dead, but Paul probably gave him
artificial respiration. Paul may even have given him mouth-to-mouth
resuscitation and cleared his lungs of the fumes. Paul must be given most
of the credit for being alert to the circumstances and doing the right thing.
Luke jumped to conclusions here as he did in Luke 8 when he said this
young man, and Jairus's daughter, were dead. Both Jesus and Paul
insisted the young people were not dead and both were revived.

Nothing supernatural occurred in this story. The natural means used
by Paul accomplished the cure.

200 *Paul's Deliverance From Conspiracy*

◆ Acts 23:1-24

> And when it was day, certain of the Jews banded together, and bound
> themselves under a curse, saying that they would neither eat nor drink
> till they had killed Paul. And they were more than forty which had
> made this conspiracy. . . . And when Paul's sister's son heard of their
> lying in wait, he went and entered into the castle, and told Paul. Then
> Paul called one of the centurions unto him, and said, "Bring this young
> man unto the chief captain: for he hath a certain thing to tell him." So
> the chief captain then let the young man depart. . . . And he called unto
> him two centurions, saying, "Make ready two hundred soldiers to go
> to Caesarea, and horsemen threescore and ten, and spearmen two
> hundred, at the third hour of the night; And provide them beasts that
> they may set Paul on, and bring him safe unto Felix the governor."

This story begins with Paul before the Sanhedrin. Paul began to defend
himself, but got nowhere, so he took another approach. What he did was
"divide and conquer."

> But when Paul perceived that the one part were Sadducees, and the
> other Pharisees, he cried out in the council, "Men and brethren, I am
> a Pharisee, the son of a Pharisee: of the hope and resurrection of the
> dead I am called in question." And when he had so said, there arose a
> dissension between the Pharisees and the Sadducees: and the multitude
> was divided. For the Sadducees say that there is no resurrection, neither
> angel, nor spirit: but the Pharisees confess both.

So now he had them against each other and the "scribes that were of
the Pharisees' part arose, and strove, saying, 'We find no evil in this man:
but if a spirit or an angel hath spoken to him, let us not fight against
God.'" That put a stop to the meeting and put Paul into protective
custody.

The next day forty Jews banded together and vowed to kill Paul. His
nephew heard about the plan and told Paul, who told the centurion, who
told the chief captain, and Paul was given a military escort to Felix the
Governor. Paul escaped death and the forty men who were involved
either starved to death or violated their "great curse." What a fascinating
story Luke tells. Now we see why on other occasions he merely uses
angels or earthquakes to free the prisoners.

As complex as the stories appear, I don't find anything miraculous in
the story. Paul was very shrewd in pitting the Sadducees against the
Pharisees, but that doesn't take a miracle. As for the vision Paul had, that
was common for Paul and it was no miracle. Paul's visions were the
natural results of hysteric hallucinations. The centurion and chief captain
were more concerned for themselves than for Paul, so the protection they
gave was no miracle.

Good strategy, an alert nephew, and cooperative military leaders were all natural elements, and no supernatural means were used to deliver Paul from the conspiracy.

201   *Paul on Malta*

◆   Acts 28:1-6

> And when they were escaped, then they knew that the island was called Melita. And the barbarous people shewed us no little kindness: for they kindled a fire, and received us everyone, because of the present rain, and because of the cold. And when Paul had gathered a bundle of sticks, and laid them on the fire, there came a viper out of the heat, and fastened on his hand. And when the barbarians saw the venomous beast hang on his hand, they said among themselves, No doubt this man is a murderer, whom, though he hath escaped the sea, yet vengeance suffereth not to live. And he shook off the beast into the fire, and felt no harm. Howbeit they looked when he should have swollen, or fallen down dead suddenly: but after they had looked a great while, and saw no harm come to him, they changed their minds, and said that he was a god.

Being shipwrecked on the Isle of Malta was quite an experience for Paul and the people on the ship. The King James Version says there were two hundred and seventy-six on the ship, but the *Codex Vaticanus* and several other old texts say about seventy-six. The first thing after they survived the sea was a greeting by some natives who had built a fire against the cold, rainy weather. Paul helped gather sticks and he was bitten by a snake. At first they said he was a murderer, but when he didn't die, they were amazed "and said that he was a god."

There are several reasons that could account for Paul's seeming miracle. One reason could be that there was no snake. Perhaps a twig stuck into his hand from a thorn, and when he held up his hand to shake off the branch it only looked like a snake. Another reason could be that it was not a poisonous snake. Another reason could be that even if it were a poisonous viper, they can bite without injecting venom. The viper has the choice of injecting no venom, all it's venom, or any amount in between. Look closely at your King James Version and you will see in Acts 28:4 that the word venomous is in italics. This indicates that the word was not in the original—it was added by the translators, so the word venomous was not the intent of the author. This seems all the more likely since there are no poisonous snakes on the Island of Malta now so there probably weren't any then either.

All in all there is not much reason to believe any thing miraculous occurred. Some may think Mark 16:18 may be of consequence here. "They shall take up serpents; and if they drink any deadly thing it shall not hurt them," but that hadn't been written in Paul's time. Even if it had it still wouldn't matter because the last verses of Mark 16 were not in the original manuscripts. Scholars are in agreement that verses 9-20 of that chapter were added years after Mark wrote his gospel. Luke may have put this story in to verify his verse, "Behold, I give you power to tread on serpents and scorpions, and over all the power of the enemy: and nothing shall by any means hurt you" (Luke 10:19). Even that wasn't known to Paul and it wouldn't have mattered anyway. John the Baptist, Stephen, James and others who had already been killed would prove that verse is of little consequence.

Paul may have been bitten by a snake, but it wasn't a poisonous snake, so there was no need for the supernatural here.

202   *Paul Cures Publius's Father*

◆ Acts 28:7-10

> In the same quarters were possessions of the chief man of the island, whose name was Publius; who received us and lodged us three days courteously. And it came to pass, that the father of Publius lay sick of a fever and of a bloody flux: to whom Paul entered in, and prayed, and laid his hands on him, and healed him. So when this was done, others also, which had diseases in the island, came, and were healed.

After about three days on the Island of Malta, Publius came to Paul with a problem: his father was sick of a fever. Paul went in, prayed, laid hands on him, and healed him.

This sounds much like the story Luke tells of Peter's mother-in-law in Luke 4:38-40. Here again a fever is a symptom of hysteria, and this time Paul calmed the man, explained the problem, and suggested a cure. Because the man had confidence in Paul, after hearing the story of the snake, he accepted the cure and the fever left. This may have been an actual event but as we have seen on many occasions, Luke was very good at making copycat stories. After Publius's father was healed, others came and were healed too. This whole scenario is very vague: they may have been counseled for hysteric illnesses or given medicines for actual sickness.

We do know there were times when Paul was unable to do things through prayer. We remember when Paul spoke of his "thorn in the flesh": "For this thing I besought the Lord thrice, that it might depart from me" (2 Corinthians 12:7-8), but it didn't depart. Paul wasn't able to help a traveling companion on another occasion: "but Trophimus have I left at Miletum, sick" (2 Timothy 4:20). We can only assume Trophimus had a real illness and not just a hysteric symptom. Nowhere were we shown any miracle of healing done for anyone with a broken bone, severed head, crushed by stoning, or any real physical problems.

Why didn't Jesus bring John the Baptist back to life? Why wasn't Stephen brought back to life? How about James the brother of John? Why didn't they pray him back to life after he was killed "with a sword"? I think there is only one reason. These were real, physical conditions. These men were actually dead. Only hysterical symptoms were cured in the Bible stories.

I trust you can now see that the overwhelming evidence presented disallows any supernatural interference in the lives of people. As we care for ourselves with natural means today, so did the people throughout the history of mankind.

There were no miracles, there are no miracles, and we need not look for miracles in the future.

Epilogue

While researching this book I gained a greater respect for the Jewish people. I learned it was they who accomplished their own survival and not some vague, supernatural force. I found the natural explanations for the stories practical because as they used nature, we also can use it to help ourselves and others. The priests demanded sacrifices, offerings and obedience to their laws because the offerings were kept by the priests. The prophets saw through this and taught a higher moral. "Wherewith shall I come before the LORD, and bow myself before the high God? Shall I come before him with burnt offerings, with calves of a year old? Will the LORD be pleased with thousands of rams, or with ten thousands of rivers of oil? Shall I give my firstborn for my transgression, the fruit of my body for the sin of my soul? He hath shewed thee, O man, what is good: and what doth the LORD require of thee, but to do justly, and to love mercy, and to walk humbly with thy God?" (Micah 6:6-8).

Jesus also deserves greater respect when we realize he used only known scientific laws and natural means to do what he did. Jesus didn't have or need supernatural assistance to help others and neither do we. Jesus said, "He that believeth on me, the works that I do shall he do also; and greater works than these shall he do" (John 14:12). If you want to do something of consequence, read Matthew 5, 6 and 7 and follow Jesus' suggestions. Most great religious leaders preached the same basic message, "Love thy neighbor as thyself" (Leviticus 19:18; Mark 12:33). Confucius, Buddha, Plato and many other philosophers taught the same precepts, and we should do our best to follow them today.

By removing the supernatural from the stories about Jesus, we see him in a new light. Jesus as man is much more convincing and compelling than Jesus as God. As Jesus was willing to do what he did for his neighbor, how much more should we do for our neighbor with what we know and what we have? As a part of my effort to help others, I wrote this book. What will you do in your lifetime to benefit mankind?

There you have it! Now that you read what I had to say, what do you think about it? Did you come away with a better understanding of the circumstances and attitudes of the Bible characters as I did?

I would appreciate hearing from you if you would like to write to me. Write in care of Eye-Opener Books, P.O. Box 1531, Santa Rosa, CA 95402.

Bibliography

Clarke, Adam. *Commentary and Critical Notes,* Cincinnati: H.S.& J. Applegate & Co, 1851

Conybeare, F.C. *The Origins of Christianity,* New York: University Books, 1958

Freud, Sigmund. *Moses and Monotheism,* New York: Knopf, 1939

Friedman, Richard Elliott. *Who Wrote the Bible?* New York: Harper & Row, 1987

Graham, Lloyd M. *Deceptions and Myths of the Bible,* New York: Bell Publishing Company, 1979

Halley, H.H. *Halley's Bible Handbook,* Grand Rapids: Zondervan, 1965

Helms, Randel. *Gospel Fictions,* New York: Prometheus Books, 1988

Josephus, Flavious. *Works of Translations* by William Wishton. New York: Holt, Rinehart and Winston.

Joyce, Donovan. *The Jesus Scroll,* New York: Signet, 1972

Lockyer, Herbert. *All the Miracles of the Bible,* Grand Rapids: Zondervan Publishing House, 1961

Schonfield, Hugh. *The Passover Plot,* Hutchinson, 1965

The Abingdon Bible Commentary, edited by F.C. Eiselen. New York: Abingdon Press, 1929

The Interpreter's Bible edited by N.B. Harmon, et al. New York: Abingdon Press, 1952

For information about presentations by Fred Acquistapace, please write to:

Eye-Opener Books
Box 1531
Santa Rosa, CA 95402

✂ -

Please send:

____ copies of *Miracles That Never Were* @ $14.95 $ _____

California residents please add sales tax: $ _____

Postage and handling:
    $2 for one book; $4 for two or more books $ _____

Total . . . . $ _____

Send check or money order to:

Eye-Opener Books
Box 1531
Santa Rosa, CA 95402

Name   _____

Address   _____

City_____ State_____ Zip _____

1

For information about presentations by Fred Acquistapace, please write to:

Eye-Opener Books
Box 1531
Santa Rosa, CA 95402

Please send:

____ copies of *Miracles That Never Were* @ $14.95 $ _____

California residents please add sales tax: $ _____

Postage and handling:
$2 for one book; $4 for two or more books $ _____

Total . . . . $_____

Send check or money order to:

Eye-Opener Books
Box 1531
Santa Rosa, CA 95402

Name _____

Address _____

City_____ State_____ Zip _____

1